WOMEN EMPOWERMENT THROUGH LITERACY CAMPAIGN

About the Author

Dr. Jaimon Varghese was awarded doctoral degree by Jamia Millia Islamia, New Delhi in 2006. He is presently serving as Assistant Professor at Centre for Studies in Rural Development—Institute of Social Work and Research, Ahmednagar, Maharashtra. He has been a keen researcher on the issue of women empowerment for the past ten years having worked with University of Delhi, Jamia Millia Islamia, Sree Sankaracharya University of Sanskrit, Kalady and IGNOU Delhi Centre. He has associated himself with eight research projects sponsored by various ministries. Two books have been co-authored by him along with Late Prof. Hajira Kumar apart from contribution of publishing several articles in journals of repute.

Women Empowerment Through Literacy Campaign

Role of Social Work

Jaimon Varghese

CONCEPT PUBLISHING COMPANY PVT. LTD.
NEW DELHI-110 059

ISBN-13 : 978-81-8069-793-7

First Published 2012

Published and Printed by

Concept
Since 1974

Concept Publishing Company Pvt. Ltd.
Regd. Office :
A/15-16, Commercial Block, Mohan Garden,
New Delhi-110059 (India)
Phones : 25351460, 25351794, *Fax* : 091-11-25357109
Email : publishing@conceptpub.com
Website : www.conceptpub.com

Editorial Office :
H-13, Bali Nagar, New Delhi-110 015, India.

Cataloging in Publication Data--*Courtesy:* D.K. Agencies (P) Ltd. <docinfo@dkagencies.com>

Varghese, Jaimon.
Women empowerment through literacy campaign : role of social work / Jaimon Varghese.
p. cm.
Originally presented as the author's thesis (Ph. D.)—Jamia Millia Islamia.
Includes bibliographical references (p.) and index.
ISBN 9788180697937

1. Women in development—India—Faridabad (District) 2. Literacy programs—India—Faridabad (District) 3. Women volunteers in social service—India—Faridabad (District) 4. Women employees—India—Faridabad (District)—Social conditions. 5. Education and state—India—Faridabad (District) I. Title.

DDC 305.420954558 23

Preface

The success of literacy campaign largely depends upon people's active participation and the involvement of NGOs. National Literacy Mission (NLM) has worked in collaboration with several grassroots NGOs throughout the country. Literacy campaign since its inception has incorporated more than eight million volunteers who come forward to take up the task of teaching the illiterate persons. 'Each one, teach one' is a popular slogan in NLM. What is the motivation for such voluntary literacy workers to join the literacy campaign? A large number of literacy workers are women. Is this voluntarism, a sign of women empowerment? Are these women literacy workers empowered due to their active participation in the voluntary literacy work? This book is a report of the research focused on some of these issues.

The book is divided into 9 chapters. Chapter 1 presents briefly the status of women in India, crime against women, concept of women empowerment and relevant literature review. Chapter 2 explains the research methodology. Chapter 3 deals with the gender and literacy status of Haryana and Faridabad District. Chapter 4 presents the socio-economic information about women literacy workers. Chapter 5 presents different dimensions of women empowerment such as social, economic and political with reference to the status of women literacy workers in each dimension. Chapter 6 highlights the relationship between literacy work and the process of empowerment. Chapter 7 sheds lights on the information regarding the problems in the path of empowerment with reference to the situation of the literacy workers. Chapter 8 deals with the long-term impacts of literacy work upon the lives of women literacy workers as well as other women participants of the National Literacy Campaign. Chapter 9 provides an overview and presents conclusions emanating from the field situation. It also attempts to offer some suggestions for up-scaling the involvement of the women voluntary workers, which is likely to yield rich dividends for the NLC, for the voluntary workers and for the society. Tools used for research and some pieces of relevant literature are given in the annexure.

Jaimon Varghese

Acknowledgements

This book is based on my Thesis submitted to Department of Social Work, Faculty of Social Sciences, Jamia Millia Islamia, New Delhi for the award of the Degree of Doctor of Philosophy in Social Work.

As a writer, I wish to gratefully acknowledge the following for a variety of assistance and help extended to me during the period of my study.

First and foremost, I wish to convey my immense gratitude to my research guide, Late Prof. Hajira Kumar, Jamia Millia Islamia, New Delhi, for her valuable, constructive and amicable guidance and inspiration given to me right from the beginning till the completion of this study.

I am really thankful to Prof. M.Z. Khan who has provided the much needed direction in the preparation of the final report. He has devoted much of his precious time in reading each and every sentence of the report and suggested the best possible way to present the ideas. I have to thank him for his selfless, patient and dedicated correction of the manuscript. I should admit that without his help this report would not have been completed in this way. Above all, I am obliged to him for the improvement in my learning while I had been discussing with him upon the thesis.

I am also grateful to Prof. A.S. Kohli, Prof. Anjali Gandhi, Dr. Archana Dassi, Dr. Habeebul Rahman and Dr. Asiya Nasreen of the Department of Social Work, Jamia Millia Islamia, for their inspiration, advice, encouragement, guidance and facilitation to complete my research in time.

I am also very thankful to the librarians of Delhi School of Social Work, Institute of Public Administration and many other NGOs who have permitted me to use their library resources for my study. In this regard I am particularly grateful to Sarojini Naidu Centre for Women's Studies.

I extend my sincere thanks to my colleagues and friends especially Rev. Dr. Joseph Kavalakkat, who have constantly supported me to pursue the study and complete the same in time.

I owe my sincere thanks to St. Joseph's Service Society (SJSS) and Rev. Dr. Sebastian Vadakumpadan, the founder President, for granting me permission to pursue my research at Chandpur, the project site of SJSS. I am also very much grateful to Rev. Fathers, Rev. Sisters and other staff members of Sanjoepuram, Chandpur who have facilitated data collection by providing accommodation, transportation and timely assistance. In this regard I am particularly grateful to Rev. Fr. Jose Edassery, President of SJSS, for giving me opportunity to undertake various university assignments, by granting leave whenever required. His kindhearted support has been immensely helpful in my professional development.

I express my gratitude to Dr. Suersh Pathare, Director, Centre for Studies in Rural Development Institute of Social Work and Research (CSRD-ISWR) for his constant support and guidance for my career as a teacher and researcher in the field of Social Work. I am also thankful to my colleagues and the support staff at my Institute for their encouragement and cooperation at various levels.

I render my sincere thanks to all the respondents of the research especially the Sarpanchas of 10 villages around Chandpur, Woman Literacy Workers, their family members and the participants of Focus Group Discussions for their cordial cooperation and sincere disclosures that were essential for the success of the study.

I thank Bobby—my wife, Alphons—my son, and Alwina—my daughter, for their moral support and facilitation in pursuance of the study. Finally, I am immensely grateful to my loving parents, Mr. Varghese and Mrs. Annie, my brothers, Mr. Jestin, Mr. Jenny, Mr. Jibu and my sister Mrs. Jiby and their family members for their continuous support and encouragement during my study.

Finally, I am very thankful to Concept Publishing Co. Pvt. Ltd. who have agreed to publish this work as it is. I am also grateful to Concept for the publication of my previous work, *'Victims of Social Injustice: A Study of Marginalised Women'* in 2008, written in association with Late Prof. Hajira Kumar.

There are many others who have directly or indirectly extended their help to me, but their names are not included here. I truly remain grateful to them all.

Jaimon Varghese

Contents

List of Tables

List of Charts

Abbreviations

AIDS	Acquired Immune Deficiency Syndrome
BDO	Block Development Officer
BSY	Balika Samriddhi Yojana
CAPART	Council for Advancement of People's Action and Rural Technology
CAW	Crime Against Women
CD	Community Development
CDP	Community Development Programme
CDPO	Child Development Project Officers
CEDAW	Convention on Elimination of Discrimination Against Women
CRC	Convention on the Rights of the Child
CSW	Commission on the Status of Women
CSWB	Central Social Welfare Board
DRU	District Resource Unit
DRDA	District Rural Development Agency
DWACRA	Development of Women and Child in Rural Areas
DWCD	Department of Women and Child Development
ECHR	European Convention on Human Rights
GDP	Gross Domestic Product
GoI	Government of India
HT	Hindustan Times
IAS	Indian Administrative Service
IAY	Indira Awas Yojana
ICDSS	Integrated Child Development Services Scheme
ICPD	International Conference on Population and Development
IFAD	International Fund for Agricultural Development
IGNOU	Indira Gandhi National Open University
ILO	International Labour Organization

IMR	Infant Mortality Rate
INC	Indian National Congress
IPC	Indian Penal Code
IPS	Indian Police Service
IRDP	Integrated Rural Development Programme
ITU	International Telecommunication Union
JRY	Jawahar Rozgar Yojana
JSN	Jan Sikshan Nilay
LPG	Liberalisation, Privatisation and Globalisation
MHRD	Ministry of Human Resource Development
MLA	Member of Legislative Assembly
MLC	Member of Legislative Council
MMR	Maternal Mortality Ratio
MSY	Mahila Samriddhi Yojana
NABARD	National Bank for Agricultural and Rural Development
NADK	Not Applicable Don't Know
NARI	National Association for Resource Improvement
NBA	Narmada Bachao Andolan
NCIW	National Council for Indian Women
NCRB	National Crime Research Bureau
NCW	National Commission for Women
NCWR	National Commission for Women's Rights
NGO	Non-Governmental Organisation
NIRD	National Institute of Rural Development
NLM	National Literacy Mission
NNP	National Nutrition Policy
NOS	National Open School
NPA	National Plan of Action
NPP	National Perspective Plan
NPPW	National Perspective Plan for Women
NREP	National Rural Employment Programme
NRY	Nehru Rojgar Yojana
NSAP	National Social Assistance Programme
NSKFDC	National Safai Karmchari Finance and Development Corporation
NSLRD	National Scheme of Liberation and Rehabilitation of Scavengers

NSSO	National Sample Survey Organization
NVTI	National Vocational Training Institutes
OBC	Other Backward Castes
PITA	Prevention of Immoral Traffic Act
PMIUPEP	Prime Minister's Integrated Urban Poverty Eradication Programme
PMLA	Pariwarik Mahila Lok Adalat
PMRY	Prime Minister's Rozgar Yojana
PMGSY	Pradhan Mantri Gram Sadak Yojana
PNDT	Pre-Natal Diagnostic Techniques
PRI	Panchayati Raj Institution
RLEGP	Rural Landless Employment Guarantee Programme
RMK	Rashtriya Mahila Kosh
RVTI	Regional Vocational Training Institute
RWDEP	Rural Women's Development and Empowerment Project
SAARC	South Asian Association for Regional Cooperation
SC/ST	Scheduled Castes/Scheduled Tribes
SEEUY	Scheme for Employment of Educated Unemployed Youth
SEPUP	Self-Employment Programme for the Urban Poor
SEWA	Self-Employed Women's Association
SHG	Self-Help Groups
SITA	Suppression of Immoral Traffic in Women and Girls Act
SJSRY	Swarna Jayanti Shahari Rojgar Yojana
SJGSY	Swarna Jayanti Gram Samridhi Yojana
SNCWS	Sarojini Naidu Centre for Women Studies
STEP	Support of Employment Programme for Women
TOI	Times of India
TRYSEM	Training of Rural Youth for Self-Employment
UBSP	Urban Basic Services for the Poor
UDHR	Universal Declaration of Human Rights
UN	United Nations
UNDP	United Nations Development Programme
UNESCO	United Nations Educational, Scientific and Cultural Organization

UNHCHR	United Nations High Commissioner for Human Rights
UNHCR	United Nations High Commissioner for Refugees
UNICEF	United Nations International Children's Educational Fund
UNICRI	United Nations Interregional Crime Research Institute
UNIDO	United Nations Industrial Development Organization
USEP	Urban Self-Employment Programme
UWEP	Urban Wage Employment Programme
WAF	Women's Action Forum
WDC	Women's Development Corporation
WDP	Women Development Programmes
WFP	World Food Programme
WHO	World Health Organization
WPR	Work Participation Rate

1

Introduction

Women and men do not enjoy equal status in terms of the possession and enjoyment of power anywhere on the globe. There is seen a marked difference both in degree and nature of power exercised by women and men. This kind of difference or discrimination in the level of empowerment is more so visible in India. Consequently, there is a considerable difference in opportunity structures. Work opportunities are gender specific. This is abundantly seen in terms of share of men and women in the workforce. It is thus hardly surprising that the men move up faster, in grabbing greater opportunities, than women. Are they handicapped by their sex or by their gender?

Status of Women in India

Comparatively the status of women in India is lower to that of men in several aspects such as sex ratio, access to health care services, participation in productive work and share in community affairs.

Sex Ratio

Some facts even the official statistics underline the state of powerlessness of women in India. Census of India 2001 brings out certain trends that are alarming. As is well known India does not fare well in the sex ratio (the number of females per 1,000 males). Among the populous countries, India's sex ratio is the lowest. Within the country, the states of Uttar Pradesh, Bihar, Jharkhand, Orissa, Chhattisgarh, Madhya Pradesh, Gujarat, Maharashtra and Tamil Nadu have mainly contributed to this downward trend. Among the states, Kerala is the only state which has a sex ratio favourable to women. It was a little above 1,000 in 1901, it has maintained it and it was 1,058 in 2001. Although there is an improvement over 1991's figure with regard to the general sex ratio, the sex ratio in the age group 0-6 decreased from the national average of 945 in 1991 to 927 in 2001. More alarming is the pace at which it has been dipping compared with the overall sex ratio. This imbalance is expected to have a cascading effect on the overall sex ratio during coming decades (Census, 2001).

Sex ratio is an important demographic indicator of gender equality. There is scientific evidence to show that, at the time of fertilisation, there is a greater chance of survival for girl-children compared to boy-children. The female zygote is heavier, healthier and more resistant to diseases. The gestation period for female foetus is on the average longer than that of male foetus. Therefore, natural tendency is that sex ratio is favourable to women. In most European countries sex ratio is favourable to women. In India the situation is otherwise. Except in Kerala, all the states in India have a sex ratio favourable to men. How do we explain it? The possibility cannot be ruled out that the female foetus is eliminated during pregnancy following pre-natal sex detection, legal provisions notwithstanding. The death rate is also higher in the case of females in the age groups up to the age of 40 after which it starts declining and is lower than male death rate. The subordinate position of women is evident from the adverse sex ratio of girls. The theme of sex ratio is a sensitive indicator, which can break through unilinear theories of the changing status of women or the state of society with its existing dominant paradigms of development or globalisation (Majumdar, 2001).

Life Expectancy

Men generally fare better than women on almost every socio-economic indicator except life expectancy (HDR, 2004). Because of biological reasons, women tend to have a longer life than men. And the neglect of women's health and nutrition is so serious that it even outweighs women's natural biological tendency to live longer than men. Her reproductive health is least taken care of. Mortality rates are higher for girls than for boys in the 0-4 age group. In a society having an overwhelming preference for male children, drastic methods of elimination of females, besides neglect and under nourishment, are being employed. Medical tests used for detection of genetic abnormalities in foetus coupled with the Medical Termination of Pregnancy Act are being utilised for eliminating unborn female babies. Female infanticide is being practised in some parts of the country. Methods for killing female babies include stuffing the baby's mouth with rice husk to choke her or administering poisonous juice from local plants or making her consume a double dose of opium (Khanna, 1998 : 71).

Discrimination in Education

In every age group, literacy figures are lower for girls and women compared to men. Schools' enrolment figures continue to be lower for girls than for boys at all stages and ages. School dropout rates are also higher for girls at every stage, from elementary to higher secondary school. Women's access to information and education is limited which in turn affects the quality of training they impart to the younger generation. Ignorance about the rights and responsibilities is the chief block in the path of empowerment. Women remain powerless due to their illiteracy.

We have a discouraging picture when we examine the literacy rate among women. Let us take a close look at figures coming up from the decennial census of 2001. Literates in India stand as 566,714,995 (65.38% of total population) of which 339,969,048 are men (75.85% of all males) and 226,745,947 are women (54.16% of all females). Male-female gap in literacy is 21.70 per cent. Three-fourths of the males and more than a half of the females aged above seven are literate. Kerala is on top with a 90.92 per cent literacy rate and the minimum gap (4.56%) in male-female literacy rates. Bihar is the lowest with 47.53 per cent of literacy rate and the gender gap is 26.75 points (male literacy rate is 60.32% and female literacy rate is 33.57%). Bihar has also the lowest female literacy rate.

Population of Scheduled Castes (SC) in 1991 was 138,000,000 i.e. 16.38 per cent of the total population. It was

14.61 per cent in 1951. The corresponding rates for the Scheduled Tribes (ST) are 8.08 per cent and 5.3 per cent respectively (Mohanty, 2004 : 408). Altogether the SC/ST population constitute 25 per cent of the India's population. Over 25 crores of people in India belong to SC/ST population. They have never been brought to the mainstream as far as the educational status is concerned. Their literacy rate is always 10 points below the general literacy rate. The literacy rate of SC in 1991 was 37.41 per cent (49.91% for male and 23.76% for female). The corresponding figures for the general population were 52.21 per cent, 64.13 per cent and 39.29 per cent respectively. Literacy rate in 1961 was 10.27 per cent (16.96% for male and 3.29% for female). The corresponding figures for the general population were 24.02 per cent, 34.44 per cent and 12.95 per cent respectively (Mohanty, 2004 : 410). Literacy rates among rural women of the STs are as low as 4 per cent in Rajasthan and 9 per cent in Andhra Pradesh. The most distressing dimension of educational disparity is that 90 per cent of the rural women belonging to Scheduled Castes and Scheduled Tribes are illiterate.

Illiteracy accounts for their lack of awareness, lack of self-esteem and self-confidence, lack of information and knowledge about markets, lack of skills, lack of job opportunities and lack of income. They remain in a state of blissful ignorance. Ignorance of one's own rights leads a person to subjugation and deprivation. So, it is essential to create awareness to establish respect for human life, equality, freedom and human dignity.

Girls and boys have differential access to formal education. In India at primary stage, 70 per cent of girl students become dropouts and only 2 per cent enter the college. Dropouts among girls outnumber boys at all stages. Important constraint to girls' education is parents' lack of interest due to girls' unrecognised role as economic supporters to their families prior to marriage. Schooling of girls undermines the visible or invisible economic gains the family earns through their unmarried daughters. Other constraints include direct cost of educating girls, concern for girls' safety and observance of certain socio-cultural traditions restricting mobility of girls. Lack of facilities in schools also contributes to the lower enrolment ratio for the girls. They include absence of women teachers, separate toilets for boys and girls, hostel facilities for girls, lack of perceived relevance of school curricula to girls' immediate needs etc.

Participation in Work

In productive and unproductive work, both in organised and unorganised sectors, there is an unjustifiable discrimination towards women. Comparisons of the work hours of men and women across geographical regions show that women work longer than men in both market and non-market activities, and that is especially true of the rural areas. The majority of women work in the unorganised sector for low wages and at low levels of skills. The agricultural workers constitute by far the largest segment of the workers in the unorganised sector. According to Census, 2001 there are about 10.7 crore agricultural labourers and 12.7 crore medium and large farmers. In spite of the fact that these agricultural workers have such numerical strength, they are extremely vulnerable to exploitation on account of their low level of literacy, low level of awareness, persistent social backwardness and absence of unionism and other forms of viable organization (www.lisd.delhi.nic.in). Women constitute a major segment in the agricultural labours in the rural sector.

Women contribution in the country's economy is 48 per cent of agricultural labour, three-fourth of animal husbandry, 80 per cent of food processing and 100 per cent of domestic work. In hill areas, search for forest products including fuel wood engages a fairly large number of women. The Government of India Country Report presented to the Fourth World Conference on Women, Beijing, 1995, observes that two to three million people in the forest and tribal belts of India earn their livelihood through head loading. Of these, 90 per cent are women. They walk long distances to sell loads of wood. It is the non-participation of women in non-agricultural paid work outside home that makes the difference in the social status of women. In spite of significant contribution to the productive work, women work-force is largely invisible. "Statistical *purdah*" created by existing concepts and the methods of measuring labour participation accounts for the invisibility of women's contribution to National Income of the country (Gopalan, 1995). For example, the census defines work as gainful economic activities but activities done for domestic consumption are not considered as work. So we find that in 1991 only 22 per cent of total female population are considered to be workers in contrast to 52 per cent of the male population though the rural areas show slightly higher female work participation rate, namely 27 per cent, than that of the total rate. In absolute terms, the number of women workers during the last four decades has more than doubled from 40 million in 1951 to 90 million in 1991 (www.indiabudget.nic.in).

As women operate in labour intensive and non-monetised economy, they have become victims of profiteers, middlemen and also of the men in their own family groups. 'If the objectives of development are to enlarge people's choices and increase people's capabilities to exercise such choices, nowhere is the challenge more daunting than in the case of poor women' (Narasimham, 1999 : 35). Conventional strategies for development address only poverty, not powerlessness or subordinate status, which are the crucial issues.

Participation in Community Affairs

The status of women has implication for several social realities. It is a significant reflection of the level of social justice in society. It can easily be concluded that gender equality is a rare phenomenon everywhere including India. Throughout the human history, it is the men who represent the family, community, most of the Governmental and non-Governmental organisations and industrial and commercial establishments. The role of men in decision-making at all levels in any institutional and organisational set-up is visible in India.

Women's political participation is more or less minimal in India. Legislatures both at state and national levels are the most powerful decision-making bodies in the country. The decisions taken at legislative assemblies are considered as the will of the people nation expressed. In India, the political participation of women is limited to the level of mass appealing such as public demonstrations, *satyagrahas*, rallies, and participation in mass movements. Their voice matters little at decision-making levels. Therefore, their participation in Legislatures has remained negligible quantitatively and qualitatively. What is more, child-rearing process is such that few women are conscious of the injustice done to them with regard to poor participation in Legislatures.

Decentralisation and redistribution of power is the chief objective of Seventy-third and Seventy-fourth Amendments of the Constitution of India. Realising the need for adequate political representation of women in the democratic machinery of India, the Constitutional Amendment of 1992 ensured the reservation of seats for women at the grassroots level of democratic set-up, beginning with villages, block to the districts. No such scheme of reservation exists for Assemblies and Parliament. As a result seldom has the representation of women among members of Parliament and State Legislatures has never exceeded 9 per cent (Narasimham, 1999 : 26).

Social learning and individual aspirations of women have a significant role in moulding their role and status in society. What people choose as their goals tends to reflect both their social positioning as well as their individual histories and preferences. The discrimination in the social status between men and women has thus become something unconscious, intrinsic and so instinctive that it uncovers itself naturally in assuming social roles beginning from the family, the nucleus of society, till the Parliament, the highest legislative body in India.

Indian culture is such that women are appreciated more for their excellence in household management rather than their public participation and discharge of public responsibilities. Even if they are successful in their professional career, if they are not able to discharge their duties and responsibilities as wife, mother, daughter-in-law, and a sister-in-law, at her husbands' house, they are not appreciated both in their home nor are they respected by the public at large in society. Women's participation in development programmes both of Governmental and non-Governmental agencies is thus severely circumscribed by cultural constraints. As a consequence, they are deprived of the benefits from such programmes. Patriarchal attitudes and assumptions have effectively made women's participation and contribution to the society invisible. Deeply rooted cultural patterns confine women largely to house and to invisible activities. Any attempt to re-examine the rationality of the traditional roles of women in society proves uncomfortable for those who benefit from women's subordination. Women empowerment in Indian context has much to do with the mental set both of men and women.

Tacitly religious and traditional values safeguard the interests of patriarchy. Patriarchal attitude operates through family norms, state policies and laws and they keep women in a subordinate position. Women's subordination is deeply embedded in the consciousness both of men and women and is reinforced through religious beliefs, cultural practices, and educational systems that assign lesser status to women. We can find a number of references in most of the religious texts where women are given a subordinate status to men. We do not have count of many religious leaders and saints who are women.

Crimes Against Women

According to National Crime Research Bureau (NCRB), Ministry of Home Affairs, crimes against women are rape, kidnapping and abduction, dowry death, torture, molestation, sexual harassment, importation of girls, indecent representation of women, crimes committed under Sati (Prevention) Act and crimes committed under Immoral Traffic (Prevention) Act (NCRB, 2004). Table 1.1 describes the statistics of crimes against women in India.

Table 1.1 : Incidence of crimes committed against women in India during 2003

Sl.No.	*Crime head*	*Total*
1	Rape	15,847
2	Kidnapping and abduction	13,296
3	Dowry death	6,208
4	Torture/cruelties by husband or family members	50,703
5	Molestation	32,939
6	Sexual Harassment/eve teasing	12,325
7	Importation of Girls	46
8	Sati (Prevention) Act	0
9	Immoral Traffic (Prevention) Act	5,510
10	Indecent Representation of Women (Prevention) Act	1,043
11	Dowry Prohibition Act	2684
	Total	140,601

Source : NCRB, *Crime in India*.

The table shows that the incidence of crimes against women is substantial in spite of growing awareness about women's rights. NCRB data brings out that at the national level, there were 15,847 rape victims. Of these, 62.3 per cent were in the age group of 18 to 30 years. Offenders were known to the victims in 87 per cent cases. Neighbours were offenders in 34.3 per cent of rape cases. Andhra Pradesh reported 13.1 per cent of total crimes committed against women followed by Madhya Pradesh (10.1%) and Uttar Pradesh (9.1%). The number of crimes committed per lakh population for crime against women reported to the police worked out to be 7.59 in 2003 (NCRB, 2005).

Crimes against women in Delhi are also on the rise. Total rape cases reported in Delhi in 2003 were 380 and molestation cases were 360. Some of the incidences of rape which attracted the media attention in the capital were : The rape of the Swiss diplomat (14th October, 2003), rape of a nurse at Shani Mukund Hospital by a sweeper boy (7th September, 2003), rape of the 17 year old girl by the President's bodyguards at Buddha Garden (October, 2003), rape of a student of the Maulana Abul Kalam Medical College (October, 2003), 16 year old patient raped by doctor for two days in the hostel of Safdarjung Hospital (TOI, 17th May, 2004). Table 1.2 presents information on rape cases during 1999-2003 in Delhi.

Table 1.2 : Rape cases reported in Delhi

Year	*Cases reported*	*Convicted*
1999	503	245
2000	591	280
2001	288	116
2002	442	98
2003	380	91

An analysis of these cases reveals that the rapists knew the victims in 95 per cent of the cases. 58 per cent of the rapists were between the 18 and 25 years. Over 30 per cent of them were school dropouts 32 per cent of them were illiterate. Only 40 per cent of the rapists were convicted. What is more disquieting is the fact that 60 per cent of the rape victims were minor. Most rapes were committed by first timers with no past criminal record (TOI, 18th October, 2003).

It may be added that the victims of rape undergo trauma that leave an indelible mark on their psyche often irrecoverable. The miseries and psychological problems they face afterwards are countless. A study conducted by Swanchetan Society for Mental Health reveals that it normally takes 13 weeks to recover from the immediate trauma. 20 per cent of the victims tend to withdraw into a shell and 35 per cent tend to rationalise their bad experiences (HT, 20th October, 2003).

Concept and Meaning of Women Empowerment

Women's empowerment primarily means having their contribution recognised and valued. In the context of empowerment of women in the domestic world, Justice Krishna Iyer remarks, 'Cooking is women's burden, home her workhouse, fuel collection is women's task, and drinking water carrying is also her job. Looking after children, sending them to school, taking care of their food and health and doing the menial jobs in the home are her responsibility. Why should it be? Sharing and caring is gender justice' (Iyer, 1993 : 20). Sharing the household responsibilities and caring for each other on equal basis are essentially the empowerment process in the family.

It was only in the latter half of the 1970s the concept of women's empowerment became a popular concern. There are several models of empowerment, viz. self-help, liberationist (feminist), managerial and market (economic) models of empowerment. It is important to recognise its regulatory as well as libratory potential (Davies, 2000 : 117). Empowerment has the potential to establish an equal status for men and women (regulatory) as well as to emancipate women from a miserable state of being (liberationist). Empowerment includes several modes of intervention. Financial intervention aims to increase women's access to credit. Enterprise development facilitates women's access to innovative technologies, skills and training in management and production packages. Marketing strategies seek to increase their knowledge about markets and ensure markets for products produced by women's groups. Bargaining strategies mobilise women to struggle for higher wages, better working conditions, job security, etc.

In this context it is important to understand the state of powerlessness women experience. There are 'three approaches for understanding women's powerlessness' (Bisnath and Elson, 2001). (i) Women are powerless due to factors beyond their control such as patriarchal forces which determine women's roles and relationships in the society. (ii) Powerlessness of women is due to factors within. It focuses on roles women prefer and assume automatically in the household or the workplace. (iii) The third approach locates the process of women's subordination in multiple domains either simultaneously or sequentially. When these approaches are analysed we can find two sets of factors that contribute to the powerlessness of women, viz. external and internal factors. There are conditions that beyond the control of women as well as there are certain stereotypes within the mindset of women that are responsible for their powerlessness.

Empowerment begins with awareness of gender inequalities. The awareness definition of women's empowerment refers to 'a process whereby women, individually and collectively, become aware of how power relations operate in their lives and gain the self-confidence and strength to challenge gender inequalities' (Xaxa, 2001 : 203). Autonomy, which is basic to democracy, comes from awareness of one's rights and responsibilities, and awareness comes from information. Information and awareness ensure that exploitation can be fought and reduced, and in that sense, awareness is empowerment. Women must recognise that they are disadvantaged, be aware of what they can do peacefully, constructively and legally to overcome their oppression. Disseminating information through a non-conventional approach, based on participatory approach, empowers women. What is important is not so much what people receive, as how much involvement they have, and what part they play in the process of growth itself. Integrating power, consciousness and learning, Gutierrez defines 'empowerment' as "...basing the helping relationship on collaboration, trust and share power; utilising small groups; accepting the client's definition of the problem; identifying and building on the client's strengths; raising the client's consciousness of issues of class and power; actively involving the client in the change process; teaching specific skills; ... experiencing a sense of personal power within the helping relationships; and mobilising resources or advocating for clients" (Gutierrez *et al.*, 1995 : 535).

Popular meaning of empowerment is individualistic and it implies a little more than feeling good or powerful. According to the country report of Government of India, empowerment means moving from a position of powerlessness to one of power. It intends to promote women's inherent strengths. One should not misunderstand that empowering women is to give them power to establish their superiority over others. To empower women is to enable them "to flower their latent talents, abilities and capacity and real identity; to enable them to develop self-dignity, to raise voice and fight against injustice, exploitation, abuse and violence done to them" (Kapur, 2001).

The concept of empowerment brings into mind an activity or an attempt of making someone powerful, helping the downtrodden to have control over their life, facilitating the weak to gain strength, to help increase one's self-esteem, to help someone to be assertive, self-confident, to enable someone to confront injustice and oppression, to support someone to fight for his/her rights, etc. Empowering women means "strengthening them to confront the traditional patriarchal forces and biases operating in family, community, caste, religion and society" (Arya, 2000 : 147). The process of empowerment facilitates the struggle for social justice and women's equality through a transformation of economic, social and political structures at national and international levels.

We need to identify power, less in terms of domination over others (which means that a gain for women implies a loss for men) and more in terms of the capacity of women to increase their self-reliance and internal strength. This implies the right to determine choices in life, to influence the direction of change, and the ability to gain control over resources. The Beijing Declaration of the United Nations has clarified the nature of empowerment in its preamble itself. "[We are determined to] intensify efforts to ensure equal enjoyment of all human rights and fundamental freedoms for all women and girls who face multiple barriers to their empowerment and advancement because of such factors as their race, age, language, ethnicity, culture, religion, or disability, or because they are indigenous people" (Beijing Declaration, 1995 : Para. 32).

Empowerment is about power, and women empowerment is nothing but balancing the distribution of power between men and women. The process of gaining control over the self, over ideology and the resources may be termed empowerment. In Indian context, women's empowerment does mean "the loss of man's traditional power and rights to control over the woman of the household" (Pamei, 2001). Empowerment of Indian woman means to constrain man of his enjoyment of undue rights over a woman of his household, viz. his control of her body and her physical mobility; his right to physically abuse or violate her; his right to spend family income on personal pleasures and vices; his right to abandon her and take other wives; and his right to take unilateral decisions which affect the whole family. Empowerment for women is facilitating her to gain the self-confidence and strength to challenge gender inequalities at the household, community, national, regional and international levels.

Woman Empowerment means enlarging the choices and productivity levels of women. Empowerment strategies intend to overturn cultural, economic and political institutions and processes, which perpetuate gender subordination. Women's empowerment is often interpreted as increased access of women to productive resources, expanded choices and participation in decision-making (www.unifem.org). Empowerment of women is defined as a process of "securing greater access to, and command over resources, access to knowledge as well as ideological shifts that bring about changes in how women perceive themselves and how they are perceived in relation to the community" (Daver, 2001 : 52).

There is close relationship between development and empowerment. Empowerment is development with justice. It means mainstreaming the neglected, underprivileged, weaker sections, and the marginalised groups into the society by providing various state-sponsored socio-economic benefits (employment, education, training, health care, water, housing, etc.). Empowerment is establishing a right-based partnership relationship with the people who are marginalized. It facilitates self-monitored development process on the part of women who are discriminated. Since the mid-eighties the development practices expressed the ideal of empowerment. "The significant point of departure here is that while the earlier discourses saw the poor people as beneficiaries, the emergent one has recognised them as partners of development" (Roy, 2001 : 14).

Empowerment involves changes in social and economic institutions, political ideologies and traditional practices. It requires a drastic change in the mindset of the marginalised people through conscientisation. The process of empowerment is directed to create a collective identity of the downtrodden for the demolition of the structure of subordination imposed on them. It will provide them with enough space in the society, access to knowledge and resources for their material and social well-being. Such process will generate a social environment free of inequalities to each member of the society required for their self-fulfilment and expression. The goals of women's empowerment are to challenge patriarchal ideology (male domination and women's subordination), to transform the institutions that reinforce and perpetuate gender discrimination and social inequality (the family, caste, class, religion, educational institutions, the media, health systems, laws and civil codes, political processes, development models, and Government institutions) and to enable poor women to gain access to, and control of, both material and non-material resources.

Changes are possible only through sustained social movements at grassroots level. By organising around immediate practical needs and facing the challenges that result, women tend to develop a deeper awareness of the necessity for more fundamental changes in power structures. Addressing practical needs means to extend social protection to the women by increasing their piece rates and wages, by reducing dependence on middleman for job orders, and by providing health, housing, education and other appropriate benefits. "An organisation of merely women of affluent rural women cannot fully represent the problems, interests, concerns or priorities of the poorest, most overworked, invisible, deprived, exploited and unprotected group of working women in the world" (Majumdar, 2001 : 149). They need their own organisations to break the barriers of inequality, invisibility and powerlessness. The overall objective of this empowerment strategy is to help the majority of women who are 70 per cent of the poor citizens of the world play an effective and meaningful role in development, not as victims or beneficiaries, but as partners and leaders.

Empowerment is an active process of self-help. It is an art of self-help. Empowerment cannot be done from the outside; it is something women need to do for themselves. Aim of women empowerment is to help develop adult women. An adult woman is a person who can look at a situation, weigh the *pros* and *cons*, take decisions and bear the consequences of these decisions with courage and without feeling guilt. There are two ways of understanding the process of Empowerment, viz. Empowerment that is externally induced involving the creation of conditions that enable women to exercise their autonomy and self-empowerment, a process where women find time and space of their own to re-examine their lives critically and collectively. "While the former process denotes the removal of barriers to, as well as the facilitation of, women's access to and control over resources, the latter emphasises women's agency in seeking higher levels of access and control" (www.unifem.org). Women's empowerment consists of acquiring knowledge and an understanding of gendered relations and developing a sense of self-worth and a belief in one's ability to secure desired changes. It recognises the right to control one's life, gaining the ability to generate choices and developing the ability to organise and/or influence the direction of social change to create a more just social and economic order. Armed with their growing strength, women begin to assert their right to control resources, including their bodies and participate equally in decisions within the family, community and village. Empowerment becomes an inevitable change, which the world around is forced to acknowledge.

Women's empowerment is to wipe out gender bias and implant positive attitudes from the minds of men, women and children so that the family and the society at large would participate in the planning process for women's advancement. When the mindset is cleared of prejudices and stereotypes, women will be able to perceive the reality, rationally and think for themselves independently. Once the women are able to think of themselves as rightful citizens to a better life, overcoming the culture of submission will become easier. And in this process it will be possible to check corruption because the women empowered will demand accountability. There will be a reduction in environmental degradation because the people who are going to be affected are the ones who will take the decisions, rather than outsiders who will look only at their own profits and convenience. Changes in laws, civil codes, systems of property rights, and legal institutions that underwrite male domination and privileges, are essential for the achievement of women's equality.

Women empowerment is a dynamic process. Empowerment is a social process or well-planned social change by-products of which are empowered women. With education comes employment and with this comes economic freedom. Empowerment presupposes primarily economic independence. In the process of empowerment, women look at old problems in new ways, analyse their situation, recognise their strengths, access new kinds of information and knowledge, acquire new skills, and initiate action aimed at gaining greater control over resources, situation and ideologies. This is a spiral process which leads to greater and greater changes and more and more empowerment. Problem identification, action for change and analysis of that action and its outcome lead to higher levels of consciousness of more fundamental problem. "Levels of Empowerment are pre-empowerment, intra-personal at micro level, interpersonal at mezzo level and institutional at macro level" (Busch and Valentine, 2000 : 92).

Savitri Bisnath and Diane Elson have presented a set of approaches to women's empowerment (www.unifem.org). These different approaches are useful to understand deeply the causes of women's powerlessness and different interventions that lead to empowerment. The integrated development approach interprets women's powerlessness as a result of their greater poverty and lower access to health care, education, and resources. Strategies under this approach aim to enhance women's economic status as well as access to public services. The economic development approach situates women's economic vulnerability at the centre of their powerlessness. It assumes that economic empowerment positively impacts every aspect of women's existence. The strategies are for strengthening women's position as workers through organising and providing them with access to support services. The consciousness-raising approach is based on unfavourable gender relations and women's status. It ascribes women's powerlessness to the ideology and practice of patriarchy. Strategies focus on organising women to recognise and challenge gender based discrimination in all aspects of their lives. Though successful in enabling women to address their strategic needs, this approach is ineffective in assisting them to meet their immediate or practical needs.

Women empowerment has both manifest and latent aspects. Some of the manifest aspects of empowerment are ownership of property and consumption of resources, better exercise of the right to avail facilities, rights over one's own body and life, the right for decision-making on crucial matters, greater mobility outside the family, reduction of infant mortality and female foeticide, reduction of morbidity and achievement of greater life expectancy of women, the right to exercise Family Planning methods and the right to limit the number of children. Some of the latent aspects of Empowerment are feeling better sense of security, improvement of self-image.

Major indicators of empowerment are autonomy to move out for recreational purposes such as exhibition, park, marriages other than that of the relatives, picnics, religious ceremonies, films etc.; individual autonomy in social and economic activities; autonomy to wear or not to wear *burkha/ purdah*; membership and freedom to participate in social organisations; visits to bank and freedom to spend money; individual autonomy to exercise franchise, i.e. the freedom to participate as a voter or a contestant; autonomy in decision-making on significant matters such as purchase of household articles, education of children, employment of children, preparation of food, marriage of children, savings, income, etc.; and autonomy to follow any hobby and a significant attitudinal change (Nayak, 1983 : 5-6).

Indicators of Empowerment of Women

Human Development Report also gives out indicators of empowerment of women are included in the Report (UNDP, 2005). The report has identified 7 indicators to map out the gender status in various countries. These include Gender Development Index (GDI), Gender Empowerment Measure (GEM), Status of Gender Equality, Gender in Political Participation, Gender in Education, Gender in Economic Activities and Gender in Work Burden and Time Allocation.

Gender Development Index (GDI) considers the comparative status of men and women in life expectancy at birth, adult literacy rate, combined primary, secondary and tertiary gross enrolment ratio (educational) and estimated earned income. There is some correspondence between the HDI ranking and the GDI ranking. Gender development has a positive correlation with Human Development. European countries are far ahead of Asian countries in both HDI as well as GDI. Life expectancy at birth is always favourable to women. It may be due to the better natural disposition of female foetus to survive. Consistently the adult literacy rate is higher for men than women in all the nations. The disparity in literacy rate is more among less developed countries compared to the countries with higher HDI status.

Table 1.3 : Gender-related Development Index (GDI)

		Gender-related development index (GDI)		Life expectancy at birth (years) 2003		Adult literacy rate(%age 15 and above) 2003	
HDI rank	*Countries*	*Rank (GDI)*	*Value*	*Female*	*Male*	*Female*	*Male*
1	Norway	1	0.96	81.9	76.8	99.9	99.9
3	Australia	2	0.954	82.8	77.7	99.9	99.9
10	United States	8	0.942	80	74.6	99.9	99.9
11	Japan	14	0.937	85.4	78.4	99.9	99.9
15	United Kingdom	15	0.937	80.6	76	99.9	99.9
16	France	16	0.935	83	75.9	99.9	99.9
20	Germany	20	0.926	81.5	75.7	99.9	99.9
85	China	64	0.754	73.5	69.9	86.5	95.1
93	Sri Lanka	66	0.747	76.8	71.5	88.6	92.2
120	South Africa	92	0.652	50.2	46.8	80.9	84.1
127	India	98	0.586	65	61.8	47.8	73.4
135	Pakistan	107	0.508	63.2	62.8	35.2	61.7
139	Bangladesh	105	0.514	63.7	62.1	31.4	50.3

Source : UNDP, *Human Development Report*, 2005.

The Gross Enrolment Ratio and the Estimated Earned Income are proportional to the HDI rank. In both the parameters generally men fare better than women in less developed countries, while the gross enrolment ratio is favourable to women in European Countries that are placed high in the GDI.

Gender status in economic activity is estimated from the women's economic activity rate, percentage of women to men rate, percentage women contributing to family workers, percentage of women workers in primary (agriculture), secondary (industry) and tertiary (services) sector. Participation of women in productive works is a significant variable for women empowerment. There is no correlation between gender inequality and the HDI ranking. Global rate of women's economic activity is 55.6 per cent. Pakistan and India have the lowest percentage of women in the productive sector, while China has the highest percentage (72.4%) women in productive sector. All the countries except China and Russia show an increasing trend of women participation in economic activity. Pakistan, which has the lowest percentage of women in economic activity, has shown the highest percentage of increase compared to the corresponding status in 1990. In no countries women contribute equal share as that of men. The global average is 89 per cent of the male rate. Pakistan and India have the corresponding rate much below the global average.

Table 1.4 : Gender inequality in economic activity

		Female economic activity rate (age 15 and above)			*Contributing family workers*	
HDI rank	*Country*	*Rate (%) 2003*	*Index (1990= 100) 2003*	*As % of male rate 2003*	*Female (as % of total) 1995-2003*	*Male (as % of total) 1995-2003*
1	Norway	60.3	111	86	63	38
10	United States	59.6	107	83	63	37
11	Japan	51.2	104	68	81	19
15	United Kingdom	53.5	106	76	68	32
16	France	49.3	108	78	—	—
20	Germany	48.0	101	71	78	22
62	Russian Federation	59.1	98	83	42	58
85	China	72.4	98	86	—	—
93	Sri Lanka	43.5	108	56	56	44
127	India	42.5	105	50	—	—
135	Pakistan	36.7	129	44	33	67
139	Bangladesh	66.5	101	76	81	19
	World	55.6	103	89	—	—

Source : UNDP, *Human Development Report*, 2005.

Gender bias operates in work burden and time allocation. Women bear greater burden in terms of workload and duration of work. Gender consideration is very much seen in the participation in market and non-market activities. Equality in work burden and time allocation is a goal to achieve globally. In all the countries, work burden is more for women. In Germany and the UK women and men share equally the work burden. There is no significant correlation between the HDI rank and the sharing of work burden. In South Africa and the

Hilly regions of Nepal the ratio of work burden between women and men is 122.

Work burden for women is less in developed countries compared to the developing and underdeveloped countries. Women spend most of their work time in non-market economic activities while men invariably engage themselves more in market activities in all the countries. In developing countries people engage mostly in market activities. In India and Japan more than 60 per cent of the total time spend by people are allotted for market activities while in Germany the corresponding figure is only 44 per cent. Market activities refer to market-oriented production activities. In India 92 per cent of total non-market activities are done by women and only 8 per cent is done by men, while 65 per cent of the market activities are done by men and 35 per cent is done by women. Equilibrium in this regard seems to be a distant goal as far as the present situation is concerned. HDI status does not seem to be a relevant factor in the time allocation of market and non-market activities between women and men.

More people in the developing and underdeveloped countries are engaged in the primary sector while more people in the developed countries are engaged in the tertiary sector. The participation of women in developed countries is more in service sector and less in industry where male participation is more than female. In the developing countries participation of women in the primary sector is more than the men and in secondary and tertiary sectors women participation is less than that of men. It is a clear indication of gender bias in the Third World Countries. Even if the data about India is not available it can be assumed that the status of India will not differ much from Pakistan, Sri Lanka and Bangladesh that show all the characteristics of the Third World Countries with regard to women's participation in economic activities. It may be estimated that as the economy grows more people will be transferred from the primary sector to secondary and tertiary sectors. The participation of women in the tertiary sector will be more than that of men who will engage themselves more in industrial activities. The contribution of women to the income of the family is not in proportion to the participation of women in economic activities which points towards another significant gender discrimination in the wage/salary structure.

Table 1.5 : Women's Political Participation

HDI rank	Countries	Year women received right [a] To vote	To stand for election	Year first woman elected (E) or appointed (A) to Parliament
1	Norway	1907, 1913	1907, 1913	1911 A
3	Australia	1902, 1962	1902, 1962	1943 E
10	United States	1920, 1960	1788[b]	1917 E
11	Japan	1945, 1947	1945, 1947	1946 E
15	United Kingdom	1918, 1928	1918, 1928	1918 E
16	France	1944	1944	1945 E
20	Germany	1918	1918	1919 E
62	Russian Federation	1918	1918	1993 E[c]
85	China	1949	1949	1954 E
93	Sri Lanka	1931	1931	1947 E
120	South Africa	1930, 1994	1930, 1994	1933 E
127	India	1950	1950	1952 E
134	Bhutan	1953	1953	1975 E
135	Pakistan	1947	1947	1973 E
136	Nepal	1951	1951	1952 A
139	Bangladesh	1972	1972	1973 E

a. Data refer to the year in which right to vote or stand for election on a universal and equal basis was recognised. Where two years are shown, the first refers to the first partial recognition of the right to vote or stand for election.

b. No information is available on the year all women received the right to stand for election. However, the constitution does not mention gender with regard to this right.

c. Refers to the year women were elected to the current Parliamentary system.

Source : UNDP, *Human Development Report*, 2005.

Gender Equality and Women's Political Participation takes into consideration the year women received right to vote and the right to stand for election, the year first woman got elected (E) or appointed (A) to Parliament, percentage of women in Government at Ministerial level and the percentage of seats held by women in Parliament. Women's participation in the medieval and ancient civilisation is not comparable with that of today's participation. Democracy is invention of the 20th century and the parameters of political participation are relevant only for the contemporary civilisation. In no countries, women had political rights before 1900 A.D. It is because the modern democracy with universal franchise and elected Parliament has become the popular form of Government only in this century.

It is interesting to see that in the USA the right to stand for election was allowed prior to the recognition of the right of women to vote. It is because of omission of gender reference in its constitution. In all the countries except Russia, Bhutan and Pakistan, women got elected to the Parliament soon after their right to stand for election was recognised. It is because in these countries democratic form of Government came into existence only recently. Therefore, gender equality in political life was recognised in Russia in 1918 but the woman to be elected to its Parliament was only in 1993. Russia was reorganised in democratic pattern only in 1991.

The percentage of women at Ministerial level and the percentage of seats held by women in Parliament are indicators of political empowerment. In European countries and the USA, women hold more than 30 per cent of Government jobs at the Ministerial level while in Asian countries the corresponding figure is just 10 per cent. It can be seen that Pakistan has a better representation in this regard, compared to India. Similar situation exists with regard to the percentage of seats in Parliament held by women. The figures are much lower compared to the previous. It is consistently seen that the women are shy to hold elected positions in the Government. The reasons are yet to be ascertained. Either the women hesitate to enter actively into political campaign or gender bias work against them in election. Whatever be the reasons, it is time to find out the reasons for their poor representation in Parliament and bring out the ratio closer to 1.

Gender Empowerment Measure takes into consideration the variables such as seats in Parliament held by women, number of senior officials and managers, number of women professional and technical workers and the ratio of estimated women to men earned income. There is little correlation between the HDI Ranking and GEM ranking. India is at 127 according to HDI ranking while seats in Parliament held by women as percentage of total is only 9.3. Pakistan at the position of 135 in HDI ranking has 20.6 per cent women representation in its Legislature. Pakistan is ahead of Sri Lanka in GEM ranking even if far behind in GDI ranking. Compared to Asian Countries, the European Countries fare better in GEM status. Participation of women in economic activities is much more than in political decision-making. The share of women in professional and technical work is higher than men in Russia and the United States. However, the estimated female share in the earned income is lower than the male share in all the countries.

Gender status in education is estimated on account of various parameters such as adult literacy rate, youth literacy rate, net primary enrolment ratio, net secondary enrolment ratio and gross tertiary enrolment ratio. Empowerment and education are related positively. The educational status of women and the gender equality in education is a relevant indicator of women empowerment. Gender inequality in Education is a reality in Asian Countries. Equality is prevalent in European and other developed countries. Equality in education is proportional to HDI ranking. Literacy rate is very poor in countries with lower HDI ranks. Countries with lower HDI ranking have also greater gender disparity in education. However, it is interesting to see that literacy rate for young women is higher, compared to that of adult women. It is a good sign that the younger generation is better educated than the older. It is because of greater gender sensitisation of educational policy makers in developing countries. The educational status is much better in Sri Lanka, compared to India. India needs to progress a lot both in raising the literacy rate of women and in bringing gender equality in education.

The net enrolment ratio is the ratio of enrolled children of the official age for the education level indicated to the total population at that age. The net enrolment ratio is lower in developing and underdeveloped countries, compared to developed countries. The ratio of females to males in net enrolment is seen favourable to women in developed countries. It is due to the favourable sex ratio in those countries for women. Gross enrolment ratio of women in South East Asian countries is very low. The situation in India is not comparable with other countries. We need an urgent strategy to bring all the girls of educable age into the school.

One of the major drawbacks of the above-mentioned indicators of women empowerment drawn from the UNDP report is that to some extent their comparative study has overlooked the cultural diversity and underestimated the impact of geographical, social and anthropological factors that affect the living style, child rearing practices, evolution of social norms, values and social frame of references, each of the international communities has set for self-evaluation and for evaluation of other cultures. The vital issue to be addressed is that whether it is proper to compare the culture and living standard of Irish or Sweedish citizen with that of India or Bangladesh upon a uniform parameter. Do the terms like freedom, autonomy and women's rights carry the same meaning and magnitude in these countries? As the physical conditions like geography and climate are different, so too the social and cultural factors vary in different parts of the World. The differences are too much to be compared upon a uniform criterion. Therefore every community has to develop culture specific indicators of women empowerment, which are relative to time and space.

Impediments for Empowerment and the Role of Social Work

There are certain impediments that come in the way of achieving women's empowerment. They include : (1) Traditions, customs, practices, rituals, dogmas, beliefs, ideologies, attitudes and mindset, social structures and oppressive institutions which snatch away their freedom and right to live with dignity; (2) Degeneration of humanitarian values such as social and family values of mutual love, respect, understanding, trust, caring and sharing, compassion, forgiveness, flexibility, truthfulness, honesty and lack of considering every person as an equally worthy human being; (3) Prevalence of values of materialism, consumerism and of accompanying motives of greed and unhealthy competitions as offsprings of LPG (Liberalisation, Privatisation and Globalisation) model of economic development; (4) Preponderance of inhuman values of violence including sexual violence, abuse, vulgar sex and cruelty; and (5) Unhealthy, negative, gender-based attitude and psyche of men, women and society towards girl children and women (Kapur, 2002 : 3).

Major constraints to women's empowerment lie in well-entrenched customs and mores, traditional, religious and cultural attitudes towards women and power relationships between men and women in the family and larger community, most of which aim to maintain the subordinate position of women. Any intervention for the reversal of women's role in the society such as, educational, legal or economic reforms inevitably brings tension in the relationship between men and women. "The tension between women's empowerment and the potential loss of privileges of men occurred when changes in land ownership was introduced to enable women to own land. Now that educated women have come out of the domestic world, problem of marital adjustment has also come to light in urban areas" (Kaldate, 1990 : 61).

The social worker has to create enabling conditions for women's empowerment, which include participatory democracy, critical self-reflection and collective action. Empowerment facilitates women to experience personal power from within and collective power from solidarity with other women or men. For empowering women solid steps are to be taken for changing positively the outlook, psyche and attitude of men, women, and society towards women. The specific steps and measures to be taken to change attitudes and behaviour towards women have not been mentioned in the national policy. For development of such positive attitudes it is rather imperative to devalue the increasingly prevalent values of materialism, greed, selfishness and consumerism. This could be done through value education. Value education for developing positive attitude towards women must start in the family, which is most basic and fundamental school for learning. Parents must set example of living values themselves and the children will automatically learn them by the process of socialisation. Socialising includes all the process by which a person acquires one's social skill, roles, norms, values attitudes and behaviour. The impact of the family is great in the development of attitudes and values.

Effective family education should be provided for healing and strengthening marriage and family relationships. This deals with a wide range of significant areas like integrated health, marriage and family relationship, gender roles, sexuality including sex education and gender issues, parenting including egalitarian child rearing skills, emotional and other needs of adolescents, communication skills, interpersonal relationships, positive attitude, family values, counselling, human rights and duties, creating positive self-image, self-confidence, self-worth and trust.

Social workers have effective role in educating women for empowerment. Education is very close to empowerment. Women, who constitute half the world population, work nearly two-third of its working hours, but receive only one-tenth of the world's income and own less than one-hundredth of the world's property. Only education can help to uplift the condition of women. Venkataiah (2001) surveys the scenario of women education in Third World Countries and emphasises the need for non-formal, primary and higher education of women. Right for access to elementary education is a fundamental right. The benefits of education are manifold. Educating women results in improved productivity, income, and economic development, as well as a better quality of life, notably a healthier and a better-nourished population. At the same time, it is clear that education empowers women, providing them with increased autonomy in every sphere of their lives. Reformers saw education as the key to mitigating the evils of child marriages, seclusion and the oppression of widows that were extremely severe within the higher castes.

Empowerment, enrichment and enlightenment of women are impossible without proper education. By education it is proved beyond doubt that men were no longer 'Gods' for women and women no longer 'dolls' for men. As a result of reawakening of women, men's supremacy becomes a thing of the past. The spread of education make them aware of their rights and privileges in the society. Educated mothers' provide better health care for the household. There is a high correlation between female literacy and life expectancy at birth. Higher literacy brings down the rate of infant mortality and the average number of children born per woman. Educated mother even while belonging to lower socio-economic strata, provide better health, nutrition and care to their children as well as to themselves. They also have better access to health facilities outside the home. Being literate saves women from being cheated by employers. It has also helped in raising their confidence and courage. With rising awareness, they have been able to 'fight corruption at different levels and have taken up the issues of unequal wages, lack of drinking water, deforestation, child labour, dowry and problems of destitute women' (Sachchidananda, 2001 : 196). Civil society at large and social workers in particular have a significant role in removing various constraints for education of women and girl children.

There is a need for innovative intervention of social workers in the field of physical empowerment of women, which deals with her equal opportunity for biological survival. Physical empowerment of women means ensuring holistic health for women especially reproductive health. Professional social workers must facilitate grassroots level organisation of women for training, advocacy and liaison services to safeguard the fundamental right of women for biological survival. Census reports over the past decades have repeatedly confirmed the growing trends of deliberately reducing the chance for the survival of girl children in India. Pre-natal sex detection tests adversely affect the survival of girl children. It makes women's lives more insecure, restrictive, and less dignified. Immediate attention is invited of the medical social workers to sensitise the medical practitioners, general public and the policy makers regarding the right of girl children to be born and live for the good of future generations.

Another field of professional social work related with empowerment of women is psychiatric social work, which deals with emotional and mental health of women. Psychological well-being is an essential requirement of women's empowerment. Ageing and retirement are important emotional concerns that come in the way of human development. Since women outlive men, ageing is more a women related issue. Ageing is a physical condition having much psychological impacts. Ageing is often accompanied by retiring from an active social and work life. Retiring includes loss of income, status, identity or supporting networks within a familiar work setting. Concern for senior women citizens is a vital part of women empowerment. They need to be assisted by social workers to become independent and self-reliant in old age. The older women need to be looked through the eyes of love, admiration, tenderness and acceptance.

Social workers and professional bodies have a significant role in creating venues for economic empowerment of women. The motivation for work for a majority of Indian women is the "sheer economic necessity" (Sherwani, 1992 : 89). Women's work participation and their relative contribution to total family income are higher in households with lower economic status. This means that the economically poorer families are more dependent upon women's productivity. It also means that in addition to viewing women as a key partner group for poverty alleviation programmes, anti-poverty policies need to "recognise and harness the strategic potential of women as critical players, in the process of moving their families out of poverty" (Devasia and Devassia, 1990 : 160). A right-based approach is essential for framing any poverty alleviation strategy.

Studies have established the phenomenon of 'feminisation of poverty'. Poverty and underdevelopment were assumed to put all members of affected households at an equal disadvantage. It is proved now that the 'costs and benefits of development are disproportionately distributed, depending on an individual member's sex, age, and relationship to the household head'. Women constitute the major share of the poor. Of the estimated 1.3 billion people living in poverty, more than 70 per cent are female. It cannot be assumed that females will automatically benefit from an increase in the "household income" (Devasia and Devassia, 1990 : 8). Any serious commitment to poverty alleviation must reflect this reality. There is an increasing awareness about the need for the economic empowerment of women below poverty line. Social workers need to use their skills and knowledge to impart skill training and training for capacity building for the cause of economic empowerment of women.

The role of professional social workers in the process of women empowerment becomes clearer when we understand the nature of empowerment, which is essentially a 'bottom-up' activity. Social workers should not play the role of an expert in their intervention because empowerment is clearly a bottom-up process and what is required is their participatory facilitation. The professional service must be based on equal relations rooted in trust, honesty, respect, reliability and openness, which will facilitate empowerment (Croft and Beresford, 2000 : 118). This egalitarian approach alone makes the social worker's role really professional.

Review of Literature

Much research has been done on violence against women, discrimination and exploitation of girl children, miseries and hardships of housewives, feminisation of poverty, under achievement of girls in education, parameters of women empowerment, empowerment of tribal women, political empowerment of women, economic empowerment of women and significance of literacy in empowerment of women. Let us take a close look.

Social Empowerment of Women

Raj Kumar Pruthi *et al.* (2001) have looked at women's plight and positions through the ages from the Vedic period down to the present times. Women achievers have been given their place of pride in their respective fields. The authors have attempted to explain various situations by quoting extensively from the *Puranas* and *Smrtis*. Their findings are that the women have always been struggling for equal recognition in society (Pruthi *et al.*, 2001). History as a record of the past brings into light of the social status of women at various points of time. History witnesses the progress of humanity from a state of nomadic, uncivilised, primitive and animal like living to a settled, civilised and modern life. At some point in history physical strength of men acquired social, political and religious sanction, which enabled them to exercise rights over women. There is no reason to believe that men and women in survival struggle during the food gathering stage were concerned about gender inequality. Equality and empowerment are considered higher needs at par with esteem needs. Economic well-being is precondition for the rise of empowerment needs if it is related with self-actualisation. However, there is historical evidence in India that the gender inequality is as old as Indian History. The Position of Women in India—right from the ancient through medieval to the modern times—has always attracted debate. Some scholars opine that women enjoyed greater freedom in the days of yore; others hold that the opposite is true.

Tribal communities in North East and South West parts of India, being matriarchal, confer more freedom and autonomy to women. However, majority of mainstream women belong to patriarchal society where women have to struggle very hard to establish their own identity. Patriarchal bias has always stood as stumbling blocks in the path of empowerment of women. Vina Mazumdar has depicted the process of Women Empowerment quoting her own experience of working with marginalised women of Bengal. 'Poor, illiterate, landless and seasonal migrant agricultural labour women in West Bengal teach of the 5 boundaries that had confined their lives, hopes, articulation, thinking and identities. They were (i) the family, (ii) the village, (iii) the caste/tribe and kin group, (iv) class and occupation, and (v) their resulting status among their neighbourhood. They say, "Before we formed our *samitis*, we had no names outside our immediate family or kin. We were only *kamins*. After organising and discovering/demonstrating our collective strength and capacities, people called us by our names. As we grew stronger and learnt about our rights under law, we became *didis*—even to local policeman and *neta*—even though we were still poor" (Mazumdar, 2002).

A study by Bisnath and Elson shows that in the accessibility to health care services there is a noticeable disparity between men and women in India. During illness, women in rural areas have neither the time nor leisure to travel to health centres for medicines or treatment. They lack mobility and childcare assistance in such situations. The study proved that in terms of food intake, women suffer greater deprivation intra familially. Women eat last, 'as part of the culture of self-effacement and service to others and if there is insufficient food, the men and children get fed first and the women do without' (Bisnath and Elson, 2001).

Bhargavi V. Davar (2001) has studied the psychological, social and political forces, which have significant impacts on women's mental health. Through examples of domestic violence and child sexual abuse she looks at the victimisation of women by violence and links it to mental health. Domestic violence coupled with sexual abuse degenerates the mental health of rural women. In women, there was "a sharp rise in neuroses in the age group of 25-39 years from the previous age group of 14-24 years, and a rise of 8 per cent, compared to 4 per cent increase in the next age group of 40-49 years" (Davar, 2001 : 47).

Indian culture and traditions have always treated women as secondary citizens in almost every sphere of life. Narasimham (1999) has studied the difference between male and female entitlements in work, employment, earnings, education, health status and decision-making powers (Narasimham, 1999 : 23).

Another tradition that prevails in Indian culture is the preference for boy child for religious sake. This unreasonable preference for the male children has resulted in crimes such as female genocide and thereby gradual widening of sex ratio. A study conducted by G.A. Siddiqui (2001) has assessed the role of socio-economic factors on women fertility differentials in Eastern Uttar Pradesh. The average age of marriage for females changed from 13.2 per cent in 1901-11 to 17.2 per cent during 1961-71. Out of 318 districts in India, in 112 districts the average age of marriage of girls was below 15 in 1961 (Siddiqui, 2001).

Literacy and Empowerment of Women

There are a several studies, which have been linking empowerment of women and educational levels. Education has a significant role to play in changing both the mental set of women and the oppressive social and political systems. Moreover education is important for all kinds of demographic behaviour, affecting mortality, health, fertility, and contraception. The study of Shireen J. Jejeebhoy (1995) has found out that in almost every setting, regardless of region, culture, and level of development, the best-educated women bear fewer children than uneducated women (Jejeebhoy, 1995). Analysis of the census reports reveals that the social, demographic and health indices such as life expectancy, infant mortality rate, sex ratio, school enrolment ratio, etc. are better in those states having higher literacy rate. Education, emancipation and empowerment are closely related. Lattice Menno (1998) has attempted to furnish the basic parameters of women's development issues in the context of awareness, emancipation, social status, sexual liberation and professional achievement (Menno, 1998).

Educational opportunities are not equally availed and utilised by women. They do not have equal access to the formal educational stream. Study of Maya Majumdar (2001) upon the difficulties of women in accessing to the existing educational system reveals that, "among the respondents who have faced difficulties/problems, a greater percentage (76.34%) has faced the problems termed as financial difficulties, followed by the problems titled resistance from family members (39.13%), lack of space in the house to pursue independent studies (29.96%), non-co-operative attitude of teachers (15.45%), eve-teasing (13.04%), harassment by co-students (9.17%) and lack of personal interest (6.77%), in this sequential order" (Majumdar, 2001 : 285).

Analysing the present system of education it can be seen that education of the young is not gender sensitive. Both formal and informal education system needs to be reformed. All India Adult Education Conference (2001) recommends various measures to transform education for women empowerment such as :

- Change in syllabus of formal education including more lessons on renowned women of the country;
- Illustration in books are to be gender sensitive;
- Train all women for income generation at home;
- Campaign for 100 per cent literacy among women;
- Formation of SHGs for women;
- Since childhood, girls/women should be involved in decision-making;
- Special efforts to build-up self-confidence and self-respect among women at family level and the society;
- Vocational training for economic uplift of women;
- Training for women to protect themselves such as judo and karate;
- *Doordarshan* programmes to promote gender equality;
- Awareness programmes related to women's rights—lecture, exhibition, discussion, folk media at grassroots levels;
- Special homes and hostels for girls in distress and income generation programmes for them;
- Women's work should be given due recognition at the national level;
- Health policies to concentrate on her whole life instead of women and child care only;
- Women are not to be made the only target of population control;
- To play political roles, proper training opportunities at the Government level (All India Adult Education Conference, 2001).

Economic Empowerment of Women

Inequality in the economic sector is very evident. Poverty and powerlessness are closely related. Lakshmi Narasaiah (2001) analyses the complex phenomenon of rural poverty and its invisible relationship to inequality and discrimination against women in rural communities. Economic dependence is one of the major factors that limit the freedom and autonomy of women in general and rural women in particular. In this context the SHG movement has to do much for economic empowerment of rural women (Narasaiah, 2001).

Economic independence which is reflected in the gaining of freedom to earn, spend, acquire property, save and invest is very important for women to establish their identity and equality in this gendered World. Unless her economic rights are recognised and respected, empowerment in true sense will never be realised. Sukanya Nihal Singh (2001) has studied the key areas of women's development—economic emancipation, enabling environment, legal framework, security of family and property, and the principle of equal opportunity (Singh, 2001).

Women lack economic power. However, their contribution to the economic production cannot be neglected. Suman Pamecha (2002) examines the issues relating to contribution of women to income, employment, work in non-marketed activities, their wage imputation and work participation. Since time immemorial, women are found to be involved in farm production in addition to their sole responsibility of managing the homes. In India, women form 46 per cent of the agricultural labour force. In spite of their fare share in building national economy their contributions have not only been underestimated and underremunerated but they have even been treated as invisible hands (Pamecha, 2002).

Breda Cranney (2001) has depicted the miseries of women of Himachal Pradesh through a selected number of case studies. Women of the lower socio-economic stratum of Himachal Pradesh lead a miserable life. A considerable part of her life in the hills is spent for fetching out drinking water. Her starvation at home is often unnoticed. Her lot is often subject matter of black magic (Cranney, 2001).

Navinder K. Singh (2001) has portrayed the various social, cultural and functional activities of women workers of tea plantations who in reality are the backbone of the tea industry in great detail. Neglected, abused and discriminated from cradle to grave, these women desperately seek a change, which is only possible through education and social empowerment (Singh, 2001).

Political Empowerment of Women

Studies have been conducted on the level of empowerment, women have achieved following the seventy-third amendment to the Constitution. It made mandatory that village, block and district *panchayats* to have women through the formal election process. It has also made it mandatory to have one-third of panchayat members in each panchayat and one-third of the chairpersons to be women. However, one should not identify political reservation with real empowerment. K.C. Vidya (1997) presents the first comprehensive empirical research work on the theme of political empowerment and has disclosed many social, economic, institutional and functional constraints that impair the functioning of women in the Panchayati Raj Institutions. Participation in the panchayats is rather passive, in the sense that women are panchayat members and chairpersons only for name, and their husbands or sons or brothers execute the administrative powers. According to K.C. Vidya, political reservation has not achieved the desired result. The study of Kaushik (2002) has also confirmed the same finding. Getting a space is only a means to empowerment. Once women get elected or selected to various positions in political structures and committees, the women should be able to exercise the power/space given to them for 'making themselves knowledgeable, skilled and empowered, utilising it for the development of women, children and the society, and eventually making use of their empowerment, to empower other women' (Kaushik, 2002 : 4).

Studies have been conducted to identify the factors of poor participation of women in politics. Some reasons for lack of political participation of women are shyness, unpreparedness, effect of *purdah* system and personal laws, impact of religion, reaction of family members, domestic responsibilities, undue interference by the male members in the work, security problem, lack of facilities, lack of incentives, political discrimination in distribution of development schemes, criminalisation of politics, official interference and corruption at grassroots level (Pande, 2001 : 222).

The foregoing review of literature brings out that few concerted studies have been conducted on women literacy workers. On the other hand a policy and a programme-oriented study of such workers is likely to go a long way in improving the educational status of people. National Literacy Mission has been underway for several logistic and operational reasons since 1986. It has been re-christened in 1991 as *'Sarva Shiksha Abhiyan'*. There are several women volunteers coming forward to participate in the programme as literacy workers. Haryana is one of the six richest states in India. With regard to literacy the status of Haryana is among the last ten. The literacy workers are the agents of social change in the rural India. No reports or research is reported so far about the empowerment of women literacy workers of Haryana. Hence the research under consideration is a pioneer study.

2

Research Methodology

Literacy Scene in India

Doubtless, female literacy is an important indicator of women empowerment. Literacy rate of India has substantially increased since independence. Literacy rate in India was 16.7 per cent in the year 1951, 52.21 per cent in 1991 and 65.38 per cent in 2001. That the literacy in the country is accelerating is indicated by the decadal growth (1991-2001), which works out to be 13.17 per cent. What is not, for the first time since independence there has been a decline in the absolute number of illiterates! In the previous decades, there has been a continuous increase in the number of illiterates, despite the increase in the literacy rates. It is right to call this period as 'literacy decade'. During the decade, the number of literate persons has increased to 562.01 million thus adding an additional 203.61 million literates in the country.

Literacy scene in the country, however, is far from being even. It varies and varies markedly from state to state. Among various states in India, Kerala has the highest literacy rate of 90.92 per cent followed by Mizoram (88.49 %) and Lakshadeep (87.52 %). Bihar has the lowest literacy rate in India (47.53 %). Other states having literacy level below 60 per cent are Jharkhand (54.13 %), Jammu Kashmir (54.46 %), Arunachal Pradesh (54.74 %) and UP (57.36 %).

The male literacy rate during the decade 1991-2001 has increased to 75.85 per cent. On the other hand, the female literacy rate has gone up to 54.16 per cent. Stated differently, it has increased by 14.87 per cent. As a consequence, the male-female literacy gap has reduced from 24.84 per cent in

1991 to 21.70 per cent in 2001. Even in this, there are regional differences. Mizoram has the minimum gender gap of (4.56%) in male-female literacy rates followed by Meghalaya (5.73%) and Kerala (6.34%). Gender disparity with regard to literacy rate is highest in Rajasthan with a gender gap in the male-female literacy levels as high as 32.12 per cent.

Literacy Level in Haryana

According to the Census Report of 2001, literacy rate in Haryana is 68.59 per cent, which is higher than national literacy level. Women literacy rate is 56.31 per cent, which is 2.15 per cent higher than national rate. Literacy level in Haryana has improved from 55.85 per cent to 68.59 per cent in 2001 with a decadal growth of 12.74 per cent. However the difference in male-female literacy levels is 22.94. There is marked differences among various districts in the state of Haryana with regard to literacy rate. Karnal has the lowest literacy rate and Ambala has the highest literacy rate in the state. Faridabad district has maintained its literacy status above the state average. With regard to female literacy level, Karnal again has the lowest figure and Ambala has the highest followed by Bhiwani and Faridabad. Faridabad is the third highest district with regard to female literacy rate. However, Faridabad occupies only 10th position with regard to male literacy level in the state. Gender gap in literacy levels in Faridabad is 15.2 per cent. The decadal growth in the literacy rate of Haryana is 28.12 and it is 22.04 per cent in Faridabad. Overall literacy status as well as women's literacy status in Faridabad is comparatively better than other districts of the state.

National Literacy Campaign (NLC)

Much progress in literacy levels could be traced to nationwide literacy campaign organised by National Literacy Mission (NLM). National Literacy Campaign (NLC) was launched by NLM in May, 1988 on the basis of a successful experiment conducted in Kerala in 1986. During the last two decades, the literacy level of Indian population has improved significantly. Literacy campaigns have visibly contributed to the process of women empowerment. The literacy movement has to its credit several achievements. Up to November 2003, literacy campaigns have been launched in 596 districts, out of which 191 districts are in Post Literacy programmes and 238 districts in continuing education phase. Literacy projects sanctioned so far under all the schemes of NLC are estimated to cover more than 150 million neo-literates in the age group of 9-35. Of them, nearly 106.64 million learners have been enrolled under literacy campaigns. More than 106.7 million have already been made literate under all programmes of NLC. 60 per cent learners are female and 40 per cent are male. 24 per cent learners belong to Scheduled Caste and 13 per cent belong to Scheduled Tribes. The cumulative number of literary volunteers mobilized since the launching of literacy campaigns exceeds 10 million. The literacy campaigns thus represent the largest ever civil mobilization in the history of the country.

National Literacy Campaign in Haryana

The progress of Literacy Campaign in Haryana was rather slow. Even when the national literacy campaign was launched in 1988, it did not flourish desirably in the state of Haryana. Within five years, the entire campaign came to a virtual standstill. It was found that lack of people's participation and absence of facilitating NGOs in the field has caused its slow progress. It was only in the year 1999 that mass literacy campaigns have been reorganised after getting inspiration from the successful experiments in the neighbouring states of Rajasthan and Uttar Pradesh (Mahila Samakhya). Literacy programmes were organised in almost all the districts of the State around August 2000.

National Literacy Campaign in Faridabad

St. Joseph's Service Society, an NGO working for the welfare of the disabled girl children and youth, has initiated literacy programmes in 2000 in Chandpur region, in Faridabad district. The organisation NGO managed to enlist the service of several women who came forward for voluntary literacy work. Perhaps women literacy volunteers get an intrinsic satisfaction from their work.

Empowerment is a process of building or sharpening of capacities, so that the people experience continuous and sustained changes or development. The research has brought out whether women literacy workers are empowered because of their involvement in literacy work. If so, how much they are empowered, what are the factors of empowerment and to what extent could literacy work be a means of empowerment for women literacy workers.

Women in Literacy Campaign

One of the great strengths of the adult education programme has been the involvement of women. As much as 62 per cent of participants in India are women. Programmes have provided illiterate adult women who have been denied access to formal schooling with great opportunity for reading, writing, increasing awareness levels and skills training. Literacy and adult education campaigns have actively promoted gender equity and have sought to empower them as to decision-making about themselves, their families and their communities.

This major strain running through the programmes has played a significant role in improving the status of women within their own families. Whereas, traditionally women in India had little say in family decision-making, they, through participation, have begun to express their newly found self-belief in having a say both within and without the family.

The effect of Adult Education on health and hygiene are indeed most significant. Raising the functional literacy level of a community leads to a demonstrable decline in fertility and infant mortality rates. Adult education has helped spread knowledge about health care and nutrition, thereby enabling mothers to keep their families in better health and to care better for their children.

Literacy Campaign and NGOs

The National Literacy Campaign (NLC) recognises the potential of NGOs in furthering its programmes and schemes. Since its inception, NLC has taken measures to strengthen its partnership with NGOs. The sheer grind and persistence that literacy campaigns involve have greatly diminished much of the enthusiasm. NLC has made all efforts to evolve both institutional and informal mechanisms to give voluntary organisations an active promotional role in the literacy movement. Under the scheme of support to NGOs, voluntary agencies are encouraged and financial assistance is provided for activities, such as running post-literacy and continuing education programmes with the objective of total eradication of illiteracy in well-defined areas; undertaking resource development activities through establishment of State; organising vocational and technical education programmes for neo-literates; promoting innovation, experimentation and action research; conducting evaluation and impart studies; and organising symposia and conferences, publication of relevant books and periodicals and production of mass-media support aids (www.nlm.nic.in).

With more and more districts having completed the post-literacy programmes, NGOs now have to diversify the scope of their activities. They are expected to take up area-specific continuing education programmes for life-long learning. This will include skill development programmes for personal, social and occupational development.

The success of literacy campaign largely depends upon people's active participation and the involvement of NGOs. NLC has worked in collaboration with several grassroots NGOs throughout the country. Literacy campaign since its inception has incorporated volunteers who come forward to take up the task of teaching the illiterate persons. 'Each one, teach one' is a popular slogan in NLC. What is the motivation for such voluntary literacy workers to join the literacy campaign? A large number of literacy workers are women. Is this voluntarism, a sign of women empowerment? Are these women literacy workers empowered due to their active participation in the voluntary literacy work?

Rationale

The year 2001 is observed as the Year of Women Empowerment with the promulgation of National Policy for Women Empowerment. During the literacy campaign in Haryana it has been found that a large number of women have come forward as literacy workers voluntarily. As against this, no study has been conducted to find out significant factors of such motivation on the part of women literacy workers in Haryana.

If literacy has any role in empowering women, the women literacy workers should themselves have been empowered for themselves before they begin to empower others. It would be therefore interesting and relevant to study how much empowerment has the women literacy workers achieved during the entire process of literacy work.

As shown in the literature survey earlier, achievement of literacy has an impact not only on women, but also on the entire community. It is, therefore, important that women literacy voluntary workers are studied in terms of their role, status and empowerment.

Given the above consideration, a study has been conducted on women literacy voluntary workers involved in the implementation of NLC in the district of Faridabad in Haryana. The study has the following main objectives.

Objectives of the Study

(a) To critically study the implementation of National Literacy Campaign in Faridabad district in the state of Haryana with particular reference to NGO contribution to the campaign.
(b) To look into the socio-economic background of women literacy workers.
(c) To evaluate the level of empowerment of women literacy workers in the district.
(d) To study the impact of National Literacy Campaign (NLC) work on the personality, life and aspirations of the women literacy workers.

(e) To ascertain the impact of voluntary work on the motivation level of the women literacy workers as denoted by the formation of self-help groups for development work in the village.

(f) To suggest measures for upgrading the involvement of women literacy workers in NLC.

Operational Definitions

(a) ***Women Empowerment*** refers to building or sharpening capabilities of women, so that, they experience continuous and sustained changes or development. Major indicators of empowerment are as follows :

(i) Autonomy to wear clothes of their preference.
(ii) To wear or not to wear *Burqa/purdah.*
(iii) Autonomy in decision-making on significant matters such as preparation of food, purchase of household articles, education of children, employment of children, savings, income, marriage of children, etc.
(iv) Autonomy to move out for recreational purposes such as picnics, exhibition, marriages other than that of the relatives, religious ceremonies, seeing films etc. (Azim, 1997 : 151).
(v) Individual autonomy in social and economic activities.
(vi) Autonomy to follow any hobby.
(vii) Healthy image and sense of efficiency.
(viii) Rights over one's own body and life.
(ix) Right to choose spouse, conception, desired number of children etc.
(x) Membership and freedom to participate in social organisations.
(xi) Autonomy to visit bank and freedom to spend money.
(xii) Ownership of property.
(xiii) Consumption of resources.

(xiv) Exercise of the right to avail facilities.
(xv) Individual autonomy to exercise franchise, i.e. the freedom to participate as a voter or a contestant.

(b) ***Personality Development*** in the context of the research is the acquisition or improvement of personality traits such as improvement of the 'self-concept' and increase in the level of 'security' by the literacy workers on account of their active involvement in the literacy campaign.
(c) ***Literacy Work*** in the context of the research refers to the organisation of literacy classes for the illiterate people particularly in villages under National Literacy Campaign in association with state level, district level and local level literacy councils and other agencies.
(d) ***Literacy Workers*** under the research refer to those volunteers who have come forward to lend helping hand in National Literacy Campaign by conducting literacy classes for the illiterate people in the village communities.

Research Design

For the present purposes, a descriptive research design has been evolved. In order to have a comprehensive assessment of the implementation of the National Literacy Campaign, attention has to be focused at the grassroots level, we have to go to villages and interact with stakeholders such as public opinion leaders, women literacy workers, and beneficiaries, namely participants in literacy classes. Observing ongoing literacy classes is likely to be much insight giving. Similarly Focus Group Discussion (FGD) with beneficiaries is likely to throw much light on the strength and weaknesses in the campaign implementation.

It must be added that the process of first hand data collection has to be supplemented with that of wide range of official information. Hopefully, such an approach of research design will fulfil the objectives of the study.

Universe and Sampling

The present study is located in the district of Faridabad in Haryana. The state is considered to be a prosperous one, and Faridabad is taken to be a vibrant and high growth district. In the region, not only are the people socially and politically alive, but also quite a few NGOs are reportedly active. To illustrate, St. Joseph's Service Society has been active in the villages for the past 13 years. The Society has been collaborating in the implementation of National Literacy Campaign in a large number of villages. In consultation with the Society, 10 villages have been selected. Table 2.4 presents relevant information.

Table 2.1 : Universe of the study

Village	*Illiterate*	*Male*	*Female*	*Literacy workers*	*Women in classes*
Alipur	102	13	89	7	70
Aruva	282	84	198	1	10
Bahadurpur	122	5	117	12	122
Chandpur	340	154	186	7	70
Dalaigharh	31	9	22	1	10
Faejpur	83	13	72	6	60
Imamudinpur	100	38	62	2	20
Nehandola	79	14	65	7	70
Raipurkalan	108	22	86	3	30
Shajapur	276	79	197	10	100
Total	1523	431	1094	56	562

For the category of opinion leaders, study has gone mainly for the *Sarpanchs* of the village Panchayats of the 10 villages. May it be noted that the sub-samples also includes 3 women *Sarpanchs*.

In the selected villages, the Society is having a large number of voluntary literacy workers. However, attention has been focused on 56 workers, who has joined hands in the year 2001. Their progress, attitudinal and personality changes have been studied over next 12 months.

Apart from literacy workers, their relatives—father, mother, husband or brother—numbering ten have been randomly selected.

Literacy classes in the selected villages have been systematically observed once every month. The total number of observation is 672.

Likewise, 10 FGDs with the participants of literacy classes—five in the beginning of the year and the other five at the end of the year—have been conducted. The overall picture of information sources in the study is :

Voluntary literacy workers	—	56
Opinion leaders	—	20
Number of observations (56 × 12)	—	672
Number of FGDs	—	10

Tools

The tools for information gathering used in the study are :

- Interview schedules
- Observation sheet
- FGD guide
- Rating scales

A brief description of various tools used in the study is given below.

Interview Schedules

Three interview schedules have been prepared for the three groups of respondents, viz. literacy workers, their family members and the *Sarpanchs*.

The interview schedule for the literacy workers has two domains. First part of the interview schedule for each of the literacy worker has been administered at the beginning of the research to understand the socio-economic background of literacy workers. It included questions on personal particulars, family background and details about the assets, life experiences and opinions. Some of the items included are age, sex, marital status, caste, religion, educational qualifications, family income, availability of amenities and the use of public amenities.

Second domain of the interview schedule has been administered before and after the literacy work on woman literacy workers to assess the level of empowerment. Items included in the interview schedules pertain to the opinion and beliefs of woman literacy workers regarding the type of education given to boys and girls, career orientation given to girls and boys, women's behaviour in the event of a marital dispute, girls' responsibility to look after their parents after marriage and their understanding about the concept of women empowerment, usefulness of literacy work, frequency of women's mobility outside their village, women's participation in village festivals, their participation in religious and social activities, their observance of *Purdah* from the elders of the village, respondents' role in the financial matters of the family, daily routine of women at home, women's participation in the decision-making at home (such as cooking food, education of children, purchase of household articles, employment of the younger members, marriage of family members, income, savings and investment), usual do's and don'ts for the womenfolk in their village, woman literacy workers' initiative to meet the civil authorities for the sake of common good, their initiative to face the emergencies of the village, women's safety in the village and finally, the response pattern of woman literacy workers in risky situations.

A similar interview schedule has been used to collect relevant data from the family members and the *Sarpanchs*. The interview schedule has been administered before and after the duration of the action on ten family members to collect their view on the changes in the behaviour of the primary respondents.

An interview schedule has been administered on ten village headmen before and after the duration of the action to collect their opinion about the changes in the behaviour of the literacy workers under study.

Observation Sheet

An **observation sheet** has been developed for a monthly observation of the changes in the personality and behaviour of the women literacy workers over a duration of 12 months. The observation sheet has the following main variables:

- Number of learners in the classroom
- Attentiveness of the learners
- Discussion of women's issues in the classroom
- Singing and dancing in the class
- Dress of the worker
- Interaction between the learners
- Reaction to the researcher
- Use of *Purdah* by the worker
- Presence of the kids in the classroom
- Confidence in the worker's behaviour

Focus Group Discussion (FGD)

Focus Group Discussion (FGD) with the participants of the literacy classes of five classes before and after the literacy work has been conducted on the basis of an FGD guide. FGD included simple and complex items. Main items are :

- Advantages of being literate,
- Topics of learning,
- Regularity and punctuality,
- Teacher's teaching method,
- Extra curricular activities conducted in the class,
- The syllabus,
- Visible changes in the ability of your teacher such as increased confidence, communicative skills, social behaviour, etc.,
- Differences of literacy workers from other women of their age and background,
- Opinion about gender equality,
- Opinion about the appropriateness of the status given to women by our society, and
- Their understanding about the term 'Women Empowerment'.

Rating Scales

Two rating scales have been used for the literacy workers before and after the literacy work.

Self-Concept Scale

The first rating scale is an adaptation of ***Self-Concept Scale*** developed by Mukta Rani Rastogi. The scale is highly suitable to assess self-concept among women literacy workers. It has been adapted for the present purposes and for the present set of respondents. The adapted rating scale has 50 self-statements (statements that describes the self) with five responses from 'Strongly Agree' to 'Strongly Disagree'. Thus the adapted scale used in the study has fifty statements pertaining to various aspects of the concept of self. The important dimensions of the 'self-concept' assessed under the study are the following :

- Emotional balance (11 statements)
- Optimism and open-mindedness (6 statements)
- Self-acceptance (6 statements)
- Self-confidence and sense of efficiency (10 statements)
- Self-esteem or sense of worthiness (5 statements)
- Sense of reality, beliefs and convictions (7 statements)
- Social competence (5 statements)

S-I (Security-Insecurity) Inventory

Second rating scale is ***S-I (Security-Insecurity) Inventory*** which has been developed by Maslow. The feeling of security and insecurity of the literacy workers before and after the duration of the literacy work has been detected and assessed by administering the Maslow's S-I Inventory. This inventory is one of the widely used tools in assessing the feeling of security and insecurity. The inventory contains 50 questions having three fixed responses—'Yes', 'No' and 'Undecided'. Maslow's S-I inventory has been used for the study with minor changes for suitable adaptation to the context.

Data Collection in the Study

The process of data collection commenced with the new batch of literacy workers joining the National Literacy Campaign in the sampled villages in Faridabad District.

Interviews

Interviews have been held at three levels in two rounds :

- Interviewing the women literacy workers,
- Interviewing family members of the literacy workers,
- Interviewing *Sarpanchs* of village Panchayats in sampled villages.

The first round of interviews have been held as soon as the literacy workers joined the literacy campaign. The second round of interviews have been held after 12 months' of literacy campaign in the villages. The researcher would visit the concerned villages with the intention of motivating village communities to join the literacy campaign being conducted under the National Literacy Campaign. He would call upon the *Sarpanchs* of the village panchayat and arrange meetings of the villagers to choose literacy workers and to choose venue and timings of the literacy classes. The *Sarpanchs* concerned have been interviewed on the basis of an interview schedule. They have been asked about the role and status of women in general of their village communities and the literacy workers in particular, the literacy status of the villages and their opinion about the voluntary literacy work by the women literacy workers.

The literacy workers would conduct the classes at their home at a time convenient for the learners who belong to her immediate neighbourhood. The learners required a lot of encouragement to come regularly for the classes. The literacy workers would go and call all the learners from their houses at the time of the class. As soon as volunteers came forward for literacy work in the concerned 10 villages, the researcher along with the agency supervisor appointed by the NGO would visit them. After some initial conversation, the timing and venue of their literacy work would be fixed. During the first two or three visits the first round of interviews have been held with them on individual basis by using the respective interview schedules. The items in the interview schedules have been explained to them whenever required. None has been compelled to disclose the required information. However the permission has been sought in advance from the *Sarpancha* and the elders of the family such as father, father-in-law, mother or mother-in-law for approaching the literacy workers personally. The participation of other family members during the data collection has been discouraged. Altogether 56 women literacy workers have been interviewed.

After completing the preliminary data collection from the literacy workers, 10 randomly selected family members have been interviewed by the use of interview schedules.

After one year, the second round of interviews have been held with the literacy workers, family members and the *Sarpanchs* using an abridged version of the same interview schedule used for the first round interviewing. Emphasis has been given to the relevant questions that pertain to changes in the attitudes and behaviour of the literacy workers due to the year-long literacy campaign.

Tape recorder has been used to record the relevant responses of women literacy workers. Tape recorder has always been used for conducting interviews with the *Sarpanchs*. The recorded interview has been very useful in analysing the information during the data processing stage.

Observation

Next, 56 selected women literacy workers have been observed over a period of 12 months with the help of an observation sheet. Monthly visits have been made to each of the 56 literacy workers. Monthly observation visits were not pre-planned and the date and time of the subsequent visit has not been informed to the literacy workers in advance. Therefore, 12 visits have been spanned in 18 to 24 months. It has been due to non-availability of the literacy worker during a particular visit (which has not been informed to women literacy workers in advance). Sometimes the literacy classes lose regularity because of sickness of the literacy worker, suspension of the literacy classes due to harvesting, festivals, some casualties such as death of somebody in the village, etc. The researcher would sit at the back seat of the literacy class and silently observes the teaching of the literacy worker. The researcher has associated with the literacy class since its beginning. He has been there to negotiate with the *Sarpanchs* for a suitable place for literacy class, to find out volunteers to run the class, to organise the illiterate participants for the literacy class and to find out a substitute in the event of leaving of one literacy worker. Therefore the presence of researcher in the literacy class has never been considered as a distraction to the class, on the other hand it has been regarded as factor or facilitation and encouragement to the literacy campaign. The monthly observation has become a routine and from the NGO's point of view it has been part of monthly monitoring and supervision schedule. The observation sheet has been filled in during the observation or soon after the observation during the transit from one centre to another.

The researcher would travel by a two-wheeler along with an agency supervisor from village to village. He has to cover at least two literacy classes per day, so that he could complete 56 visits in a month. Literacy classes are usually arranged in the afternoon hours that is between 1.00 p.m. to 3.00 p.m. during which women in the household are free to attend the classes. In some of the villages, classes have been organised in the evening hours so that working class women could attend the classes. Apart from the syllabus (*Jatan Bhag* 1, 2 and 3) discussions about some women's issues or about some common problems of the villages have also been included in the literacy classes. Participants of the class enjoyed singing together and also dancing some traditional folkways in special occasions or upon invitation.

Although formal observation of literacy workers has been rounded off at the end of the year, the informal observation has continued for quite some time. The participation of literacy workers in the formation of self-help groups, income generation programmes and participation in various other social activities have been recorded and these informations would assess the long term aspects of women empowerment. In the informal observation it has been found that some of the literacy workers have really come up in the path of women empowerment. They have started actively participating in various social activities organised by the NGO in the villages such as organising *balmelas,* conducting *balwadi,* organisation of Self-Help Groups (SHGs) and participation in various social awareness and training programmes. Some of them rose to the leadership roles of women's Self-Help Groups (SHGs). Now there are over 90 SHGs in the concerned villages. Most of them are linked to NABARD and have started income generation activities. These SHGs have secured a marketing outlet in Tigaon, a growing town in Faridabad District with the assistance of NABARD and the NGO. One can easily observe that commencement of literacy campaign and the active participation of women literacy workers in the campaign has been the real beginning of the process of women empowerment in the concerned villages.

Focus Group Discussions (FGDs)

Five literacy classes out of 56 have been randomly selected for conducting FGDs. Five FGDs have been held in the beginning of the year and five here have been held by the end of the year. Since the researcher has been visiting each of the classes on a monthly basis, the visit for conducting FGD has not been pre-planned. FGD has been conducted in such a way that the literacy worker would be absent during the session. FGD has been conducted on such days when the literacy worker would become absent on account of visiting doctor, going out of village for attending some programmes or being busy with some guests at home. FGD would not have been effective if literacy worker has been present for the session, because all the unstructured questions thrown for the discussion were regarding the performance of the literacy worker, right from her appearance in the classes to her communicative skills, teaching methods, interest in extra curricular activities, concern for the syllabus, sociability, friendliness etc. Since the researcher has to engage the class during the absence of the literacy worker, there has been no suspicion on the part of the participants of the literacy class. 8 to 10 participants would be present for FGD. The purpose of FGD has been hidden to the participants. It has also been conducted in a very informal way as if some monitoring is going on about the progress of literacy classes in general. No responses have been recorded in front of women literacy workers. The documentation of the FGD has been done immediately after the FGD. Sometimes tape recorder (walkman) has been used to record the responses. As soon as the literacy worker reach the scene, the FGD has been closed instantly and the class has been handed over to the volunteer. The FGD has been continued in a latter occasion.

Rating Scales

Two rating scales have been used for information gathering from the literacy workers : Adapted 'Self-Concept Scale' of Mukta Rani Rastogi and Maslow's of SI (Security-Insecurity) Inventory. They have been used twice—first round in the beginning of the year and second round by the end of the year.

Soon after the first round interview of the literacy worker, she has been given the adapted *Self-Concept Scale* of Mukta Rani Rastogi. She has been asked to fill in the particulars required at the top of the scale. Women literacy workers have been requested to read each statement in the rating scale and indicate their position by putting a tick mark on the pre-coded codes, namely 'Strongly Agree', 'Agree', 'Undecided', 'Disagree' and 'Strongly Disagree'. They were assured that their responses would be kept confidential while helping us and giving their responses, they should not omit any item.

After the administration of Self-Concept Scale, Maslow's **SI Inventory** (adapted) has been given to her. She has been asked to fill in the particulars required at the top of the inventory. Then she has been asked to read carefully the general instructions given at the top of the inventory.

"This is not a test. Answer all questions being sure to choose only one answer 'Yes', 'No', or 'Can't Say'. Put a cross on the answer that is true for you. Your answers and any comments you may wish to add will of course be considered strictly confidential. There are no right or wrong answers. There is also no time limit. 90 per cent of the ordinary people will usually finish the test in about 10 minutes. Unless you give your frank, honest and genuine responses the result will be useless. Don't omit any of the items." Woman literacy worker has been asked to give her responses in a separate answer sheet according to the instruction given above.

Unlike the interviewing, the rating scales have been found more effective to conduct in a small group situation. Five or six literacy workers of a village have been gathered in a common place and the instructions have been given commonly. Since the rating scales used were meant for university level students, village level workers who were mostly plus two levels did not easily understand them. Most of the items in both the scales has to be explained to them in detail. The lecturing upon the items of the scales has been interesting. In a small group situation, the instructions were effective. However, the filling up of the scaling has been done individually. Analysis has not been done in public. In fact the result has not been informed to them at all. It has been used only for the purpose of research. It has been assumed that the revelation of the result would lead to unwanted comparison and frustration among some of woman literacy workers. It has been informed to them that the above-mentioned tests are part of their self-evaluation and self-assessment of their psychological well-being. After completing the first round of the tests in all the 56 respondents, it has been announced to all women literacy workers that they have been found psychologically fit to undertake the literacy work. It has also been announced that the second round testing would take place in the next. Once the second round testing has been over, it has been informed to the literacy workers that all of them have shown significant improvement in their 'self-concept' as well as their sense of security and psychological well-being.

Data Analysis

Both the quantitative and qualitative data have been collected. Quantitative data have been collected both from the primary and the secondary sources. Best possible effort has been applied to quantify all the data collected. Quantitative data has been collected by socio-economic survey schedule and from the documents available from reliable sources. Qualitative data have been collected by observation and semi-structured interview schedule. Findings of personality rating scales have been quantified by summated scoring technique. Data have been analysed by using appropriate statistical techniques. Data have been tabulated, presented in the form of tables (one way and two-way tables) and charts. Statistical Package for Social Sciences (SPSS), a software for social research is used for data analysis.

With regard to rating scales, standardised scoring procedure has been followed. The results have been interpreted according to the scoring key. After completion of the test of 'Self-Concept Scale', the responses have been scored according the scoring instruction given below.

Table 2.2 : Interpretation of the Scoring of Self-Concept Scale

	Levels of Self-Concept				
Various Aspects of Self-Concept	*I*	*II*	*III*	*IV*	*V*
A. Emotional Balance	45 to 55	34 to 44	23 to 33	12 to 22	1 to 11
B. Optimism and Open-mindedness	25 to 30	19 to 24	13 to 18	7 to 12	1 to 6
C. Self-Acceptance	25 to 30	19 to 24	13 to 18	7 to 12	1 to 6
D. Self-Confidence and Sense of Efficiency	41 to 50	31 to 40	21 to 30	11 to 20	1 to 10
E. Self-Esteem (Sense of Worthiness)	21 to 25	16 to 20	11 to 15	6 to 10	1 to 5
F. Sense of Reality, Beliefs and Convictions	29 to 35	22 to 28	15 to 21	8 to 14	1 to 7
G. Social Competence	21 to 25	16 to 20	11 to 15	6 to 10	1 to 5
Over All Level Of Self-Concept	**201 to 250**	**151 to 200**	**101 to 150**	**51 to 100**	**1 to 50**

I. Very good self-concept, very positive, high level of empowerment
II. Good Self-concept, positive, gaining empowerment
III. Average level of self-concept, rather confused, need to gain empowerment
IV. Poor Self-Concept, rather negative self-image, low level of empowerment
V. Very poor self-concept, lowest level of empowerment, needs great encouragement

After completion of the test, which used Maslow's S-I Inventory, the responses of the women literacy workers have been scored according to the scoring instruction. The sum of all the items is women literacy worker's score. High score indicated feeling of insecurity and low score indicated feeling of security. From the score it has been found whether women literacy worker has feeling of security or insecurity.

Table 2.3 : Interpretation of the Scoring of S-I Inventory

Score	*Explanation*
1 to 25	Highly secure, self-confident, gaining empowerment
26 to 50	Secure, moderately confident, marching towards empowerment
51 to 75	Less Secure, not so confident, lower self-image, moving slowly towards empowerment
76 to 100	Insecure, Non-confident, very poor self-image, not moving towards empowerment
Above 100	Highly Insecure, Abnormal, Powerless, Disorganised, At the verge of breakdown

Report

The report of the research is divided into 9 chapters. Chapter 1 of the report is introductory, which includes the present status of women in India, crime against women, concept of women empowerment and relevant literature review. It is based on secondary data collected and analysed. Chapter 2 explains the research methodology including the narration of the research setting. Chapter 3 deals with the gender and literacy status of Haryana and Faridabad District. This chapter is also based on the secondary data such as published reports and statistics.

Chapter 4 presents the socio-economic information about women literacy workers. Chapter 5 presents different dimensions of women empowerment such as social, economic and political with reference to the status of women literacy workers in each dimension. Chapter 6 highlights the relationship between literacy work and the process of empowerment. Chapter 7 sheds lights on the information regarding the problems in the path of empowerment with reference to the situation of the literacy workers.

Chapter 8 is the record of the follow up study, which deals with the long-term impacts of literacy work upon the lives of women literacy workers as well as other women participants of the National Literacy Campaign. Empowerment is a long-term process. To identify some long term aspects of this process as well as to open up the future scope of the research on the observation of the changes in the villages especially with regard to the participation of women in various events and developmental activities continued till date. Much change in the direction of empowerment has been found out in the long run and some of these positive trends are narrated in Chapter 8.

Chapter 9 provides an overview and presents conclusions emanating from the field situation. It also attempts to offer some suggestions for the effective implementation of the National Literacy Campaign as also for up-scaling the involvement of the women voluntary workers which is likely to yield rich dividends for the NLC, for the voluntary workers and for the society.

3

National Literacy Campaign and Gender Status in Faridabad District of Haryana

Literacy Programmes in India

Literacy work has been emphasised since the time of independence because of its latent and manifest impact upon social progress. The socio-economic and health indices have always been associated with literacy rate. Education is the chief means of empowerment especially of women. Women are progressing faster than men in the field of education (Khanna, 1998 : 80). Improvement of women literacy level is a significant indicator of women empowerment.

Major experiments of literacy education for women are the following :

- Adult Education Programme, launched during the Third Five-Year Plan, has been renamed as Functional Literacy Programme in 1965, giving emphasis to farmers' functional literacy. It became Rural Functional Literacy in 1970.
- National Adult Education Programme is formally inaugurated on 2nd October, 1978.
- Non-Formal Education Programme for children (6-14) launched in 1979-80 has 2.97 lakhs NFE centres out of which 1.17 lakhs are only for girls.
- DPEP (District Primary Education Programme) is launched in 163 districts of 14 states since 1994 for universalisation of Primary Education.

- Operation Blackboard is launched in 1987-88 for appointment of two teachers and for securing essential teaching learning equipment in all primary schools. It has been revised in 1993-94 for the appointment of a third teacher for all the schools having above 100 children.
- Lok Jumbish (People's Movement for Education for All) in Rajasthan is a successful educational experiment in the field of Non-formal education, women's group formation, and establishment of primary schools.
- Mid-day Meals Scheme is introduced on 15th August, 1995.
- Mahila Samakhya has been launched in 1989 with the objective of Education for Women's Equality. Education means empowerment. The Union Government has clarified this concept by the institution of 'Mahila Samakhya'. Mahila Samakhya is the pilot programme of the Department of Education, Ministry of Human Resource Development, Government of India. It has been born out of the emphasis given in the New Education Policy of 1986 to the need for education programmes to play a "positive interventionist role" in bringing about women's equality. It sees education as a dynamic process of learning, where women receive meaningful information, engage in critical reflection and act as a collective to change the material and social conditions of their existence. Mahila Samakhya is a women's empowerment project, which not only aims at service delivery but also seeks to bring about a change in women's perception about themselves and that of society in regard to women's traditional roles. It endeavours to create an environment for women to seek knowledge and information in order to make informed choices and create circumstances in which women can learn at their own pace and rhythm. The centrality of education in the struggle to achieve equality is an important focus of Mahila Samakhya. The programme has been launched in Gujarat, Karnataka

and Uttar Pradesh. Despite the many educational and developmental programmes undertaken by the Government over the past four decades, women remain exploited and oppressed. The worst affected are the poor rural women. They play no role in designing the welfare and development schemes but remain merely the passive 'beneficiaries'. The objective of Mahila Samakhya is to reverse this process. The basic strategy is the building of village level collectives or *sanghs* which are activity oriented. *Sangh* enable women to recognize their own strengths and improve their self-confidence.

- Other major programmes for the mass education are Integrated Education for Disabled Children (1974), National Open School (1989), Navodaya Vidyalaya (1986), Indira Gandhi National Open University (1985), and National Literacy Mission (1988).

The importance of universal literacy has been recognised only recently in India. The nineties witnessed the emergence of mass literacy campaigns as the societal response both at the level of official efforts and at the level of people's movements. Abraham Taisha and Malashri Lal (1995) have studied the impact of literacy programmes in rural communities of the Jaipur district of Rajasthan. In particular, the authors address the issues of women empowerment, human rights and dignity within a contextualised framework. Local responses to innovative literacy programmes launched by Lok Jumbish, Women's Development Project, Sandhan, Vishakha, State IDARA, IEC and other agencies are examined. The analysis also takes note of research conducted by the Institute of Development Studies. Further, Abraham and Lal give a useful account of culturally coded learning materials such as word-centred modules, numeric units and primers. The detailed field interviews determine the impact 'of literacy in terms of attitude towards girl-child education, marriage age, dowry and sati.' This subject is significant because Rajasthan has specially targeted the girl-child as a potential agent of change.

National Literacy Mission

During the past two decades, the literacy level of Indian population has improved significantly due to the efforts of National Literacy Mission (NLM). NLM, set up in May 1988 has a three-tier structure (Chart 1).

Chart 1 : Structure of National Literacy Mission

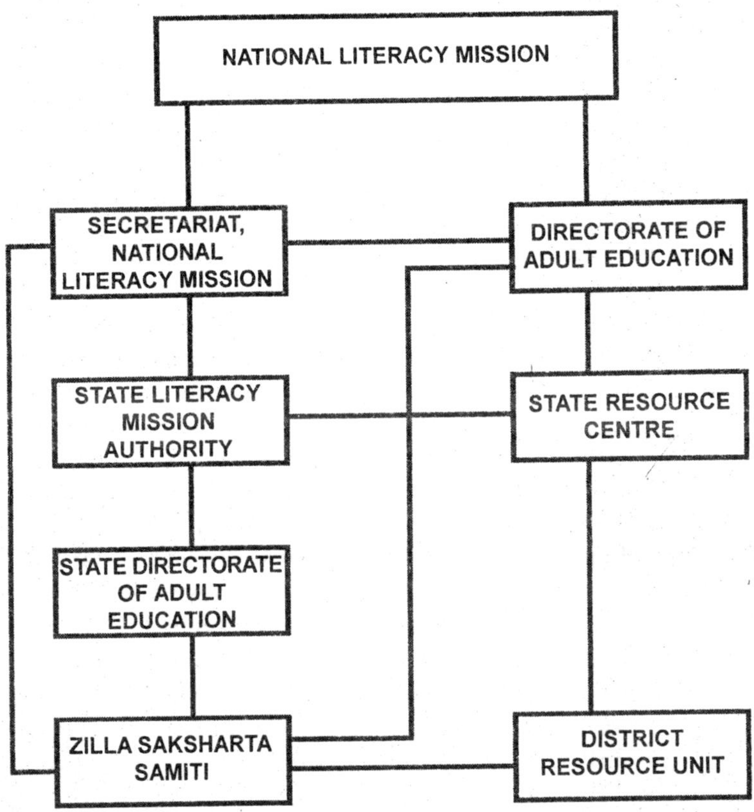

Source : www.nlm.nic.in

At the apex is the National Literacy Mission Authority supported by the Directorate of Adult Education, which controls the programme at the national level. The State Literacy

Mission Authority directs activities at the state level, supported by the State Directorate of Adult Education. Finally, the Zilla Saksharta Samiti helps make the programme a reality in villages all over India. In urban areas, Nagar Palikas are being encouraged to take up the challenge. The Zilla Saksharta Samitis are registered under the Societies Registration Act as independent and autonomous bodies so that they may provide a forum for individuals and organizations to work together. All sections of society are duly represented in the planning and implementation of the programme.

The Directorate of Adult Education, which is a subordinate office of the Department of Elementary Education and Literacy, Ministry of Human Resource Development, has been functioning as the National Resource Centre for Adult Education and Literacy Programmes in the country. It is the 'functional arm' of the National Literacy Mission, which is responsible for monitoring and evaluation of various schemes launched under the aegis of National Literacy Mission.

The Directorate of Adult Education is entrusted with the task of developing model learning materials for illiterates and neo-literates. For this purpose the Directorate harnesses all kinds of media facilities. It also provides professional, academic and technical guidance for the effective functioning of Jan Shikshan Sansthans (Previously known as Shramik Vidyapeeths). The Directorate provides financial assistance to National and Regional Documentation Centres on Population and Development Education set up in Hyderabad, Rajasthan and New Delhi.

The main activities of various Units of the Directorate are provision of academic and technical resource support for implementation of various programmes of the National Literacy Mission, development of teaching-material, organisation of training and orientation programmes keeping in view the needs of ongoing programmes in the field, monitoring of the progress and status of literacy campaigns, production of learning materials by harnessing of all kinds of electronic, print, traditional and folk media, printing and publishing of different literacy campaigns success stories, coordination, collaboration and networking with all the resource centres and other organizations and agencies, analysis of the findings of the evaluation and research activities concerning the literacy campaigns, professional, academic and technical guidance concerning literacy activities and monitoring of Jan Shikshan Sansthans (JSSs), implementing UNFPA assisted project, namely "Population and Development Education in Post Literacy and Continuing Education" through State Resource Centres.

Since 1988, NLM under the supervision of the Directorate of Adult Education has led a vigorous literacy campaign all over the country during the last two decades and remarkable improvement in the literacy level of the nation has been seen. The analysis of the recent reports and statistics published by NLM (www.nlm.nic.in) confirms this progressive trend.

Status of National Literacy Campaign in India

Literacy campaigns have visibly contributed to the process of women empowerment. The literacy movement has several achievements to its credit. Up to November 2003, literacy campaigns have been launched in 596 districts (Table 3.1), of which 191 districts are in Post Literacy phase and 238 districts in Continuing Education phase.

Literacy projects under all the schemes of NLM conducted so far have covered more than 150 million illiterates/neo-literates in the age group of 9-35. Of them, nearly 106.64 million learners have been enrolled under literacy campaigns. More than 106.7 million have already been made literate under all programmes of NLM.

UNESCO has awarded 'Noma Prize' to the National Literacy Mission of India for its wonderful performance over the past two decades. It has also received the Nehru Literacy Award in 2001. The programmes are still going on in all the states of the country. An integrated approach regarding literacy, post-literacy and continuing education programmes is taken up in the new millennium.

Table 3.1 : Status of National Literacy Campaign in India

Sl. No.	*Name of States/UTs*	*No. of Districts*	*TLC*	*PLP*	*CEP*	*Total Districts covered*	*Uncovered Districts*
1.	Andhra Pradesh	23	0	2	21	23	0
2.	Arunachal Pradesh	15	15	0	0	15	0
3.	Assam	23	13	10	0	23	0
4.	Bihar	38	19	17	2	38	0
5.	Chhattisgarh	16	3	12	1	16	0
6.	Delhi	9	9	0	0	9	0
7.	Goa	2	2	0	0	2	0
8.	Gujarat	25	0	0	25	25	0
9.	Haryana	19	10	8	1	19	0
10.	Himachal Pradesh	12	0	11	1	12	0
11.	Jammu & Kashmir	14	13	0	0	13	1
12.	Jharkhand	22	14	6	2	22	0
13.	Karnataka	27	0	2	25	27	0
14.	Kerala	14	0	0	14	14	0
15.	Madhya Pradesh	45	0	17	28	45	0
16.	Maharashtra	35	5	13	17	35	0
17.	Manipur	9	9	0	0	9	0
18.	Meghalaya	7	6	1	0	7	0
19.	Mizoram	8	0	0	8	8	0
20.	Nagaland	8	8	0	0	8	0
21.	Orissa	30	10	17	3	30	0
22.	Punjab	17	9	7	1	17	0
23.	Rajasthan	32	0	4	28	32	0
24.	Sikkim	4	4	0	0	4	0
25.	Tamil Nadu	29	0	6	23	29	0
26.	Tripura	4	0	0	4	4	0
27.	Uttaranchal	13	1	10	2	13	0
28.	Uttar Pradesh	70	16	41	13	70	0
29.	West Bengal	19	0	6	13	19	0
30.	A and N Islands	2	0	0	0	0	2
31.	Chandigarh	1	0	0	1	1	0
32.	D and N Haveli	1	1	0	0	1	0
33.	Daman and Diu	2	0	1	0	1	1
34.	Lakshadweep	1	0	0	1	1	0
35.	Pondicherry	4	0	0	4	4	0
	Total	**600**	**167**	**191**	**238**	**596**	**4**

Source : www.nlm.nic.in

Literacy Status in India

Since independence there has been a steady progress in the literacy rate (Table 3.2). Female literacy rate has increased from 8.86 per cent in 1951 to 54.16 per cent by 2001 while male literacy rate has gone up from 27.16 per cent to 75.85 per cent.

Table 3.2 : Growth of Literacy Rate in India

Year	Persons	Male	Female
1951	18.33	27.16	8.86
1961	28.31	40.40	15.34
1971	34.45	45.95	21.97
1981	43.56	56.37	29.75
1991	52.21	64.13	39.29
2001	65.38	75.85	54.16

Source : www.nlm.nic.in

Table 3.3 presents the information regarding the increasing number of literates in India. Till 1981 literacy has been estimated upon the population of the age group of 5 plus. Since 1991 literacy rate is estimated upon the population above 7 years of age. The difference in both the estimates is obvious from the figures of 1981.

Table 3.3 : Number of Literates and Non-literates in India : 1951-2001

Year	Total Population (All Ages)	Age Group	Total Population	Non-literates	Literates
1951	361.09	—	—	300.09	60.19
1961	438.93	5+	372.84	267.32	105.52
1971	548.16	5+	468.60	307.19	161.41
1981	665.29	5+	581.78	340.75	241.03
1981	665.29	7+	541.04	305.31	235.73
1991	846.30	7+	688.16	328.88	359.28
2001	1027.01	7+	866.85	300.14	566.71

Source : www.nlm.nic.in

There is significant disparity between the literacy rates of men and women in India. Table 3.4 presents the gender gap in the literacy rates in India. There is an average of 20 points difference in the rates of male-female literacy rates over the years. Since 1951 the male literacy rate has increased by 48.69 per cent while the increase in female literacy rate is 45.3 per cent.

Table 3.4 : Male-Female gap in literacy rate in India

Census Year	*Persons*	*Males*	*Females*	*Male-Female gap in literacy rate*
1951	18.33	27.16	8.86	18.30
1961	28.30	40.40	15.35	25.05
1971	34.45	45.96	21.97	23.98
1981	43.57	56.38	29.76	26.62
1991	52.21	64.13	39.29	24.84
2001	65.38	75.85	54.16	21.70

Source : www.nlm.nic.in

There is also pronounced rural-urban difference with regard to literacy rates in India. Table 3.5 shows the urban-rural disparity with regard to literacy levels. The rural-urban gap with regard to literacy rate is as wide as 31.97 points in 1961. It has come down to 20.85 points by 2001 showing a trend of gradual decrease except in the year 1971 where a marginal increase in the rural-urban gap is seen. It is obvious that urban population has better educational opportunity. In other words,

Table 3.5 : Urban-Rural Differential in Literacy Rates in India : 1961-2001

Year	*Age Group*	*Literacy Rate Urban Areas*	*Literacy Rate Rural Areas*	*Difference in rural/urban areas (%age points)*
1961	5 and over	54.43	22.46	31.97
1971	5 and over	60.22	27.89	32.33
1981	5 and over	64.85	34.04	30.81
1981	7 and over	67.20	36.00	31.20
1991	7 and over	73.08	44.69	28.39
2001	7 and over	80.06	59.21	20.85

Source : www.nlm.nic.in

social infrastructure is better in the urban areas compared to rural areas. It is seen that with regard to population above 7 years of age the rural-urban difference in literacy rate is more compared to the age group of people above 5 years in the year 1981 which shows that there is opportunity for children of the age group of 5-7 years for elementary education in the villages.

Literacy Rate Among Scheduled Castes and Scheduled Tribes

Literacy level of SC/ST population is much lower compared to the general population in India. The Caste-wise data regarding literacy rate is available latest for the year 1991 (Table 3.6).

As per 1991 census the literacy rate of Scheduled Castes and Scheduled Tribes is 37.41 per cent and 29.60 per cent respectively. Literacy rate of SC females compared to general population is much lower in the states of Bihar (7.07%), Rajasthan (8.31%) and Uttar Pradesh (10.69%). Literacy rate of ST females is extremely low in Rajasthan (4.4%). As per 1991 census the literacy rate for SCs is the lowest in Bihar (19.49%) and highest in Kerala (79.66%) and for STs the lowest is in Andhra Pradesh (17.16%) and highest in Mizoram (82%).

District-wise analysis of the literacy status reveals that Lalitpur district of Uttar Pradesh has the lowest literacy of 4.74 per cent for STs in the country. For ST males the literacy is lowest in Mau district of UP (3.85%) and for females it is Jalore district of Rajasthan (0.55%). Literacy rate of STs is more than the SCs in the states of Bihar, Meghalaya, Mizoram, Sikkim, and Uttar Pradesh. In general the SCs are ahead of the STs in literacy. But in urban areas the STs are ahead of SCs. The percentage of learners of SCs and STs under literacy Campaigns are 23.85 per cent and 12.34 per cent respectively. The share of expenditure in implementation of literacy campaigns between the Centre and States in tribal areas is 4 : 1 instead of 2 : 1 in other areas.

Table 3.7 presents the data regarding the progress in the literacy rates of SC/ST population in India.

Table 3.6 : Literacy Rates for SC/ST Population by Sex (1991)

Sl. No.	India, State or Union Territory	Persons			Males			Females		
		Total	S.C.	S.T.	Total	S.C.	S.T.	Total	S.C.	S.T.
	INDIA	52.21	37.41	29.60	64.13	49.91	40.65	39.29	23.76	18.19
1.	Andhra Pradesh	44.09	31.59	17.16	55.13	41.88	25.25	32.72	20.92	8.68
2.	Arunachal Pradesh	41.59	57.27	34.45	51.45	66.25	44.00	29.69	41.42	24.94
3.	Assam	52.89	53.94	49.16	61.87	63.88	58.93	43.03	42.99	38.98
4.	Bihar	38.48	19.49	26.78	52.49	30.64	38.40	22.89	7.07	14.75
5.	Goa	75.51	58.73	42.91	83.64	69.55	54.43	67.09	47.51	29.01
6.	Gujarat	61.29	61.07	36.45	73.13	75.47	48.25	48.64	45.54	24.20
7.	Haryana	55.85	39.22	0.00	69.10	52.06	0.00	40.47	24.15	0.00
8.	Himachal Pradesh	63.86	53.20	47.09	75.36	64.98	62.74	52.13	41.02	31.18
9.	Karnataka	56.04	38.06	36.01	67.26	49.69	47.95	44.34	25.95	23.57
10.	Kerala	89.81	79.66	57.22	93.62	85.22	63.38	86.13	74.31	51.07
11.	Madhya Pradesh	44.20	35.08	21.54	58.42	50.51	32.16	28.85	18.11	10.73
12.	Maharashtra	64.87	56.46	36.79	76.56	70.45	49.09	52.32	41.59	24.03
13.	Manipur	59.89	56.44	53.63	71.63	65.28	62.39	47.60	47.41	44.48
14.	Meghalaya	49.10	44.27	46.71	53.12	54.56	49.78	44.85	31.19	43.63
15.	Mizoram	82.27	77.92	82.73	85.61	77.54	86.67	78.60	81.25	78.74
16.	Nagaland	61.65	0.00	60.59	67.62	0.00	66.27	54.75	0.00	54.51
17.	Orissa	49.09	36.78	22.31	63.09	52.42	34.44	34.68	20.74	10.21
18.	Punjab	58.51	41.09	0.00	65.66	49.82	0.00	50.41	31.03	0.00
19.	Rajasthan	38.55	26.29	19.44	54.99	42.38	33.29	20.44	8.31	4.42
20.	Sikkim	56.94	51.03	59.01	65.74	58.69	66.80	46.69	42.77	50.37
21.	Tamil Nadu	62.66	46.74	27.89	73.75	58.36	35.25	51.33	34.89	20.23
22.	Tripura	60.44	56.66	40.37	70.58	67.25	52.88	49.65	45.45	27.34
23.	Uttar Pradesh	41.60	26.85	35.70	55.73	40.80	49.95	25.31	10.69	19.86
24.	West Bengal	57.70	42.21	27.78	67.81	54.55	40.07	46.56	28.87	14.98
25.	Andaman and Nicobar Islands	73.02	0.00	56.62	78.99	0.00	64.16	65.46	0.00	48.74
26.	Chandigarh	77.81	55.44	0.00	82.04	64.74	0.00	72.34	43.54	0.00
27.	Dadra and Nagar Haveli	40.71	77.64	28.21	53.56	88.03	40.75	26.98	66.61	15.94
28.	Daman and Diu	71.20	79.18	52.91	82.66	91.85	63.58	59.40	67.62	41.49
29.	Delhi	75.29	57.60	0.00	82.01	68.77	0.00	66.99	43.82	0.00
30.	Lakshadweep	81.78	0.00	80.58	90.18	0.00	89.50	72.89	0.00	71.72
31.	Pondicherry	74.74	56.26	0.00	83.68	66.10	0.00	65.63	46.28	0.00

Source : www.nlm.nic.in

Table 3.7 : Increase in Literacy Rate of SC/ST population during 1961-1991

Year	*Scheduled Caste (% Increase)*			*Scheduled Tribe (% Increase)*			*Total Population (% Increase)*		
	Total	*Male*	*Female*	*Total*	*Male*	*Female*	*Total*	*Male*	*Female*
1961	10.27	16.96	3.29	8.53	13.83	3.16	28.31	40.40	15.34
1971	14.67	22.36	6.44	11.30	17.63	4.85	34.45	45.95	21.97
	(42.84%)	(31.83%)	(95.75%)	(32.47%)	(27.48%)	(53.48%)	(21.69%)	(13.74%)	(43.22%)
1981	21.38	31.12	10.93	16.35	24.52	8.04	43.56	56.37	29.75
	(45.74%)	(39.18%)	(69.72%)	(44.69%)	(39.08%)	(65.77%)	(26.44%)	(22.67%)	(35.41%)
1991	37.41	49.91	23.76	29.60	40.65	18.19	52.21	64.13	39.29
	(74.98%)	(60.38%)	(117.38%)	(81.04%)	(65.78%)	(126.24%)	(19.86%)	(13.77%)	(32.07%)

Source : www.nlm.nic.in

It can be seen from the table (Table 3.7) that the female literacy rate for ST is as low as 18.19 per cent in 1991 while the corresponding figure for the total population is 39.29 per cent. However, the increase in the female literacy rate with reference to the rates of 1981 is 126.24 per cent for ST women and only 32.07 per cent for total population. Similar finding is seen in the case of SC women too. It shows that there is gradual growth in the literacy levels of SC/ST women.

Literacy and Women Empowerment

Literacy campaigns have visibly contributed to the process of women empowerment. In all the literacy programmes, 60 per cent learners are female and 40 per cent are male. 24 per cent learners belong to Scheduled Castes and 13 per cent belong to Scheduled Tribes. The cumulative number of literary volunteers mobilized since the launching of literacy campaigns exceeds 10 million. The literacy campaigns thus represent the largest ever civil and military mobilization in the history of the country.

The achievements of National Literacy Mission's Total Literacy Campaign have been discussed in All India Adult Education Conference (2001) and are summarised as follows :

(a) Awakening of masses for empowerment (encouraging voluntarism especially of women literacy workers) in the Society. Anti-arrack agitation of Nellore in Andhra Pradesh by neo-literate women is a demonstration of empowered women.

(b) *Promotion of Social Integration* : Untouchability and feuds on account of caste and communal considerations have become issues of the past.

(c) *Gender equality and women empowerment* : Development of Mahila Mandals and women's organisations.

(d) *Better utilisation of franchise* : Between 1984 and 1989, number of invalid votes came down from 12683 to 7857 in Ernakulam district, Kerala.

(e) Lower birth rate and infant mortality, better immunisation programmes.

(f) Greater Public Health awareness, AIDS awareness and greater response to polio vaccination programmes.

(g) *Greater Environmental Awareness* : 1500 smokeless *chulhas* have been installed by neo-literate women's organisations at Ramanathapuram.

(h) *Higher rate of enrolment and retention in Primary schools* : 25 per cent of increase in enrolment of children of neo-literate parents compared to non-literate parents (Indian Adult Education Association, 2001 : 22).

The single biggest characteristic of the literacy campaigns has been their ability to galvanize entire communities into believing that learning must become an integral port of their lives. The *modus operandi* has been to create and build on environment conducive to learning by accessing communities through their cultural roots and traditions. All manner of tools have been used such as cultural processions, street plays, local theatre, puppetry, folk songs, etc.

The Adult Education Programme has contributed in a significant way to better enrolment of children in schools. Study findings in India show that enrolment of boys and girls in the age group of 5-15 years is significantly higher in neo-literate households as compared to children in illiterate households. 2 out of 3 boys in neo-literate households are enrolled in schools compared to 3 out of 4 in participant households. In the case of girls this difference is even more enhanced—58 per cent for non-participants and 72 per cent for participants (www.nlm.nic.in).

India recorded heightened social awareness regarding the importance of education both for themselves as well as for their children. The biggest achievement of the adult education movement has been its impact on girls' education. The confidence of the girls as they perform their scholastic and extra-curricular roles is the result of the awareness among neo-literate parents that girls need to be educated and outgoing. The need to provide equal opportunity to both girls and boys has also had the effect of generating greater demand for the quantity and quality of primary schooling.

Haryana State

The study is conducted in the state of Haryana. Haryana is the home of the legendary Bharata Dynasty. Kurukshetra, the ground of epic Mahabharat battle, is in Haryana. During the medieval period the historical importance of Haryana gradually declined. During the Mughal era, Delhi occupied the Central place of India's political history. Haryana remained almost anonymous till 1857. Several heroes have emerged during the rebellion of 1857. When the British army crushed the rebellion, the rulers of Haryana had to forfeit their land and property. Consequently the Nawab of Jhajjar, Nawab of Bahadurgarh, Raja of Ballabhgarh and Rao Tula Ram of Rewari were deprived of their territories. All these territories were in turn, handed over to the rulers of Patiala, Nabha and Jind. Till 1966, Haryana remained as the part of Punjab. While reorganising Punjab, Haryana has been formed as a separate state on 1st November, 1966. It has an area of 44,212 sq. km. It is the 16th largest state in India. Its population is 2,10,82,989. Density of population of Haryana is 477, while the national density is 324 (Census, 2001).

According to the Census report of 2001, literacy rate in Haryana is 68.59 per cent, while all India rate is 65.38 per cent. Women literacy level is 56.31 per cent, which is 2.15 per cent higher than all India rate. The percentage of Scheduled Castes population in Haryana is 19.75 per cent while their share in

India's population is 16.48 per cent. Scheduled Tribes is *nil* in the state of Haryana. Rural-urban population ratio in the state is 74.3 : 25.7. Haryana has 1749 industrial model townships. Four-fifth of country's total passenger car production is from Haryana. Two-third of motorcycles, one-fourth of cycles and sanitarywares are produced in Haryana. Paniput is known as the "weavers' city". Cyber city at Gurgaon is the first of its kind in the country. Haryana is the first state to achieve 100 per cent rural electrification by 1970. The state has pioneered the lift irrigation system in India with the construction of Western Yamuna Canal, Bhakra Canal and Gurgaon Canal. All villages are inter-connected with metalled roads. Haryana is industrially very forward but urbanisation of Haryana is not proportionate. The rural Haryana seems to be typically traditional and caste ridden.

Economic Status of Women in Haryana

Haryana is known for dairying and dairy products. Women are the chief stakeholders in dairying. Contribution of woman to dairying ranges from collection of fodder, to milking of animals, cleaning and taking care of animals. They get up as early as 2 : 30 am for preparing animals for milking. However, it is observed that women hardly have any say in owning the animals or the income obtained from the sale of milk (Ahlawat, 1995 : 68).

On account of deeply entrenched social customs, taboos and prejudices, women's work in Haryana continues to be invisible and confined more to non-monetary activities. In Haryana, women are mainly engaged as self-employed workers largely in home based activities where their work intermixes with their household duties. Therefore, the productivity of their work as well as their status as workers remains invisible. There are several activities like collection of fodder and fuel, maintaining of dairy, looking after cattle, food processing, sewing, weaving, etc. which women are engaged in and increase the household's command over the necessities. The household would have to spend a lot of money in procuring these services, if the women refuse to render them. In Haryana, women work for longer hours and contribute more than men in terms of total labour energy spent by the household members. The average hours of unpaid work done by married women outside the home in Rohtak town varied from 6.13 to 7.43 hours per day (Ahlawat, 1995 : 63).

Gender Status in Haryana

Literacy level of women is an indicator of women empowerment. There is considerable difference between men and women with regard to literacy level in the country. The situation is not different in Haryana. On the other hand gender disparity is more acute in the state. Lower literacy level of women indicates their unequal opportunity for basic education. The high incidence of illiteracy amongst females constitutes one of the greatest barriers to their development. It limits the scope of their training, employment, utilization of health facilities and exercise of legal and constitutional rights. There is significant correlation between female literacy and other demographic indices. The census data reveal several such correlations. Female literacy rate is positively related with mean age at marriage. Female literacy is strongly and negatively related with infant mortality rate, percentage of married females aged 14-24, crude birth rate, and total fertility rate.

Table 3.8 reveals the comparative gender status of Haryana among other states of India with regard to literacy rate and sex ratio.

Statistics shows gender discrimination in literacy level and sex ratio in the state of Haryana. Table 3.1 shows the comparative literacy status of different states of India. Literacy level in Haryana has improved from 55.85 per cent to 68.59 per cent in 2001 with a decadal growth of 12.74 per cent. However the difference in male-female literacy levels is 22.94. This difference is highest in Rajasthan with 32.12 per cent followed by Jharkhand, Uttar Pradesh, Bihar and Madhya Pradesh. Gender gap in literacy level is lowest in Mizoram with 4.56 per cent.

Table 3.8 : Gender status of Haryana

	State	Literacy Rate (2001 Census) (In %)			Lite-racy Rate	Change in Lite-racy Rate	SexRatio Ratio	
		Persons	Males	Fe-males	(1991 Cen-sus)	(1991-2001)	General	(0-6 Yrs)
1	Andhra Pradesh	61.11	70.85	51.17	44.09	17.02	978	964
2	Arunachal Pradesh	54.74	64.07	44.24	41.59	13.15	901	961
3	Assam	64.28	71.93	56.03	52.89	11.52	932	964
4	Bihar	47.53	60.32	33.57	37.49	10.04	921	938
5	Chhattisgarh	65.18	77.86	52.40	42.91	22.27	990	975
6	Delhi	81.82	87.37	75.00	75.29	06.53	821	865
7	Goa	82.32	88.88	75.51	75.51	06.81	960	933
8	Gujarat	69.97	80.50	58.60	61.29	08.68	921	878
9	**Haryana**	**68.59**	**79.25**	**56.31**	**55.85**	**12.74**	**861**	**820**
10	Himachal Pradesh	77.13	86.02	68.08	63.86	13.27	970	897
11	Jammu and Kashmir	54.46	65.75	41.82	NA	NA	900	937
12	Jharkhand	54.13	67.94	39.38	41.39	12.74	941	966
13	Karnataka	67.04	76.29	57.45	56.04	11.00	964	949
14	Kerala	90.92	94.20	87.86	89.81	01.11	1,058	963
15	Madhya Pradesh	64.11	76.80	50.28	44.67	19.41	920	929
16	Maharashtra	77.27	86.27	67.51	64.87	12.39	922	917
17	Manipur	68.87	77.87	59.70	59.89	08.97	978	961
18	Meghalaya	63.31	66.14	60.41	49.10	14.21	975	975
19	Mizoram	88.49	90.69	86.13	82.27	06.22	938	971
20	Nagaland	67.11	71.77	61.92	61.65	05.45	909	975
21	Orissa	63.61	75.95	50.97	49.09	14.52	972	950
22	Punjab	69.95	75.63	63.55	58.51	11.45	874	793
23	Rajasthan	61.03	76.46	44.34	38.55	22.48	922	909
24	Sikkim	69.68	76.73	61.46	56.94	12.61	875	986
25	Tamil Nadu	73.47	82.33	64.55	62.66	10.81	986	939
26	Tripura	73.66	81.47	65.41	60.44	13.22	950	975
27	Uttar Pradesh	57.36	70.23	42.98	40.71	16.65	898	916
28	Uttaranchal	72.28	84.01	60.26	57.75	14.53	964	906
29	West Bengal	69.22	77.58	60.22	57.70	11.52	934	963
	INDIA	65.38	75.96	54.28	51.63	13.75	933	927

There are 861 women per 1000 men in Haryana. Only five states have the sex ratio below 900. They are Delhi, Haryana, Punjab, Sikkim and Uttar Pradesh. Sex ratio of Haryana is lower than all India figure of 933. Haryana state has the second lowest sex ratio in India. Delhi alone has the sex ratio lower than Haryana. Compared to the neighbouring states of UP, MP, Punjab and Rajasthan, Haryana has lower sex ratio. It clearly indicates the overriding preference for male children in the families of Haryana state.

It can be seen from the table that the child sex ratio (0-6 years of age group) in India is lower than that of general sex ratio. The child sex ratio in Haryana is 820. It is lower than the general sex ratio of Haryana. It is also lower than the All India figure of 927. Five states having child sex ratio below 900 are Punjab, Haryana, Delhi, Gujarat and Himachal Pradesh. Punjab has the lowest child sex ratio of 793 followed by Haryana. Compared to the neighbouring states of Delhi, UP, MP and Rajasthan, Haryana has lower child sex ratio. It is again an indication that the communities of Haryana state prefer male children to female ones. Lower sex ratio of the younger age group points towards the trend of widening the gender gap in the state. Over the past forty years, there has been a gradual decline in the sex ratio of the state of Haryana. This increasing gender gap is made clearer from Table 3.9.

Table 3.9 : The sex ratio of Haryana for the past 40 years

Year	*Haryana*	*India*
2001	861	933
1991	865	922
1981	878	933
1971	887	930
1961	888	941

Over the past 40 years, the gender gap in the state has increased from 112 to 139 per 1000 population. Even if the literacy level has increased tremendously over these decades, the gender gap has kept on widening. Haryana is one of the rich states in the country. However, it is poorer in gender balance. The progress in economic and educational fields has not reduced the gender discrimination in the state.

Gender Status in Faridabad District

Faridabad district, where the research is undertaken, is the largest district in Haryana in terms of population. It has an area of 2,151 sq. km. with a population of 21,93,276 (Census, 2001). The study is undertaken in 10 villages in Chandpur region of Haryana state. Chandpur is situated in Faridabad district, 12 kilometres away from Delhi-Mathura Road. Ballabhgarh is the nearest railway station, which is situated 13 kilometres far from Chandpur. It is 20 kilometres far from Faridabad town and 55 kilometres far from New Delhi railway station. Faridabad district, being closer to New Delhi, has benefited from the industrial and economic growth of the region. Setting up of new industries and expansion of residential quarters on both sides of Mathura Road have contributed to process of the gradual modernisation of the district. Industrialisation and urbanisation are changing the face of the village communities in the district. Rural-urban migration is also on the fast track. The Census Report of 2001 has given out the district-wise demographic data. The gender status with regard to sex ratio and literacy ratio in the district of Faridabad is reflected in Table 3.10.

Faridabad district, which had the lowest sex ratio in 1991, has become third from the lowest in 2001. Panchkula has the lowest sex ratio of 823 in the state. Only two districts have the sex ratio above 900. They are Mahendragarh and Rewari. The child sex ratio (age group of 0-6 years) of Faridabad is 807. The lowest child sex ratio is in the district of Fatehabad followed by Jind. Five districts in Haryana have child sex ratio below 800. They are Fatehabad, Jind, Bhiwani, Gurgaon and Paniput. Faridabad is seventh district from the low end with regard to child sex ratio. None of the districts in Haryana has the child sex ratio above 900. The wide disparity between the general sex ratio and the child sex ratio is a serious concern today.

Table 3.10 : Gender status of Faridabad District

	State/District	*Sex ratio*		*Sex ratio 2001*	*Literacy Rate 2001*			*Female Literacy Rate*
		1991	*2001*	*(0-6 years)*	*Persons*	*Males*	*Females*	*1991*
1	Ambala	903	869	837	76.54	82.74	68.98	56.17
2	Bhiwani	878	880	784	76.2	83.01	68.48	56.78
3	**Faridabad**	**828**	**839**	**807**	**72.2**	**79.28**	**64.08**	**50.16**
4	Fatehabad	877	886	770	70.04	78.23	60.76	46.56
5	Gurgaon	871	874	789	59.5	69.81	47.6	28.78
6	Hisar	853	852	808	68.2	76.74	58.42	41.92
7	Jhajjar	861	848	807	69.75	79.16	58.48	42.78
8	Jind	838	853	783	73.71	83.95	61.65	45.74
9	Kaithal	853	854	818	62.8	74.69	48.97	29.86
10	Karnal	864	864	830	58.16	68.71	46.4	29.77
11	Kurukshetra	879	866	818	61.2	70.93	50.31	34.02
12	Mahendragarh	910	919	830	65.85	77.62	52.09	33.41
13	Panchkula	839	823	838	68.17	81.19	53.5	35.07
14	Panipat	852	830	796	74.56	84.29	63.19	48.25
15	Rewari	927	901	805	72.48	83.26	59.88	46.12
16	Rohtak	849	847	814	70.43	85.31	54.61	36.75
17	Sirsa	885	882	814	75.75	89.04	61.25	46.34
18	Sonipat	840	839	863	63.64	77.11	48.29	34.94
19	Yamunanagar	883	863	856	70.79	82.49	56.8	42.12
	Haryana	865	861	820	68.59	79.25	56.31	40.47

District-wise demographic features showing gender difference is presented by Table 3.10. Faridabad district has maintained its literacy status above the state average. With regard to female literacy level, Karnal again has the lowest figure and Ambala has the highest followed by Bhiwani and Faridabad. It is worthy to note that Bhiwani has a high female literacy rate and very low child sex ratio. Faridabad is the third highest with regard to female literacy rate. However, Faridabad occupies only 10th position with regard to male literacy level in the state. Gender gap with regard to literacy rate is lowest in Ambala with 13.76 per cent and highest in Rohtak with 30.7 per cent. Gender gap in literacy levels in Faridabad is 15.2 per cent, which is comparatively low. The decadal growth in the literacy rate of Haryana is 28.12 and it is 22.04 in Faridabad.

The decadal growth is lowest in Bhiwani and highest in Rohtak. Overall literacy status as well as women's literacy status in Faridabad is comparatively better than other districts of the state.

Concluding Remarks

Analysing the available statistics and published reports, it is seen that rapid progress is achieved in the literacy level of the nation since independence. National Literacy Campaign launched in 1988 has significantly contributed to the improvement in the literacy level of the nation. However, regional disparity is vivid. The Scheduled Castes and Scheduled Tribes lag behind with regard to literacy level and their women are far behind the national average in this regard. Sex ratio continues to be declining especially with industrialised states. Haryana is above average in literacy level compared with the national literacy rate but is below average concerning sex ratio. Faridabad district where the study is held is better in literacy level, but poorer in sex ratio in comparison with the state averages.

4

Socio-Economic Profile of Women Literacy Workers

Socio-economic profile refers to demographic, economic and social identity of women literacy workers. This information helps us to locate the basic socio-economic status of women literacy workers in the wider context of the nation. Understanding the primary identity of women literacy workers is essential to analyse the magnitude of empowerment they have achieved due to their active participation in the literacy work.

Empowerment is a relative phenomenon. No social development can be defined in absolute terms. Empowerment is a relative improvement in the basic socio-economic status of women literacy workers. The level of empowerment achieved by the rural women will be significantly different from the level of empowerment achieved by their urban counterpart. In urban set up women get better access to education, health care, and vocational training. But in a rural set up the situation is rather unfavourable to women. In this chapter an attempt is made to explore into the demographic, economic and social profile of women literacy workers.

Demographic Profile

Demographic profile is the essential aspect of socio-economic status of women literacy workers. Demographic profile of women literacy workers includes the native place of women literacy workers, age group, marital status, religion and caste of women literacy workers. These are the pieces of information that make the first level of understanding of an individual. This data allows us to form the first impression about women literacy workers. This data is also the basis for placing the limits for our expectation regarding the level of empowerment achievable by women literacy workers. All women literacy workers belong to a cluster of ten villages. These villages are situated in Faridabad district of Haryana State, 20 kilometres distant from the town of Faridabad. Six of these villages are lying on the bank of the river Yamuna. The population of these villages ranges from 500 to 2000. Most of the villagers are farmers. These villages have primary schools run by the Panchayats. The educated members of the rural folks migrate almost permanently to the industrial centres of Haryana and Delhi. The status of women who are residing permanently in these villages is very low. Progress of literacy programmes is very slow in these villages. When SJSS, an NGO, started working in these villages the officials of the block level development agencies informed about the twice-failed attempts to educate the illiterate women of these villages. After continued efforts of the dedicated social workers of SJSS, 56 women came forward as volunteer literacy workers.

It can be seen from the following analysis that women literacy workers are a typical sample of rural women of Haryana.

Table 4.1 : Village of women literacy workers

Sl. No.	*Particulars*	*Frequency*	*Percentage*
1	Alipur	7	12.50
2	Aruva	1	1.79
3	Bahadurpur	12	21.43
4	Chandpur	7	12.50
5	Dalaigarh	1	1.79
6	Imamudinpur	6	10.71
7	Faejpur	2	3.57
8	Nehandola	7	12.50
9	Raipurkalan	3	5.36
10	Shajapur	10	17.86
	Total	**56**	**100.00**

We see considerable differences in voluntarism among the villages. There are several factors accounting for these differences. In Aruva and Dalaigarh we find one literacy worker each while in Bahadurpur we see 12 literacy workers. Aruva and Dalaigarh are relatively small villages. Literacy programmes did not appeal effectively to these village communities who found it almost impossible to spare some time for attending adult education classes.

Table 4.2 : Age Group of women literacy workers

Sl. No.	*Particulars*	*Frequency*	*Percentage*	*Cumulative Percentage*
1	15 to 20 Years	33	58.93	58.93
2	21 to 25 Years	11	19.64	78.57
3	26 to 30 Years	3	5.36	83.93
4	31 to 35 Years	4	7.14	91.07
5	36 to 40 Years	3	5.36	96.43
6	41 to 45 Years	2	3.57	100.00
	Total	**56**	**100.00**	

Nearly 60 per cent of woman literacy workers are below 20 years of age. Almost 80 per cent of women literacy workers are below 25 years of age. It has been observed that most of women literacy workers are high school or higher secondary students. They are at home preparing for their marriage. They have joined as literacy workers partly as time pass and partly as social service. It is easy to motivate them compared to the married women. Since the married women are originally from other villages, they are forced to use *Purdah* and seldom come forward for social service. Comparatively the married women are less educated. Some of women literacy workers who are educated and unmarried have joined as literacy workers with the hope of getting a better place in the society. Meanwhile most of them have expressed their willingness to take up an outdoor job in the village or town.

Table 4.3 : Marital Status of women literacy workers

Sl. No.	*Particulars*	*Frequency*	*Percentage*
1	Married	22	39.29
2	Single (unmarried)	34	60.71
	Total	**56**	**100.00**

Over 60 per cent of women literacy workers are unmarried. Marital status is a significant factor in voluntarism. Voluntarism is less appropriate to the married women than the unmarried. Married women find little time and convenience for sparing for voluntary service. Unmarried girls are comparatively free either for studies or for social service. Unmarried girls get greater opportunities to pursue their studies and get higher educational qualifications. Higher education for women does not prepare them for a gainful employment but facilitate for a better suit in marriage. To get involved voluntarily in literacy work has been found very much satisfying for them. This intrinsic reward is the primary motivation for the unmarried and educated women to come forward as literacy workers.

Table 4.4 : Religion of women literacy workers

Sl. No.	*Particulars*	*Frequency*	*Percentage*
1	Hindu	49	87.50
2	Muslim	6	10.71
3	Any other	1	1.79
	Total	**56**	**100.00**

Most of the women literacy workers are Hindu by religion. Majority of the rural population belong to Hindu religion and the number of literacy workers is proportional to the total population of the villages. It is observed that in two villages the majority of the population belong to Muslim religion and the literacy workers in those villages are Muslim. Asma from Alipur has combined Urdu classes with literacy classes. She is running a tailoring centre too. She has taught literacy to all the trainees in her tailoring centre. It is also observed that Hindus and Muslims have attended the literacy classes regardless the religious background of the literacy workers.

Table 4.5 : Caste of women literacy workers

Sl. No.	*Particulars*	*Frequency*	*Percentage*
1	Brahmin, Sharma or Pandit	5	8.93
2	Kshatriyas (Thakur, Rajput or Jat)	24	42.86
3	Shudra (Dalit, Gujar, Gadariya or Nai)	18	32.14
4	Any other	3	5.36
5	NA/DK	6	10.71
	Total	**56**	**100.00**

Over 30 per cent of women literacy workers belong to Scheduled Caste. At least 10 per cent of women literacy workers are Muslims and caste discrimination is not relevant in this community. It is observed that there is a greater initiative on the part of Dalits with regard to literacy work. At least four of the villages have a considerable number of Dalit population. Many of them have regular employment either in public limited companies or in Government departments. Educationally, Dalit communities are found better qualified and this account for their better initiative in literacy work.

Economic Profile

Economic profile deals with the income, earnings, employment, accommodation and amenities of women literacy workers. Haryana is sixth richest state in India in terms of GDP. Both agriculturally and industrially, Haryana is ahead of most of the states in India. Villages are small in size and settlements are clustered. The concerned villages of Faridabad, being closer to industrial units located on Delhi-Mathura Road, have availed the employment opportunities in the industrial sector. Even if agriculture is the chief occupation of the villagers, landless workers are many in these villages and the income earned from non-agricultural occupations is very significant. In this section the economic status of women literacy workers is analysed.

Table 4.6 : Land in possession of women literacy workers' family

Sl. No.	Particulars	Frequency	Percentage
1	Own land	27	48.21
2	Rented	5	8.93
3	Landless	24	42.86
	Total	**56**	**100.00**

Over 48 per cent of women literacy workers possess cultivable land, 9 per cent of women literacy workers have rented plots for cultivation and remaining women literacy workers are landless. It is observed that the landless families depend chiefly upon non-agricultural occupation. Rural-urban linkage is high in landless households and they tend to migrate almost permanently to the nearby towns like Faridabad and Ballabhgarh. General trend in these villages is to look for an industrial or non-agricultural occupation of regular nature. Cultivation is not only seasonal but also part time occupation. Unless one has a large plot of land his/her family cannot survive on this type of seasonal occupation.

Table 4.7 : Financial Status of women literacy workers

Sl. No.	Particulars	Frequency	Percentage
1	Below Poverty Line (BPL), i.e. Per Capita Expenditure (PCE) below Rs. 300 per month	1	1.79
2	Lower middle class—PCE between Rs. 300 to Rs. 1,000 per month	55	98.21
	Total	**56**	**100.00**

It is seen that all women literacy workers except one belong to lower middle income group. Since monthly income is found difficult to be estimated due to the seasonal nature of occupation, economic status is determined on the basis of monthly expenditure or per capita consumption. It can also be inferred that greater initiative is found among the lower middle class group with regard to literacy work. There are certain high middle class families, but voluntarism is perceived among the lower middle class group. It may be due to the higher level of aspiration found among the lower middle class group. Greater economic and educational mobility is visible among the lower middle class compared to the lower income group and the higher income groups.

Table 4.8 : Agricultural activities of women literacy workers

Sl. No.	*Particulars*	*Frequency*	*Percentage*
1	Agricultural activities	28	50.00
2	Non-agricultural activities	28	50.00
	Total	**56**	**100.00**

Dependence upon the primary sector for livelihood is an indication of traditionalism. The ratio of agricultural occupation among women literacy workers is below the state average, which proves that the village communities under the study are typically traditional societies and the voluntarism emerging in these communities is unexpected. Half of women literacy workers are engaged in agriculture related occupations while the other half is engaged in non-agricultural occupations. We have seen from Table 4.6 that over 57 per cent of women literacy workers have own or rented agricultural land. Thus we can see that 7 per cent of women literacy workers who have own cultivable land do not prefer agricultural occupation. This is a trend of urbanisation where we see a gradual shift of earning members from primary sector to secondary sector.

Table 4.9 : Earnings of the family besides agriculture

Sl. No.	*Particulars*	*Frequency*	*Percentage*
1	Below Rs. 2,000	24	42.86
2	Between Rs. 2,000 to Rs. 5,000	18	32.14
3	Above Rs. 5,000	2	3.57
4	Nil	12	21.43
	Total	**56**	**100.00**

Over three-fourth of women literacy workers do have non-agricultural earnings while only 21 per cent of women literacy workers are purely dependent upon agriculture for survival. This data confirms the previous finding of the apparent shift of earning population from agricultural to non-agricultural occupations (Table 4.8). There are some earning members who are engaged in non-agricultural occupations in most of the households. Educated youth are seeking non-agricultural occupations. The initiative shown by women literacy workers is also an indicator of their aspiration for non-agricultural engagements.

Table 4.10 : Nature of Employment of the Head of the Family

Sl. No.	*Particulars*	*Frequency*	*Percentage*
1	Business	6	10.71
2	Government Service	13	23.21
3	Private Service	8	14.29
4	Daily Wage	18	32.14
5	Any other	11	19.64
	Total	**56**	**100.00**

Over one-third of the heads of the family are regular service holders in Government or private sector. Nearly one-third are daily wage labourers. Almost 10 per cent are in business. Nearly one-fifth of the heads of the family are engaged only in agricultural activities. Service holders seem to be more mobile.

It is observed that service holders are more educated and belong to lower middle class. They seem to be more hard working and show greater initiative with regard to literacy work. Daily wage labourers belong to low-income group. It is observed that they are landless labours and have taken up literacy work with the hope of getting a regular service in some Government or private concerns. It is seen that the literacy workers are easily motivated to join for self-help group movement. The women who are below poverty line have benefited from several grant-giving schemes of Government.

Table 4.11 : Unemployed or underemployed members in the family

Sl. No.	*Particulars*	*Frequency*	*Percentage*
1	Unemployed	9	16.07
2	Underemployed	19	33.93
3	Both	6	10.71
4	None	18	32.14
5	Any other	4	7.14
	Total	**56**	**100.00**

Over 60 per cent of women literacy workers have reported the prevalence of unemployment or underemployment or both in their households. It is another indication of the presence of qualified manpower, which is unutilised or under-utilised. Unemployment or underemployment of the educated youth is the characteristic of a gradually urbanising community. Such youth are comparatively free and easily get motivated to join literacy work. Educated but unemployed girls have found out a useful time-pass in the literacy work until they get married or a better and gainful employment. Another observation is that most of the households do not expect women literacy workers to look for a gainful employment.

Table 4.12 : Nature of the Housing of women literacy workers

Sl. No.	*Particulars*	*Frequency*	*Percentage*
1	Thatched	3	5.36
2	Katccha	7	12.50
3	Semi-Pucca	15	26.79
4	Pucca	31	55.36
	Total	**56**	**100.00**

More than 80 per cent of women literacy workers are living in *pucca* or semi-*pucca* houses. It is observed that almost all women literacy workers (54 out of 56) live in own houses. The remaining two are staying on rent. Over one-fifth of women literacy workers are living in thatched or *Katccha* houses. Housing is a significant factor of economic status. Sometimes in rural areas *Katccha* houses do not necessarily the indicator of poor economic status. The custom of investing for securing *pucca* accommodation is an urban characteristic. Semi-*pucca* houses are more popular in the villages than 100 per cent *pucca* houses. *Katccha* structures are attached to *pucca* structure to accommodate cattle. Cattle sheds erected in *Katccha* or semi-*pucca* style stand in front of every house in the villages of Haryana either for necessity or for decoration.

Table 4.13 : Space in the house of women literacy workers

Sl. No.	*Particulars*	*Frequency*	*Percentage*
1	Hut	4	7.14
2	Single room	16	28.57
3	Two rooms	28	50.00
4	Three rooms	3	5.36
5	Four rooms	4	7.14
6	Five or more rooms	1	1.79
	Total	**56**	**100.00**

Nearly two-third of women literacy workers live in houses having two or more rooms. Over one-third of women literacy workers live in single room or hut like accommodation. It is seen that most of the rural houses in Haryana consist of two rooms with separate kitchen and wide-open veranda. Most of these houses have separate bathing space not attached to the house. The front yards of most of the houses have facilities to accommodate cattle. Houses with four or more rooms are constructed in modern style. A few of them are multi-storey. They are purely *pucca* houses with modern toilets. Some of their family members are settled in the towns and are exposed to modern living style. Their earnings in the cities are invested to build up palatial houses. One of the houses of women literacy workers is almost like a farmhouse.

Table 4.14 : Toilet and Bathing Space in the house of women literacy workers

Sl. No.	*Particulars*	*Frequency*	*Percentage*
1	Available	11	19.64
2	Semi-modern	23	41.07
3	Not available	22	39.29
	Total	**56**	**100.00**

Almost 60 per cent of women literacy workers have toilet facilities attached to their houses while 40 per cent of women literacy workers do not have adequate toilet facilities. They use open fields for toilet services. It is observed that even if rural households in India have toilet facilities they do not often use them. Only women and guests use the toilet facilities. Traditionally the male members use the open fields, agricultural land, and the riverbanks for toileting. This practice is very much common in rural areas everywhere in the country and the use of modern toilets is an urban characteristic. Awareness about sanitation, health and hygiene is an essential component of literacy programme.

Table 4.15 : Amenities at home of women literacy workers

Sl. No.	*Assets of the Family of women literacy workers*	*Yes, for less than Two years*	*Yes, for 2 to 5 years*	*Yes, for more than 5 years*	*Yes: but do not remember*	*No*
1	Television	8	6	7	19	16
2	Cycle	13	5	11		27
3	Radio	2	2	4	9	39
4	Motorcycle	3	3	1	4	45
5	Bullock cart	1	1	2	6	46
6	Refrigerator	6		2	2	46
7	Tractor	1	2	2		51
8	Washing machine	1		1		54
9	Car				1	55
10	VCR/VCP				1	55
11	Any other :	5				51

Television and cycle are the most popular assets of women literacy workers. Compared to TV, radio is rare. Motorcycle and Bullock cart are the other popular assets. Compared to Bullock cart, motorbike is a recently acquired asset. Refrigerator is more popular than washing machine. Cycle, motorcycle, and refrigerator are the assets acquired by women literacy workers more recently while TV, Radio, Bullock cart and Tractor are the ancient household assets. It can be seen that trends of urbanisation and modernisation are clearly visible from the pattern of acquisition of modern assets by women literacy workers. TV has become the most popular asset and is gradually becoming a necessity in every household having electricity. Radio is popular in the houses where there is no electricity. Bullock cart and tractors are essentially agricultural equipment and indicate the prevalence of large-scale cultivation.

Table 4.16 : Fuel used at the houses of women literacy workers

Sl. No.	*Fuel used at home*	*Frequency*	*Percentage*
1	Cowdung cake only	21	37.5
2	Firewood only	11	19.6
5	Both the above	19	33.9
3	Kerosene	5	8.9
4	Gas	5	8.9
6	More than one (Traditional and Modern)	8	14.3

More than 90 per cent of the women literacy workers use traditional fuel like cowdung cake (*Upala*) or firewood or both. Nearly 15 per cent of women literacy workers use modern fuel at home. Firewood and cowdung cake are available in plenty and are cheap in the rural areas compared to modern fuel like gas. Cowdung cake is the most popular fuel and the way the villagers in Haryana prepare this fuel is an attractive scene for the visitors. *Upala*, the cowdung cake, is dried and stored for the use in rainy seasons. Since most of the villagers possess cattle, cowdung is very much available. Preparation of *upala* is one of the chief duties of the women of the household.

Table 4.17 : Accommodation for animals in the house of women literacy workers

Sl. No.	*Particulars*	*Frequency*	*Percentage*
1	Not available	11	19.64
2	Attached to home	21	37.50
3	Separate place	24	42.86
	Total	**56**	**100.00**

More than 80 per cent of women literacy workers have accommodation for animals at home. Haryana is known for the best quality of milch animals. Karnal dairy has a variety of good quality milch animals. Buffalos are the valuable assets for the villagers of Haryana. Milch animals are the source of supplementary income in terms of nutrition and fuel. Villagers in Haryana have appreciated the economic value of buffalos and are proud of showing these animals just in front of their houses. At least 37.5 per cent of women literacy workers have cattle sheds attached to their houses. Cultivation in Haryana is seasonal, while dairying is an all-season economic activity.

Social Profile

Social profile of women literacy workers refers to educational status, family size and family type of women literacy workers, civic amenities and social infrastructure available in the villages. Understanding the social profile of women literacy workers is important to understand the nature and scope of empowerment attained by women literacy workers. Education of both women literacy workers and the heads of the family is a significant factor of empowerment. Better educational status facilitates achievement of empowerment. Type and size of the family is another important social factor in the empowerment of women at the level of family. Civic amenities and social infrastructure refer to the availability of school, hospital, water supply, power supply and communication facilities. Social development greatly depends upon these social infrastructure and these amenities facilitate empowerment of women in many ways. The freedom available at home to move out of home for better education and career is not availed unless opportunities and suitable infrastructure are not available in the society. Haryana claims the credit of connecting all the villages with *pucca* roads and covering all the villages with power supply. Unless facilities are provided in each village for education and primary health care human resource development and women empowerment is difficult to achieve.

Table 4.18 : Education of women literacy workers

Sl. No.	Particulars	Frequency	Percentage
1	Primary School	3	5.36
2	High School	46	82.14
3	College up to Graduation	6	10.71
4	Graduation	1	1.79
	Total	**56**	**100.00**

Nearly 95 per cent of woman literacy workers are educated up to high school or higher level. Over 11 per cent of women literacy workers are graduates or post-graduates. Since literacy work demands certain level of educational status, women literacy workers who are below high school level of education might find it difficult to successfully conduct the programme. Women with lower educational qualifications are neither encouraged to conduct the literacy programme nor are they liked by the women participants of the programme. Literacy workers as the educators are expected to be facilitators of empowerment. Therefore, it is expected from the literacy workers that they are better educated than the ordinary womenfolk of the villages.

Table 4.19 : Education of the Head of the Family of women literacy workers

Sl. No.	Particulars	Frequency	Percentage
1	Illiterate	8	14.29
2	Primary School	13	23.21
3	High School	29	51.79
4	Graduation	5	8.93
5	Post-Graduation	1	1.79
	Total	**56**	**100.00**

As many as 85 per cent of the heads of the family are literate and more than 60 per cent of the heads of the family are educated up to high school or higher level of education. Only less than 15 per cent of the heads of the families are illiterate. Literacy of the heads of the family is facilitating factor for mobility and empowerment of women. Educated parents tend to treat both the girls and boys on equal foot. They would provide equal educational and career orientation to girl children. The average educational level of the heads of the families of women literacy workers is above the state as well as the national average. It means that the voluntarism and initiative shown by women literacy workers have some relationship with the educational level of the heads of the family. Educated parents are capable of preparing a facilitating environment for women empowerment.

Table 4.20 : Family members of women literacy workers

Sl.No.	*Family Members of women literacy workers*	*Frequency*	*Percentage*
1	Families having children below 5 years	19	33.9
2	Families with children between 5 to 12 years	26	46.4
3	Families with school-going children (13 to 19 years)	40	71.4
4	Families with youth (20 to 30 years)	31	55.4
5	Families with adults (31 to 60 years)	50	89.3
6	Families with senior citizens (60 years and above)	5	8.9

One-third of the families have kids at their home, 46 per cent families have children in the age group of 5 to 12, 71 per cent of the families have school-going children at home and only 8.9 per cent of the families have senior citizens at home. The high incidence of school-going children in the families of women literacy workers justifies a previous finding of greater number of women literacy workers who are adolescent. The adolescent girls who are motivated to join the literacy work have completed high school or higher secondary level of education. Literacy classes are usually conducted at the houses of the literacy workers. It is seen that the number of families having small children as well as senior citizens is less. This finding does not reflect the reality. Conducting literacy classes in the families with little kids is not successful. Therefore, the presence of little kids is a significant factor in the initiative and voluntarism shown by the literacy workers.

Table 4.21 : Number of Family Members of woman literacy workers

Sl. No.	*Particulars*	*Frequency*	*Percentage*
1	Below 4 members	10	17.86
2	4 to 6 members	35	62.50
3	7 and above	11	19.64
	Total	**56**	**100.00**

Nearly two-third of women literacy workers belong to medium sized families. Nearly 20 per cent of the families are large families with more than 7 members. Only 18 per cent of women literacy workers are from small families. The average size of the family is 5. This finding reflects the typical rural situation of Haryana. In the urban areas the average family size is below 5. In small families women will not be free to spare time for literacy work. In large families where there are several women to share the domestic chores, some women will be free to spare time for literacy work. It is observed that other women of the households do help woman literacy workers to render substitute service in conducting literacy classes. Therefore, larger families are found more favourable for voluntarism of the literacy workers.

Table 4.22 : Type of the Family of woman literacy workers

Sl. No.	*Particulars*	*Frequency*	*Percentage*
1	Only one couple (single family)	39	69.64
2	More than one couple (Vertical)	13	23.21
3	More than one couple (Combined)	1	1.79
4	Widow	3	5.36
	Total	**56**	**100.00**

From the above table, it is seen that nearly 70 per cent of women literacy workers belong to nuclear families with single couple and their children. Almost 5 per cent of women literacy workers are widows. One-fourth of the families are joint families. Even if majority of the families are nuclear families a significant number of families are joint families. Type of the family does not seem to be a significant factor for voluntarism and initiative for literacy work. Whether it is joint or nuclear, the size of the family is more significant with regard to literacy work. Larger the family greater the opportunity for women to spare time for social service is. However the finding of this table reflects the growing trend of shift from joint to nuclear in the families of rural Haryana.

Table 4.23 : Family members of women literacy workers

Sl. No.	*Relationship with women literacy workers*	*Frequency*	*Percentage*
1	Father-in-law	43	76.8
2	Mother-in-law	43	76.8
3	Husband	20	35.7
4	Son	16	28.6
5	Daughter	13	23.2
6	Brother-in-law	31	55.3
7	Sister-in-law	20	35.7
8	Any other	2	3.6

This table gives information about the family members of woman literacy workers. We see from the table that 76 per cent of women literacy workers live with their parents. Over one-third of women literacy workers are living with their husbands. Nearly 28 per cent of women literacy workers have sons and only 23 per cent of women literacy workers have daughters. More than half of women literacy workers have brothers or brother-in-law at home while only 35 per cent of women literacy workers have sisters or sister-in-law at home. The predominance of sons over daughters and brothers over sisters is clearly seen in the table. This finding confirms the general gender status of Haryana, which is highly favourable for men. The rural families in Haryana give an overriding preference for boys to girls. The unfavourable sex ratio is a dis-empowering factor and the gender sensitisation in families of rural Haryana is the need of the time.

Table 4.24 : Civic amenities in the village of women literacy workers

Sl. No.	*Access to Public Utility Services*	*Yes, below Two Kilometres*	*Yes, between 2 to 5 Kilometres*	*Yes, above 5 Kilometres*	*No*
1	Primary School	56			
2	Water supply	56			
3	Health care	29	7	20	
4	Bus terminal	23	6	27	
5	Taxi/auto stand	9	47		
6	Electricity	53			3
7	PDS Shop	27			29
8	Telephone	16			40

From above table we get information about the access of women literacy workers to various social infrastructures. We see that all women literacy workers have access to primary school. All of them have access to potable drinking water within 2 kilometres of distance. All women literacy workers have access to primary health care within a distance of maximum five kilometres. The nearest bus terminal for women literacy workers is situated within a distance of five kilometres. Similarly auto or taxi stand is available at a close distance. Only three women literacy workers do not have electricity at home. 29 women literacy workers do not have access to PDS shop and 40 women literacy workers do not have access to telephone. It is observed that the situation has changed recently. During the progress of the data collection three of the villages got telephone connections and all women literacy workers do not have access to telephone within a distance of 5 kilometres.

Concluding Remarks

While analysing the demographic profile of women literacy workers, it is observed that the literacy workers are from ten villages, mostly below the age of 25 years, unmarried and Hindu by religion. Among them, significantly large section is Dalit literacy workers. Analysing economic profile of women literacy workers, it is found that most of them belong to lower middle class families. Majority of women literacy workers live in semi-*pucca* or *pucca* houses with two or three rooms, have own agricultural land, have non-agricultural source of income, use traditional fuels for cooking, have traditional and modern assets and possess milch animals. Majority of women literacy workers have in their house, toilet facilities. Quite a few households have members who are either underemployed or unemployed. Majority of women literacy workers as well as the heads of the family are educated up to High School level. Most of the families of women literacy workers have school going children. Most of the families are medium size, i.e. is 4-6 members. Majority of women literacy workers belong to nuclear families. Most of the families are male dominated. Most of women literacy workers have access to various social infra-structural facilities like primary school, primary health centre, water supply, power supply, tele-communication media and public distribution system.

5

Empowerment : Social, Economic and Political

Empowerment of women is a multi-dimensional concept. The primary aspects of women empowerment are social, economic and political. Social empowerment refers to attitudinal changes at the level of family, participation in decision-making at home, progressive changes in the educational status and increasing participation in various social activities. Economic empowerment refers to greater participation of women in the economic activities, control over the earnings of women and freedom to pursue an occupation of own choice. Political empowerment of women refers to equal participation in political decision-making and the exercise of the right to represent at every level of Democratic Government on equal footing with men.

Intra-personal dimension of empowerment is a significant aspect of social empowerment. Women empowerment is a development process, taking place within a person. Intra-personal dimension of empowerment refers to right cognition, beliefs, thoughts, values, attitudes and other mental dispositions. These characteristics may be grouped into cognitive (intellectual) domain, affective (emotional) domain and psychosocial domain. Cognitive domain refers to conceptual aspects of empowerment. Affective domain refers to feelings, attitudes and values related with empowerment. Psychosocial refers to social attitudes of women literacy workers. These are the mental dispositions having wide social implication. These attitudes define their social participation and social behaviour.

Empowerment at Personal Level

Several questions have been included in the interview schedule to understand the concept of women empowerment. It is not easy to know the level of empowerment women literacy workers have really achieved by simply analysing their opinions and ideas about empowerment. What women literacy workers think and say about empowerment is sometimes different from how they behave. A proper understanding of the concept of empowerment is however the starting point of real empowerment in life. Unless women have a right perception about empowerment, they will not be able to act out in real life situation with enlightenment. Action without the conceptual basis is only exception. After showing proper convictions, if women are not able to show proper actions, it may be due to suppression or due to lack of opportunities available to them in the society. What women literacy workers understand by the term 'empowerment' is analysed in the following tables.

Table 5.1 : Opinion of women literacy workers on differences in do's and don'ts for men and women

Sl. No.	*Particulars*	*Frequency*	*Percentage*
1	Difference in do's and don'ts	21	37.50
2	Can't say	3	5.36
3	No difference in do's and don'ts	31	55.36
4	NA/DK	1	1.79
	Total	**56**	**100.00**

An item of interview schedule administered to women literacy workers is what they think about the difference in do's and don'ts for men and women. Majority of woman literacy workers think that there is no difference. Only 37 per cent of women literacy workers believe that there is some difference in what men and women should do and should not do in the society. Nearly 55 per cent of women literacy workers believe in equality of men and women and express that there should not be any difference in do's and don'ts for men and women in the society. We see later, what women literacy workers actually do with regard to the do's and don'ts. There we do not find much correspondence between what they think and what they do. Either they are restricted to act in accordance with their will or there are little opportunities to express their will.

Table 5.2 : Differences in do's and don'ts and education of women literacy workers

	Education of women literacy workers	*Difference in do's and don'ts*				*Total*
		Yes	*Can't say*	*No*	*NA/DK*	
1	Primary School	2		1		3
2	High School	16	2	27	1	46
3	College up to Graduation	2	1	3		6
4	Graduation	1				1
	Total	**21**	**3**	**31**	**1**	**56**

It is seen from this table that majority of women literacy workers who are educated up to high school believe that there should not be any difference between men and women in the code of conduct. This reveals the effect of higher education for the attainment of conceptual clarity about equality and empowerment. Education widens the mental horizon of women. Empowerment begins with conceptual clarity with regard to equality between men and women in all respects. Opinion about the prevalence of separate code of conduct for men and women is the indicator of discrimination and disempowerment.

Table 5.3 : Differences in do's and don'ts and marital status of women literacy workers

	Marital status of women literacy workers	*Difference in do's and don'ts*				*Total*
		Yes	*Can't say*	*No*	*NA/DK*	
1	Married	10	2	10		22
2	Single (Unmarried)	11	1	21	1	34
Total		**21**	**3**	**31**	**1**	**56**

This table reveals the difference between married and unmarried women with regard to their belief in the difference in do's and don'ts for men and women. It is interesting to note that majority of the unmarried women literacy workers do not admit the difference while 50 per cent of the married woman literacy workers admit the difference. Married women are closer to the realities of life. We see later that majority of the unmarried woman literacy workers are educationally better qualified compared to those woman literacy workers who are married. Married women start believing what they experience in day-to-day living and admit that there is a significant difference in the code of conduct for men and women. It may be due to the prevalence of more restrictions for the married women literacy workers compared to those who are unmarried. Therefore, majority of the unmarried women literacy workers think that there should be equality between men and women with regard to do's and don'ts.

Table 5.4 : Self-concept of women literacy workers

Sl. No.	*Self-concept of women literacy workers*	*Highly secure, self-confident, gaining empowerment*	*Secure, moderately confident, marching towards empowerment*	*Less Secure, not so confident, lower self-image, moving slowly towards empowerment*	*Insecure, Non-confident, very poor self-image, not moving towards empowerment*	*Total*
1	Emotional Balance	2	18	30	6	56
2	Optimism and Open mindedness	2	43	11	0	56
3	Self-acceptance	2	8	45	1	56
4	Self-confidence and Sense of efficiency	2	49	5	0	56
5	Self-esteem and Sense of worthiness	7	37	12	0	56
6	Sense of reality or Beliefs and Convictions		41	15	0	56
7	Social Competence		18	32	6	56

Table 5.4 shows the level of self-concept of women literacy workers. Self-concept is further analysed under various traits such as emotional balance, optimism and open mindedness, self-acceptance, self-confidence and sense of efficiency, self-esteem and sense of worthiness, sense of reality or beliefs and convictions and social competence. Emotional balance is the ability of women literacy workers to manage situations of high emotional upheavals such as sorrows, excitements, anxiety, worries and fears. Optimism refers to the positive thinking and approach to life. High level of optimism and open mindedness enable women literacy workers to face difficulties of life with constructive attitude.

Self-acceptance is the disposition to understand and accept the strengths and weakness of own personality. Self-confidence is the belief in the effectiveness of self in various situations of life. Self-esteem is the belief in essential goodness of own personality and the belief in the usefulness of living. Sense of reality, beliefs and convictions refers to the realistic vision of life. This helps an individual to develop proper beliefs and convictions regarding life and the world around. Social competence refers to that quality of an individual, which makes him/her effective in interpersonal relationships and participate well in various social activities.

Table 5.4 shows that majority of women literacy workers are secure and moderately confident with regard to optimism and open mindedness, self-confidence and sense of efficiency, self-esteem and sense of worthiness and sense of reality or beliefs and convictions while they are less secure and not so confident with regard to emotional balance, self-acceptance and social competence. At conceptual level most of the women literacy workers are gaining empowerment with regard to sense of reality, self-esteem and self-confidence but require more attention with regard to emotional balance and social competence.

The table below shows that the proportion of married women with 'good' self-concept is less compared to those who are unmarried. 'Good' refers to the score estimated by administering 'Self-concept scale'. More unmarried women literacy workers have realistic beliefs and convictions. This indicates the prevalence of an unexpected change in the perception of reality before and after the marriage. Married women see the World more pessimistically or they are forced to perceive so. After marriage they tend to live with a narrow outlook about the reality outside home. We see later that the unmarried women literacy workers are educationally more qualified. Their better self-concept may be due to their better educational status rather than marital status.

Table 5.5 : Sense of reality or beliefs and marital status of women literacy workers

	Good concept, gaining empowerment	*Average level of concept, and need to gain empowerment*	*Total*
Married	12	10	22
Unmarried	29	5	34
Total	**41**	**15**	**56**

Empowerment at Personal Level : Emotional and Attitudinal

Emotional or attitudinal factor of women empowerment refers to feeling proud of being woman, emotional balance, self-acceptance, self-confidence, optimism and feeling self-esteem and sense of worth. Feeling a sense of power is essentially an emotional and attitudinal phenomenon. Psychological well-being is a significant aspect of women empowerment. An emotionally ill-balanced person cannot achieve a desirable level of empowerment. Literacy workers are expected to be persons of emotional integrity and of well-balanced personality. Psychological well-being is essentially a feeling of boldness and is expressed as courage and confidence in decision-making and maintaining balanced temperament in times of crisis. This feeling of inner power is essential to become independent in decision-making and therefore, it is inseparable from the state of empowerment.

The process of empowerment renders emotional strength and confidence. An emotionally well-balanced person can be a good teacher. An emotionally balanced teacher is affectionate and understanding of the needs of the students they teach. Emotional balance and psychological strength can be estimated by administering self-rating scales. Several items have been included in the interview schedule to estimate the magnitude of emotional strength of women literacy workers.

Psycho-social dimension refers to those attitudinal components which enable women to behave socially competent way. Social competence is a trait achieved by social learning and exposure to various social situations. Social competence is affected by educational, occupational and marital status. Educational institutions are the primary institutions of socialisation and higher education offers greater chance for girls for socialisation in a wider social context. The following tables give information about the social competence of women literacy workers.

Table 5.6 : Feeling no shame or guilt for being a woman

Sl. No.	Particulars	Frequency	Percentage
1	No guilt feeling of being women	45	80.36
2	Can't say	3	5.36
3	Guilt feeling of being women	4	7.14
4	NA/DK	4	7.14
	Total	**56**	**100.00**

It is seen from the table that 80 per cent of women literacy workers do not have guilt feeling of being women. Majority of the women literacy workers feel that a woman is not to regret over her womanhood, on the other hand, they should feel proud of being women. Almost 12 per cent of women literacy workers are confused or did not respond to this query. They have been undecided or of the opinion that being man or woman is just a matter of chance and there is nothing to feel guilt or pride. Only 7 per cent of women literacy workers do feel guilt of being born as women. They are disappointed with the kind of lives they lead in contrast to the men of their household. Feeling proud of being woman is a matter of self-esteem. Empowerment of women must begin with this understanding of self-image. Literacy workers who are mediators for social change are expected to have positive self-image and high self-esteem. It is seen that majority of women literacy workers have good self-esteem.

Table 5.7 : Sense of security of women literacy workers

Sl. No.	*Particulars*	*Frequency*	*Percentage*
1	Highly secure, high level of empowerment	11	19.64
2	Secure, gaining empowerment	45	80.36
	Total	**56**	**100.00**

It is found that all women literacy workers are above average with regard to sense of security. Four-fifth of women literacy workers are socially secure and gaining empowerment. Feeling of security is a sign of social competence. Nearly 20 per cent of women literacy workers are found to be highly secured as far as sense of security is concerned. This feeling of high level of security is not the sign of high level of empowerment as far as the social behaviour is concerned. It is seen later that women literacy workers differ in their behaviour pattern from their thinking pattern. Either the social customs or the situational factors prevent them to be socially active and competent members of the society.

Table 5.8 : Security and Marital Status of women literacy workers

	Highly secure, high level of empowerment	*Secure, gaining empowerment*	*Total*
Married	1	21	22
Unmarried/single	10	24	34
Total	**11**	**45**	**56**

Married women are supposed to be more socially competent. Even if all women literacy workers are above average with regard to the sense of security, it is seen that unmarried women are more secured than the married women. Out of 11 highly secured woman literacy workers 10 are unmarried and only one is married. It shows that the married women feel less secure at the house of the husband or marriage brings many restrictions for her freedom and mobility. In rural Haryana, the situation of newly married women is very pathetic. Until they become mother-in-law, their position is very low and her freedom for mobility is restricted. She is forced to hide herself from the public. They feel less secure.

Table 5.9 : Social Competence and Education of women literacy workers

Self-Concept of women literacy workers	*Good concept, gaining empowerment*	*Average, level of concept, and need to gain empowerment*	*Poor self-concept, low level of empowerment*	*Very Poor self-concept, lowest level of empowerment*	*Total*
Primary School		3			3
High School	14	26	4	2	46
College up to Graduation	4	2			6
Graduation		1			1
Total	**18**	**32**	**4**	**2**	**56**

The table shows that majority of women literacy workers have average level of self-concept as far as social competence is concerned and they need to gain empowerment. Nearly one-third of women literacy workers have good concept regarding social competence and are gaining empowerment. We can see from the table that the proportion of college educated women have a better self-concept regarding social competence in comparison with woman literacy workers who are educated up to secondary level of education. Out of 6 woman literacy workers who have attended college level of education, 4 have good self-concept and a better level of social competence. While out of 46 women literacy workers who are educated up to secondary level of education only 14 have similar level of self-concept and social competence.

Social Empowerment at the Level of Family

Empowerment of women begins at home. The essence of domestic empowerment is in participating in decision-making in key affairs of the family. Empowerment of women at home begins with recognizing the value of the household duties and responsibilities. Empowerment of women at home means equal sharing of domestic chores, absence of gender based restrictions and creative participation of women in all the decisions affecting the economic and social life of the family. Women empowerment at the level of family has much to do with the ways the boys and girls are socialised in the family, career orientation given to the girl children in contrast to the orientation given to the boy children. Various domestic factors of women empowerment are analysed in the following tables.

Table 5.10 : Role of women literacy workers in decision-making at home

Sl. No.	*Participation in Decision making at home*	*Very often*	*Often*	*Some-times*	*Rare-ly*	*Never*	*Any Other*	*NA/DK*	*Total*
1	Kind of food and the mode of its preparation	22	7	19	2	3	1	2	56
2	Education of the children	35	5	7	5	3		1	56
3	Purchase of house-hold articles	28	4	14	1	5	2	2	56
4	Employment of the younger members	22	8	17	1	4		4	56
5	Marriage of family members	23	4	12	5	5	2	5	56
6	Income, savings and investment	19	5	17	6	2	1	6	56

It is seen that majority of women literacy workers are consulted by the heads of the families with regard to most of the decisions taken at home either very often or sometimes. Comparatively women literacy workers are not consulted with regard to marriage of family members and income, savings and investment of family property as frequently as the other domestic affairs. However, the overall finding is very much favourable to women literacy workers. It is observed by the researcher that women literacy workers are the best educated member of the family and their role in the decisions of the family is welcome. Their voice is heard and respected. It is once told by a family member, 'Why should I consult with her regarding these affairs? She herself is managing everything and is consulting occasionally with us just not to offend us.'

Table 5.11 : Decision-making at home and age group of women literacy workers

	15 to 20 Years	*21-25 Years*	*26 to 30 Years*	*31 to 35 Years*	*36 to 40 Years*	*41 to 45 Years*	*Total*
Self	2	3			1	1	7
Husband	2	3	3	4	2	1	15
Father	20	4					24
Mother	7	1					8
Any other	1						1
NA/DK	1						1
Total	**33**	**11**	**3**	**4**	**3**	**2**	**56**

It is asked to women literacy workers who take the key decisions at home. Most of women literacy workers replied that their fathers take the decisions at home. In 15 families the husbands are the decision-makers. In 15 families either women literacy workers or their mothers are the decision-makers. It can be seen from the table that fathers are the decision-makers in the houses of literacy workers who are below the age of 20 years and husbands are the key decision-makers in the house of literacy workers who are above 20 years of age. Most of the women literacy workers below the age of 20 years are unmarried and the parents take the decisions at home. It is observed that in houses where the women take key decisions, the male members are either old or infirm or away from home most of the days. The decisions taken by the women are informed and approved by the elder men of the household. It can be observed that in majority of the houses men are the decision-makers and the role of women is secondary and supplementary and never has it been complementary.

Table 5.12 : Decision-making at home and marital status of women literacy workcrs

	Married	*Unmarried/single*	*Total*
Self	5	2	7
Husband	15		15
Father	2	22	24
Mother	2	6	8
Any other		1	1
NA/DK		1	1
Total	**24**	**32**	**56**

It can be seen from the table that most of the decision-makers in the houses of the married women literacy workers are the husbands and in the houses of unmarried women literacy workers the decision-makers are the fathers. This information supports the previous finding (Table 5.11). There are certain interesting findings in this table. There are two women literacy workers who are unmarried but are the decision-makers at home. There are two households where the mothers-in-law take the decisions at home. There are two houses where the fathers-in-law are the decision-makers. Even if in some families, women are the decision-makers majority of the families have male decision-makers.

Table 5.13 : Decision-making at home and family size of women literacy workers

	Below 4 members	*4 to 6 members*	*7 and above*	*Total*
Self	4	3		7
Husband	3	9	3	15
Father	2	15	7	24
Mother	1	6	1	8
Any other		1		1
NA/DK		1		1
Total	**10**	**35**	**11**	**56**

It can be seen from the table that in smaller families, women literacy workers or their husbands are the decision-makers while in larger families the parents are the decision-makers. Out of the 10 small families, women literacy workers are the decision-makers in four families. In these families the husbands are away from home for the sake of job in the cities. In nuclear families women get better opportunity for participating in decision-making. Non-availability of male members gives opportunities for the women in nuclear families to take decisions for the family. Women are found to have significant role in at least 25 per cent of the families of women literacy workers. This is an important finding. Generally what is observed is that men are the decision-makers and women have only delegated power for decision-making. In this particular finding we see that at least 25 per cent of women literacy workers have boldly admitted that in their families either their mothers or they themselves are the decision-makers. It can be observed that voluntarism for literacy work is encouraged in families headed by women.

Table 5.14 : Decision-making at home and employment of the Head of the family

	Business	*Government Service*	*Private Service*	*Daily Wage*	*Any other*	*Total*
Self	2	1	1	2	1	7
Husband	2	3	3	5	2	15
Father	1	7	3	6	7	24
Mother		1	1	5	1	8
Any other	1					1
NA/DK		1				1
Total	**6**	**13**	**8**	**18**	**11**	**56**

It is seen from Table 5.14 that in 18 families where the heads of the family are daily wage labourers, 7 decision-makers are women. In these families, the male members are away from home most of the day time. They struggle to earn some money and hand over whatever they earn to the women of the household. Women in such houses, get more opportunity to manage the family affairs. In most of these families women are also employed. They have been proved to be efficient to manage the family Budget with a meagre income. In these families women are found better educated than the men and more responsible with regard to the education, career and marriage of the children.

Table 5.15 : Decision-making at home and employment of women literacy worker

	Business	*Agri-culture*	*Daily wage Labourer*	*Private Service*	*Any other*	*Total*
Self		1		3	3	7
Husband		5	1	3	6	15
Father		18			6	24
Mother	1	3			4	8
Any other		1				1
NA/DK					1	1
Total	**1**	**28**	**1**	**6**	**20**	**56**

It is seen from the table that in families where women literacy workers are engaged in non-agricultural occupations, women get greater participation in the decision-making process. Where the women are engaged in traditional occupation of agriculture, their participation in decision-making of the family matters is very much limited. Agricultural occupation does not bring out the tangible income for the women workers. Work of women in agricultural sector is not effectively estimated in terms of monetary gains. Usually women work in the field and the men do marketing of the agricultural produce. When women are engaged in non-agricultural occupations their income is made known to everyone in the family and their presence in the family is counted. Whenever any decision involving financial investment is taken, they are consulted. They sometimes rise into prominent position to take independent decisions in the family, especially when she is regularly employed.

Table 5.16 : Decision-making at home and Family Type

	Only one couple (single family)	*More than one couple (Vertical)*	*More than one couple (Combined)*	*Widow*	*Total*
Self	2	2		3	7
Husband	9	6			15
Father	19	4	1		24
Mother	7	1			8
Any other	1				1
NA/DK	1				1
Total	**39**	**13**	**1**	**3**	**56**

It is from the above table that most of the families are nuclear families and 9 nuclear families have women as decision-makers. Only 3 medium size families have women in the role of decision-making. It shows that nuclear families give better opportunities for women to play important role in the families. There will be many occasions where the women are compelled to take up the leading role in nuclear families. It is found that in three joint families, the leading role is played by women. This is an encouraging trend with regard to women empowerment.

Table 5.17 : Decision-making at home and sex ratio in the family

	More Women	*More Men*	*Total*
Self	4	3	7
Husband	5	10	15
Father	10	14	24
Mother	3	5	8
Any other	1		1
NA/DK		1	1
Total	**23**	**33**	**56**

It can be seen from the above table that decision-making and the sex ratio do not have significant relationship. In most of the families male members are the decision-makers. Out of the 15 women decision-makers, 7 are from the houses with higher ratio of women. Among women literacy workers who are the key decision-makers at home, the majority are from the families with more women. Comparatively fathers are the key decision-makers in the families with more women and husbands are the key decision-makers in the families with more men. The significant fact derived from this finding is that the numerical strength of women in the families does not affect the patriarchal power structure.

Table 5.18 : Married women, looking after the parents

Sl. No.	*Particulars*	*Frequency*	*Percentage*
1	Girls must look after their parents after marriage	35	62.50
2	Can't say	5	8.93
3	Girls need not look after their parents after marriage	15	26.79
4	NA/DK	1	1.79
	Total	**56**	**100.00**

The opinion of 62 per cent of women literacy workers as seen from the table shows that the married women have the responsibility to look after their own parents even after marriage. They have added that the responsibility of women to look after their aged and infirm cannot be ignored even if they are married. According to them, women should look after their parents especially when the aged parents do not have male children or the other male members are minors or if they do not have any source of income for survival. Over one-fourth of women literacy workers have the opinion that in no circumstances the parents would stay with their daughters after marriage. This is the general observation and the women who supported the counterview have shown the sign of empowerment.

Table 5.19 : Observing *Purdah* from the elders of the family

Sl. No.	*Particulars*	*Frequency*	*Percentage*
1	Observe *Purdah*	34	60.71
2	Can't say	4	7.14
3	Do not observe *Purdah*	8	14.29
4	NA/DK	10	17.86
	Total	**56**	**100.00**

In many parts of the country, here are several gender-based restrictions for women at home such as observing *Purdah*. *Purdah* is the system in some Muslim and Hindu societies by which women live in a separate part of a house or cover their faces so that men do not see them. It is customary in Haryana that all the married women observe *Purdah* from the elders of the family as well as the strange men of the villages. *Burqa* is popular among Muslims, while using a face cover (screen) or just covering the face except eyes with the end portion of the *saree* they wear is the common custom in Haryana. Using a separate shawl as *Purdah* is also seen in several villages. In Haryana and several other states in North India, women do not observe *Purdah* in their own villages but only in the villages of their husbands. *Purdah* is the symbol of seclusion. *Purdah* symbolises restriction to public appearance, public speaking, mobility, and many more. It is seen from the table that over 60 per cent of women literacy workers observe *Purdah*. 18 per cent of woman literacy workers are unmarried and have not responded, because this question is not applicable to them. Nearly 14 per cent of women literacy workers do not observe *Purdah* from the elders of the family. In other terms the elders of these families do not enforce them to observe *Purdah*.

Table 5.20 : Observing *Purdah* and Age group of women literacy workers

	Observe Purdah	*Can't say*	*Do not observe Purdah*	*NA/DK*	*Total*
15 to 20 Years	14	3	7	9	33
21-25 Years	9	1		1	11
26 to 30 Years	3				3
31 to 35 Years	4				4
36 to 40 Years	3				3
41 to 45 Years	1		1		2
Total	**34**	**4**	**8**	**10**	**56**

It is seen from the table that almost all women literacy workers who do not observe *Purdah* belong to the age group of 15 to 20 years of age. These women literacy workers are unmarried and the custom of *Purdah* is not enforced upon them.

It is also true that the younger women literacy workers are better educated and are willing to question the customs.

Table 5.21 : Wish to leave *Purdah*

Sl. No.	*Particulars*	*Frequency*	*Percentage*
1	Wish tc leave *purdah*	9	16.07
2	Can't say	6	10.71
3	No wish to leave *purdah*	31	55.36
4	NA/DK	10	17.86
	Total	**56**	**100.00**

It is seen from the table that above 55 per cent of women literacy workers do not wish to leave the custom of *Purdah* as if this custom has been proved useful for their safety while moving around the villages. Only 16 per cent of women literacy workers wish to do away with custom of *Purdah*. *Purdah* is not considered as a means to restrict the freedom of women by majority of woman literacy workers. On the other hand, it is regarded as a precaution to protect women from eve teasing and various other kinds of sexual harassment.

Table 5.22 : Walking out at times of marital dispute

Sl. No.	*Particulars*	*Frequency*	*Percentage*
1	Wives must leave home in dispute	3	5.36
2	Wives must not leave home in dispute	52	92.86
3	Any other	1	1.79
	Total	**56**	**100.00**

Nearly 93 per cent of women literacy workers are of the opinion that wives should not leave their home in times of marital disputes. This finding reflects the value system of rural India. Whatever the circumstances are, wives stick to their husbands' home. According to Indian tradition, 'marriages are held in heaven and men are not to break marital bond'. Separation and divorce are not popular in India and a married woman staying at her own house is considered a disgrace to the family. Women are thus bound to the home of their husbands. They bear all the torture and troubles at the home of their husbands. This concern for marriage and family is in a way very much helpful for the upbringing of children. The values of solidarity and integrity of home are considered more important than personal freedom and happiness by woman literacy workers.

Social Empowerment and Education

Education is an important variable with regard to social empowerment. Educated women do not easily get exploited by others. Literacy workers are the best-educated members of the family. Having better educational background, the literacy workers are regarded as more empowered than other female members of the family. Giving equal opportunity to both the boys and girls in the school is essential for empowerment of women. All the woman literacy workers have opined that equal educational opportunity should be given to both boys and girls.

Table 5.23 : Education of the best qualified member

Sl. No.	*Particulars*	*Frequency*	*Percentage*
1	Illiterate	3	5.36
2	Primary School	46	82.14
3	High School	6	10.71
4	Graduation	1	1.79
	Total	**56**	**100.00**

Educational status of the best-qualified member other than women literacy workers is described in the table. It can be seen that 82 per cent of women literacy workers have the best-qualified member other than themselves as literate and educated up to primary level. We have seen from earlier that over 90 per cent of women literacy workers are educated up to high school or higher level of education. Women literacy workers are the best-qualified members of the family. This better educational status is a sign of higher level of empowerment.

Table 5.24 : Usefulness of Literacy Programmes

Sl. No.	*Particulars*	*Frequency*	*Percentage*
1	Help them to read, write and count	9	16.07
2	Educate them about diseases	11	19.64
3	Makes her alert and curious to learn more	3	5.36
4	Gives them knowledge and makes them better qualified	8	14.29
5	Help them to live well, to manage home and savings	3	5.36
6	Renders self-confidence and power	4	7.14
7	Any other	1	1.79
8	NA/DK	17	30.36
	Total	**56**	**100.00**

Nearly 70 per cent of woman literacy workers are aware of the effectiveness of literacy programmes in the lives of women in one way or the other. Over 19 per cent of women literacy workers believe that literacy programme educate the women about diseases. Over 20 per cent of women literacy workers have opined that literacy programmes enable women read, write and count, renders them knowledge and make them better qualified for better occupation. Almost 12.5 per cent of women literacy workers believe that literacy programmes help them to manage home, learn savings, renders self-confidence and power and live well.

Table 5.25 : Educational status of literacy workers and the best-qualified member of the family

	Primary School	*High School*	*College up to Graduation*	*Graduation*	*Total*
Illiterate	3				3
Primary School		46			46
High School			6		6
Graduation				1	1
Total	**3**	**46**	**6**	**1**	**56**

Table 5.25 presents a significant finding. There is a close relationship between the educational status of the best-educated member other than the literacy worker and the

educational status of women literacy workers. Nearly 46 women literacy workers who are educated up to high school have the best-educated member of the family who have reached up to primary level of education. Almost 6 women literacy workers who are educated up to graduation have their best-educated family members educated up to high school. This finding shows that the aspiration of the best-educated member of the family is to educate the next generation at least one-step higher.

Table 5.26 : Residing away from home for education and employment

Sl. No.	*Particulars*	*Frequency*	*Percentage*
1	Girls can stay far for job or study	47	83.93
2	Can't say	1	1.79
3	Girls should not stay far for job or study	6	10.71
4	NA/DK	2	**3.57**
	Total	**56**	**100.00**

It is seen from the table that nearly 84 per cent of women literacy workers approve the stay of girls far away from home in pursuit of study or job. Only 10 per cent of women literacy workers do not approve the same. Generally it is found that girls in rural areas are restricted to move out of the native village to stay in far off places for the purposes of study or jobs. Even if women literacy workers are not staying away from home for the sake of studying or working, they have expressed their willingness to stay away from home for academic or vocational purposes by approving the same.

Table 5.27 : Residing away from home and marital status of women literacy workers

	Yes	*Can't say*	*No*	*NA/DK*	*Total*
Married	15	1	5	1	22
Unmarried/Single	32		1	1	34
Total	**47**	**1**	**6**	**2**	**56**

It can be seen from the above table that women literacy workers who are unmarried are more willing to move out of home the married ones. Out of 34 women literacy workers who are unmarried, 32 are ready to go far off places for higher studies or for job while only 15 out of 22 women literacy workers who are married are willing to do the same. Out of 6 women literacy workers who are not ready to stay away from home for study or job 5 are married ones. Either the attitude of women drastically changes after marriage or unreasonable restrictions are imposed upon women of rural areas who are married by custom or by the elders of the family. It may be due to other reasons like the lower educational status of the married women literacy workers compared to the unmarried ones. Married women are often overburdened with household duties like cooking, cleaning, washing, looking after the children and the elderly ones and do not think of staying away from home for any reasons.

Social Empowerment : Mobility and Participation

Mobility and participation in various social activities inside and outside the villages are significant indicators of social empowerment. Mobility refers to women literacy workers' actual movement outside village for seeing film or attending any festivals, worship, *Melas* etc. It does not include visiting relatives or friends or going to school. Use of communication media and the frequency of their use is also indicator of mobility and social participation. Using various communication media like telephone, e-mail, postal and telegraph services indicates the interest of women literacy workers in relating with people and shows their meaningful participation in social life.

Table 5.28 : Going out of village to see film or any festival

Sl. No.	*Going out of village to see film or any festival (Mobility)*	*Frequency*	*Percentage*
1	Very often	1	1.79
2	Often	1	1.79
3	Sometimes	27	48.21
4	Rarely	5	8.93
5	Never	22	39.29
	Total	**56**	**100.00**

It is seen from the table that nearly 40 per cent of women literacy workers never go out of the village for seeing a film or attending any festivals. Over 60 per cent women literacy workers do go outside the village but the frequency varies. Nearly 50 per cent of women literacy workers go out for festivals or watching movies sometimes. Only 2 per cent of women literacy workers go out of village often. The level of mobility of women literacy workers is average and moving out of village for any festivals or films is not encouraged by other family members.

Table 5.29 : Going out of village for films and marital status of women literacy workers

Marital Status	*Going out of village for films and marital status of women literacy workers*					
	Very often	*Often*	*Sometimes*	*Rarely*	*Never*	*Total*
Married	1	1	13	3	4	22
Unmarried/single			14	2	18	34
Total	**1**	**1**	**27**	**5**	**22**	**56**

It is seen from the table that the frequency of moving out of village for watching a movie or attending any festivals and *Melas* is more for married women compared to the unmarried ones. Out of the 22 women literacy workers who have never gone out of village for film or festivals, 18 are unmarried and only 4 are married. Almost 18 out of 22 married women literacy workers have gone out of village for any recreational purposes at least once while only 16 out of 34 unmarried women literacy workers have gone out of village for any recreation. When this finding is compared with the previous one, one can understand that the married women are reluctant to stay away from home for study or job but can go casually out of village for film or festivals. More women literacy workers who are unmarried are willing to stay away from home for study or job, but their freedom to go out of village for film or festivals is more restricted than the married ones. The parents hesitate to send their unmarried girls out of village for any recreational purposes for fear of unexpected troubles. Parents feel that the adolescent girls at home are to be guided carefully, because anything that affects their reputation would affect their marriage and their future. Therefore, casual flirting of girls for watching movies outside the village is permissible only after marriage and they would go along with their husbands only.

Table 5.30 : Taking part in social activities such as a village festival or a religious ceremony

Sl. No.	*Taking part in village festivals or religious ceremonies*	*Frequency*	*Percentage*
1	Very often	8	14.29
2	Often	17	30.36
3	Sometimes	21	37.50
4	Rarely	6	10.71
5	Never	3	5.36
6	NA/DK	1	1.79
	Total	**56**	**100.00**

It can be seen from the table that the frequency of mobility of women literacy workers inside the village for any religious or village festivals is more compared to their mobility outside village for watching film or attending *Melas*. Over 93 per cent of women literacy workers have attended the religious or village festivals in the village at least once. Usually the family members go together to such religious festivals in the village. Only 6 per cent of women literacy workers have not attended any festivals in the village. Mobility within the limit of the village is more permissible than mobility outside the village. Even some of the women literacy workers have not attended any festivals in their own villages. It shows that the restriction for mobility is very severe in some families.

Table 5.31 : Use of modern communication media

Use of communication media	*Always*	*Often*	*Some-times*	*Rarely*	*Never used/DK*	*Total*
1 Telephone		4	41	5	6	56
2 Post office	1	9	35	3	8	56
3 Telegraph		1	7	5	43	56
4 E-mail :				2	54	56

It can be seen from the table that telephone is the most popular means for communication followed by postal services. Nearly 90 per cent of women literacy workers have used telephone and postal services for communication. Since woman literacy workers are the best-educated members of the family they do manage all the correspondence on behalf of their family members. E-mail is the means of communication rarely used. It is observed that two women literacy workers who have used e-mail have relatives in the town and have decided to go to the city for higher education.

Economic Empowerment

Economic empowerment ensures equal opportunities for women in economic activities in terms of paid work outside home, equal opportunity to earn, save, invest and spend. It also means equal participation in the decision-making process regarding sale and purchase of land property, acquisition of movable properties, and above all, the right for holding and transfer of properties. Economic empowerment begins with career orientation for girls in the family. Some of the findings related with economic empowerment of women literacy workers are presented below.

Table 5.32 : Career orientation of the girls in relation to boys

Sl. No.	*Particulars*	*Frequency*	*Percentage*
1	Equal job orientation	54	96.43
2	Unequal job orientation	2	3.57
	Total	**56**	**100.00**

Over 96 per cent of women literacy workers have registered their opinion that equal job orientation is to be given to both boys and girls. In rural areas it is generally observed that the parents prefer to give career orientation to boys and orientation for a married life to the girls. Since all the women literacy workers are educated up to high school, they are already been given orientation for a better career and they believe that equal job orientation for both girls and boys is the need of the time.

Table 5.33 : Employed women in the family

Sl. No.	*Particulars*	*Frequency*	*Percentage*
1	Employed women in the family	11	19.64
2	No employed women in the family	45	80.36
	Total	**56**	**100.00**

It is found from the table that nearly 20 per cent of the families of women literacy workers have working women. Over 80 per cent of the families do not have working women at home. It is the observation of the researcher that nearly 70 per cent of the families of women literacy workers are agricultural families and the engagement in agricultural operation in one's own farm is not considered as a productive economic activity. Only 20 per cent of women literacy workers are engaged in non-agricultural employment.

Table 5.34 : Employment and age group of women literacy workers

Age group of women literacy workers	*Occupation of women literacy worker other than domestic*					
	Business	*Agriculture*	*Daily Labour*	*Private Service*	*Any*	*Total*
15 to 20 years	1	20			12	33
21 to 25 years		5		1	5	11
26 to 30 years		1	1		1	3
31 to 35 years				3	1	4
36 to 40 years		1		1	1	3
41 to 45 years		1		1		2
Total	**1**	**28**	**1**	**6**	**20**	**56**

It can be seen from the table that 50 per cent of women literacy workers are agricultural labourers. Nearly 40 per cent of women literacy workers are students. Another 10 per cent of women literacy workers are engaged in private service like *balwadi* teachers, tailors, daily wage labour and business (shop).

Over 60 per cent of women literacy workers are undertaking multiple activities such as domestic and household duties on the one hand and the agricultural and non-agricultural responsibilities on the other. Domestic duties are invariably the responsibility of women in rural households.

Table 5.35 : Role of women literacy workers in deciding financial matters

Sl. No.	Role in family economy	Frequency	Percentage
1	Very much	8	14.29
2	Enough	36	64.29
3	Very little	6	10.71
4	Information only	2	3.57
5	NA/DK	4	7.14
	Total	**56**	**100.00**

Nearly 80 per cent of women literacy workers have disclosed that they have significant role in deciding financial matters of the family. Since women literacy workers are the best educated members of the family they are consulted for most of the decisions taken at home. Since women literacy workers are taking literacy classes for 10 to 20 women of the neighbourhood, they are already popular in the villages, especially among the women. They are considered as role models in the villages and their role in decision-making at home has been welcomed.

Table 5.36 : Status of household work in relation to other occupation

Sl. No.	Particulars	Frequency	Percentage
1	Equal status of household works	55	98.21
2	Unequal status of household works	1	1.79
	Total	**56**	**100.00**

Almost all women literacy workers have expressed that the household work should be treated as an occupation equal to any other occupation. This view appears to be a radical one in the villages, but has become much appealing to women literacy workers who readily agreed to it. But in reality none of the women literacy workers have recognised their household duties as an occupation. Agricultural activities are recognised as an important occupation, while the household work is considered only as a daily routine or the integral part of rural lifestyle.

Table 5.37 : Taking care of monetary affairs of the family

Sl. No.	*Looking after income and expenditure*	*Frequency*	*Percentage*
1	Self	7	12.50
2	Husband	15	26.79
3	Father	24	42.86
4	Mother	8	14.29
5	Any other	1	1.79
6	NA/DK	1	1.79
	Total	**56**	**100.00**

It is seen from the table that in almost 70 per cent of the families, men are taking care of monetary affairs of the family. Over 25 per cent of the families have women as caretakers of monetary affairs. This is an encouraging finding. In 12.5 per cent of the families women literacy workers are taking care of the monetary affairs like saving and spending at home. A close observation of these families has shown that these families are headed by women and the male members in these families are aged or minors. Sometimes they are away from home. In three families the decision-making women are widows.

Political Empowerment

Political empowerment of women refers to equality in political representation and their exercise of the political rights like the right to vote, right to contest, right to attend Gram Sabha, right to appeal to civil authorities etc. A few items are included in the interview schedule to find out the level of political empowerment of women literacy workers. The tables given below explain the behaviour of women literacy workers with regard to their active participation in democracy.

Table 5.38 : Going to attend Gram Sabha meetings

Sl. No.	*Attending Gram Sabha*	*Frequency*	*Percentage*
1	Very often	5	8.93
2	Often	9	16.07
3	Sometimes	7	12.50
4	Rarely	3	5.36
5	Never	31	55.36
6	NA/DK	1	1.79
	Total	**56**	**100.00**

It is seen from the table that over 55 per cent of women literacy workers have never attended Gram Sabha meetings. Nearly 45 per cent of women literacy workers have attended the local level meeting at least once. One-fourth of women literacy workers have been attending the meeting often. Women attending Gram Sabha meeting is a rare event in Haryana. It is observed that out of the 10 villages, where the study is undertaken, three villages have women as *Sarpanch*. The literacy programme has originally been the assignment of the village panchayats. The literacy workers are mostly the relatives and the close friends of the *Sarpanch*. Therefore, the literacy workers are encouraged to participate in the local meetings.

Table 5.39 : Attending Gram Sabha and age group of women literacy workers

Age group of the respondents	*Attending Gram Sabha*						
	Very often	*Often*	*Some-times*	*Rarely*	*Never*	*NA/DK*	*Total*
15 to 20 years	1	4	4	1	22	1	33
21 to 25 years	1	1	1		8		11
26 to 30 years	2			1			3
31 to 35 years		2	1		1		4
36 to 40 years		2		1			3
41 to 45 years	1		1				2
Total	**5**	**9**	**7**	**3**	**31**	**1**	**56**

It can be seen from the table that all women literacy workers who have not attended the Gram Sabha are the younger ones. Almost 30 out of the 31 women literacy workers who have never gone to attend the Gram Sabha meetings are below the age of 25 and 22 of them are below the age of 20. Since 18 years of age is a must for political participation, it is expected that women literacy workers below this age would not attend the meeting. All women literacy workers except one above the age of 25 have attended the Gram Sabha meetings at least once. It can be said that women literacy workers are quite active in village level governance, as far as the attendance in the Gram Sabha meetings is concerned. It is assumed that the involvement in literacy work has made them popular in the village and their participation in village level meetings is encouraged to some extent.

Table 5.40 : Freedom to participate as a voter in election

Sl. No.	*Particulars*	*Frequency*	*Percentage*
1	Freedom to vote	54	96.43
2	No freedom to vote	2	3.57
	Total	**56**	**100.00**

Over 96 per cent of women literacy workers have the opinion that women have equal right to caste vote. Women literacy workers being educated up to high school are aware of their political rights. This awareness is not reflected in their activity. It is observed that women literacy workers who have cast their vote are very few. Some of them are not even aware of their right for contesting in election.

Table 5.41 : Freedom to contest and age group of women literacy workers

Age group of woman literacy workers	*Freedom to stand for election*			
	Yes	Can't say	No	Total
15 to 20 years	18	5	10	33
21 to 25 years	6	3	2	11
26 to 30 years	3			3
31 to 35 years	3		1	4
36 to 40 years	2		1	3
41 to 45 years	2			2
Total	**34**	**8**	**14**	**56**

Nearly 70 per cent of women literacy workers have expressed that women have freedom to stand in election. One-fourth of women literacy workers believe that women do not have equal right to contest in an election. Even if there are 3 women *Sarpanchs* the awareness is yet to reach among all women literacy workers about the equality of women in political participation. At least one-fourth of women literacy workers still believe that only men can contest in the election and become the leaders of the nation. It is observed that the women *Sarpanchs* are elected in the reserved quota and in fact the administration of the Panchayat is still in the hands of the husbands of the women *Sarpanchs*. Woman *Sarpanch* is only for signing the documents while the key role in the political decision-making is still played by men. Under these circumstances, women are forced to believe that political leadership is more suitable for men.

Table 5.42 : Meeting the civil authorities to solve a common problem

Sl. No.	*Leadership to appeal in civil offices*	*Frequency*	*Percentage*
1	Yes, always ready	37	66.07
2	If necessary, we'll do	12	21.43
3	Can't say unless a situation comes	6	10.71
4	NA/DK	1	1.79
	Total	**56**	**100.00**

It is seen from the table that 66 per cent of women literacy workers are always ready to meet the civil authorities to address a common problem. Over one-fifth of women literacy workers are ready to meet the authorities if it is found necessary. Most of the women literacy workers are ready to take the leadership in solving a common problem of the villagers. It is further observed that most of these answers are expression of a wish or a dream of women literacy workers and they do not reflect the real situation. However, they have preferred to respond positively to this question. It is observed that the literacy workers have a lot of initiative and interest for social service. Since they are already engaged in a voluntary service of literacy work, they have learnt the significance of voluntarism. They have been accepted by the villagers as the teachers of the illiterate and they have started looking upon themselves as leaders in the events of any common problem.

Table 5.43 : Meeting an unexpected casualty in the village

Sl. No.	*Leadership to face natural calamities*	*Frequency*	*Percentage*
1	Yes, always in the forefront	40	71.43
2	I will help others	8	14.29
3	Can't say unless a situation comes	5	8.93
4	NA/DK	3	5.36
	Total	**56**	**100.00**

It is seen from the table that 71.4 per cent of women literacy workers have shown their willingness to take the leadership to face a natural calamity or any other casualty in the village. Over 23 per cent of women literacy workers are also conditionally ready to take the leadership in such a situation. This finding proves the social and political initiatives of women literacy workers. Women literacy workers are willing to risk their lives for rescue operations and help others whenever such situation arises. This initiative is rarely found among rural women. The literacy workers are seen above average in the realm of social and political initiative.

Concluding Remarks

Empowerment of women is a multi-dimensional concept. Social empowerment refers to development in attitudinal changes at the level of family, participation in decision-making at home, higher educational status and increasing participation in various social activities. Economic empowerment refers to the participation of women in the paid work outside home. Political empowerment of women refers to their participation in political decision-making in the community and their representation at different levels of Democratic Government, i.e. in Panchayat, Assembly and Parliament. Women literacy workers are found to be above average with regard to social empowerment and average with regard to economic and political empowerment.

6

Role of Literacy Work for Achievement of Empowerment

The research is conducted for a period of one year, observing the behavioural changes in women literacy workers on a monthly basis and administering the interview schedules to the literacy workers before and after the year-long literacy work. It is found that the literacy work has not significantly contributed to the achievement of empowerment among women literacy workers. However some signs of improvement are visible. Empowerment is a long-term process, the progress of which is not visible within a short duration of one year. It is seen that a certain level of empowerment is required for the entry into the voluntary literacy programme. In this sense, women literacy workers are more empowered compared to other women of the neighbourhood.

Social Empowerment

Social empowerment in the present context refers to progressive changes in the attitudes, concepts, beliefs, values, behaviour at home and participation in social activities over a period of one year during which women literacy workers have been actively involved in literacy work. The tools for data collection have been administered twice for women literacy workers, the family members and the *sarpanch* with an interval of one year. During this period women literacy workers have been involved in literacy work. Any changes in the responses of the literacy workers in comparison to their previous responses are regarded as the impact of their involvement in literacy work.

Participation in decision-making at home refers to the significant role played by women with regard to the selection of the kind of food items prepared at home, education of the children, purchase of household articles, employment of the younger members, marriage of the family members, income and savings and investment of the family property. The role of women literacy workers in these key domestic affairs is enquired about both before and after their involvement in literacy work.

Respondents refer to women literacy workers. Some change in the opinion of women literacy workers regarding their participation in the decision-making of various family related matters like kind of food and mode of its preparation, education of children, marriage of family members and income, savings and investments are found.

It is observed that in most of the families, literacy worker is the best-educated member of the family. Other members, either out of the fear of unwelcome reaction or out of respect for her higher educational status, consult her almost all the matters pertaining family. The literacy workers have realised their prominent position after the year-long literacy work. In most of the families women literacy workers are the key persons in the kitchen. They are careful to prepare meals that are acceptable to all the members of the family. Cooking, cleaning and collecting fuel have been regarded as the undisputed duties of women in the villages. For doing these household works, they do not require any special permission or consultation in the family. They have been doing these domestic duties with direct or indirect permission. By their interaction with other women in the literacy classes they have become more aware of the situation in the houses of other women and they have realised the significant role they have been playing in the domestic affairs.

Table 6.1 : Participation of women in decision-making at home-opinion of women literacy workers

Participation in decision-making at home	*Respondents (N = 56)*	
	Before	*After*
1 Kind of food and the mode of its preparation	32	36
2 Education of the children	35	44
3 Purchase of household articles	28	24
4 Employment of the younger members	22	23
5 Marriage of family members	23	30
6 Income, savings and investment	19	23

It is noticed that women literacy workers have shown increased autonomy with regard to savings but little improvement is visible with regard to purchase and ownership of property. This is due to their membership in the micro-credit union of women. Several Self-Help Groups (SHG) for women have been started in the villages and many a literacy worker have joined the groups that promote savings in the bank and mobilisation of credit through inter-loaning. Even if SHGs have helped women to exercise greater power with regard to savings, it is observed that they take loans at the suggestions and the demand of their husbands.

Table 6.2 : Usual do's and don'ts for women of the villages—opinion of women literacy workers

Usual do's and don'ts for women	*Respondents (N = 56)*	
	Before	*After*
1 Not moving out very often	21	26
2 Not going to (own) parents' house frequently	17	20
3 Not socialising with personal friends	21	23
4 Not interfering with financial matters	37	27
5 Observing *Purdah*	53	42

It is observed that the family members, mostly the parents of women literacy workers, have expressed that the literacy workers have a very important role in the decision-making of various family affairs (not shown in the table). All the family members reported that women literacy workers have the full discretion with regard to the kind of food to prepare and its mode of preparation. Almost 90 per cent of the family members have admitted the significant role of women literacy workers in the family matters before as well as after literacy work.

It can be seen from Table 6.2 that there is some improvement in the concept and attitude of women literacy workers regarding the code of conduct for women. More women literacy workers have realised the existence of restrictions on the freedom and mobility of women in rural areas. With regard to *Purdah,* the number of women literacy workers who supported for its observation prior to the involvement in literacy work has come down afterwards. After much interaction with several women of the village, woman literacy workers have realised that *Purdah* is not as prevalent as they thought it has been earlier. They have now started positively interfering with financial matters of the family after the literacy work. Some of the literacy workers along with the participants of the literacy work have formed SHGs. SHGs have been established in all the villages soon after the literacy campaign. These groups mobilised credit out of the savings of their members and started inter-loaning. Access to credit made women literacy workers realise that they have better participation in the financial matters of their family.

Table 6.3 : Observation of do's and don'ts by women literacy workers

Observation of do's and don'ts (code of conduct) by women literacy workers	*Respondents (N = 56)*	
	Before	*After*
1 Not moving out very often	20	15
2 Not going to (own) parents' house frequently	18	17
3 Not socialising with personal friends	23	20
4 Not interfering with financial matters	38	16
5 Observing *Purdah*	38	25
6 Convincing people about your problems	47	47

Table 6.3 shows information about the observation of the 'code of conduct' by woman literacy workers. More women literacy workers have started moving out of village often. The number of women literacy workers observing *Purdah* has come down after one year of literacy work. No change is visible with regard to visiting parents' home. It is seen from the table that

80 per cent of women literacy workers have been trying to convince people about the problems of women before as well as after the literacy work.

Table 6.4 : Differences in do's and don'ts for men and women—Opinion of women literacy workers

Differences in do's and don'ts (code of conduct) for men and women	*Respondents (N = 56)*	
	Before	*After*
1 There is difference in do's and don'ts for men and women	21	30
2 Can't say	3	11
3 There is no difference in do's and don'ts for men and women	31	12
4 Any other		3
5 NA/DK	1	

It is seen from the table that more women literacy workers have admitted the prevalence of differences in the 'code of conduct' for men and women after the literacy work. It can be assumed that before the participation in the voluntary literacy work, women literacy workers have been expressing their wish that there is no difference in the code of conduct for men and women. After active participation in social service, they have realised the existence of restriction to their mobility and freedom in various forms. Realisation of the prevalence of difference and discrimination in the treatment of women at various social, economic and political fields is an indicator of positive change in the mindset of women literacy workers.

Table 6.5 : Preparedness of women literacy workers to meet any casualties in the villages

Preparedness to meet any casualties in the villages	*Respondents (N = 56)*	
	Before	*After*
1 Yes, always in the forefront	40	46
2 I will help others	8	6
3 Can't say unless a situation comes	5	2
4 NA/DK	3	2

It is seen from Table 6.5 that more women literacy workers have expressed their willingness to come to the forefront and meet any casualties in the villages after the participation in literacy work. Taking regular non-formal classes to the women of the villages, the literacy workers have acquired leadership skills and have realised for themselves that they are being accepted as the representatives of women of the neighbourhood. Even before the participation in the literacy work, 70 per cent of women literacy workers have shown this leadership trait and after the literacy work the number has rose to 80 per cent. This preparedness on the part of women literacy workers is better to be considered as a precondition for volunteering for the literacy work. It may be assumed that the literacy workers have gained greater self-confidence and courage after the participation in the literacy work.

Table 6.6 : Usefulness of literacy programme—Opinion of women literacy workers

Usefulness of literacy programme	*Respondents (N = 56)*	
	Before	*After*
1 Literacy enables women read, write and count	9	8
2 Educate them about diseases	11	9
3 Makes her alert and curious to learn more	3	3
4 Gives them knowledge and makes them better qualified	8	6
5 Help them to live well, to manage home and savings	3	0
6 Renders self-confidence and power	4	12
7 Any other (Time pass)	1	10

It can be seen from the table that more women literacy workers have realised the empowering role of literacy programmes in the life of women. Before the participation in literacy work, only 4 women literacy workers had the opinion that literacy work renders self-confidence and power to the women, after the literacy work the number of women literacy workers who subscribed for this option has raised to 12. It is also observed that more family members and the *Sarpanch* have realised that the literacy programmes help women to read, write and count, make women alert and curious to learn, educate them about diseases, and help them to live well and manage home and savings and render self-confidence and power. It seems that before the beginning of literacy programmes the family members and the *Sarpanch* were not very much aware of the usefulness of literacy programmes and only after the year-long literacy programmes, they have been able to realise the utility of the programme. The literacy workers were aware of the usefulness of the programme beforehand. It may be due to the orientation given by the District Literacy Mission prior to the implementation of the programme.

Table 6.7 : Observation of *Purdah* by women literacy workers

Observation of Purdah	*Respondents (N = 56)*	
	Before	*After*
1 Observe *Purdah*	34	20
2 Not observing *Purdah*	4	30
3 Observe *Purdah* partially	8	2
4 NA/DK	10	4

It is seen from the table that there is considerable decrease in the number of women literacy workers who are using *Purdah* in the villages. The custom of *Purdah* cannot withstand the teaching job. How can a person teach others hiding her face behind the veil? And it is obvious that the literacy workers are not using *Purdah* while taking literacy classes. They are addressing the public on a daily basis and this public interaction gave them courage to do away with *Purdah* in other social situations. It is also significant to note that the number of woman literacy workers who explicitly refused to observe *Purdah* has risen from 4 to 30. This observation supports the assumption that *Purdah* is a symbol of restriction upon the mobility and freedom of women and the empowered women would like to deny observing *Purdah*.

Table 6.8 : Concept of Women Empowerment of women literacy workers

Concept of Women Empowerment	*Respondents (N = 56)*	
	Before	*After*
1 Household work is to be considered as important as a career	55	56
2 Same type of education is to be given to boys and girls	56	56
3 Girls are to be as career minded as boys	54	54
4 For education or for employment girls could stay away from home	47	49
5 In case of marital dispute a woman should walk out of the family	3	4
6 Whether girls should look after their parents even after their marriage	35	36

With regard to the concept of women empowerment of women literacy workers, it is seen from the table that they have a fairly good concept regarding the empowerment of women before as well as after the literacy work. The changes visible are with regard to the behaviour rather than conceptual level. It is observed that women literacy workers have answered the questions, which are very simple, straightforward and appealing to their rationality. Women literacy workers are impressed by the ideas presented in the questions and have been expressing their wish in their responses rather than the reality. They are answering what the empowerment should be rather than what it is at present. These opinions are not carried out in their life. None of them have mentioned household work as their occupation in the question of their employment status. All women literacy workers have upheld the solidarity and sanctity of the institution of marriage and a very few of them have the opinion that women might leave the home of their husbands in the event of a dispute. Over 60 per cent of women literacy workers are of the opinion that women have the responsibility of looking after their parents even after the marriage. Iswardevi, the lady *sarpanch* of Shajapur, has expressed that the married women have to look after their own aged parents, if they do not have any sons, or their sons are minors or are abandoned by their sons. She held the same view after the duration one year of literacy work.

It is seen from Table 6.9 that there is some improvement in the concept of woman empowerment and of freedoms associated with empowerment after their participation in the literacy work. More women literacy workers have admitted that women must have more freedom to wear any dress of their choice; freedom to follow any hobby like embroidery, drawing, photography, etc.; freedom in decision-making on significant matters such as purchase of household articles, education of children, employment of children, marriage of children, savings, income etc.; freedom for ownership of property; freedom to earn and save; freedom for consumption of resources; freedom to visit bank and freedom to save or spend money freedom to avail facilities; and freedom to exercise rights over one's own body and life after the duration of literacy work. The involvement of literacy workers in the voluntary literacy work has widened their understanding of freedom a woman must have. Women literacy workers did not show any change in their opinion regarding the freedom to participate as a voter in election, the freedom to participate as a contestant in election, freedom to participate in social organisations, freedom to exercise family planning methods, freedom to limit the number of children and freedom to feel proud of being a woman. They retained their old position with regard to these freedoms. The number of women literacy workers who have subscribed for certain other freedoms associated with empowerment has virtually come down after the literacy work. These freedoms are the freedom to move out for recreational purposes such as going to exhibition, park, marriages, picnics, films etc. This is due to certain undesirable implication of the question. Most of women literacy workers have misjudged the implication of the term 'recreational purposes'. In fact the mobility of women outside the village is very much restricted especially in the case of unmarried ones. Women literacy workers have not perceived anything strange in this undisputed custom. Therefore, women literacy workers have become closer to reality when they declined to admit this freedom associated with empowerment.

Table 6.9 : Freedoms associated with Women Empowerment—Opinion of women literacy workers

Freedoms associated with Women Empowerment	*Respondents (N = 56)*	
	Before	*After*
1. Freedom to move out for recreational purposes such as going to exhibition, park, marriages, picnics, films etc.	33	26
2. Freedom to participate as a voter in election	54	56
3. Freedom to wear any dress	19	41
4. Freedom to participate in social organisations	50	52
5. Freedom to visit bank and freedom to save or spend money	32	45
6. Freedom to participate as a contestant in election	34	33
7. Freedom in decision-making on significant matters, such as purchase of household articles, education of children, employment of children, marriage of children, savings, income etc.	30	40
8. Freedom to follow any hobby like embroidery, drawing, photography, etc.	47	52
9. Freedom for ownership of property	31	48
10. Freedom to earn and save and Freedom for consumption of resources	35	43
11. Freedom to avail facilities, rights over one's own body and life	46	52
12. Freedom to exercise Family Planning methods and Freedom to limit the number of children	37	36
13. Freedom to feel proud and not shame or guilt for being a woman	45	47

It is seen from Table 6.10 that there is a significant change in the exercise of the freedom of mobility by women literacy workers after the literacy work. Before the participation in the literacy work only 50 per cent of women literacy workers have gone out of the village at least once. After the literacy work it is found that 75 per cent of women literacy workers have gone out of the village at least once. It was observed that the celebration of literacy day is attended by the literacy workers at the block office Ballabhgarh. The literacy workers have also attended the training programme organised at a common place in one of the villages. They have also been invited to attend the cultural programme held for the literacy workers at a common place. Most of the literacy workers attended the programme where they have been distributed some gifts for their voluntary work. Thus literacy work gave women literacy workers more opportunities to move out of their own villages for attending various social and cultural programmes. Even if their concept of freedom for mobility for women did not change significantly their mobility in reality has improved significantly.

Table 6.10 : Freedom for Mobility of women literacy workers

Freedom for Mobility	*Respondents (N = 56)*	
	Before	*After*
1 Moving out of village for film or any other festival	29	42
2 Taking part in social activities such as a village festival or a religious ceremony	46	52

The participation of literacy workers in the village level social activities like *balmela* (children's summer festival) and religious festivals has also improved. Participation in literacy work has enhanced the self-confidence of literacy workers and they started participating in various public programmes held at village and block levels. Since the literacy workers are moving as a group to various common programmes along with other supervisory staff, the family members did not object to their moving out of village.

Table 6.11 : Self-concept of women literacy workers

Self-concept of women literacy workers	*Respondents (N = 56)*	
	Before	*After*
1 Emotional Balance	20	28
2 Optimism and Open-mindedness	45	39
3 Self-acceptance	10	55
4 Self-confidence and Sense of efficiency	51	54
5 Self esteem and Sense of worthiness	44	47
6 Sense of reality or Beliefs and Convictions	41	40
7 Social Competence	18	33

The notion of self-concept is a useful one to conceptualise behaviour in terms of a single, unified process. Self-concept may be simply defined as the total collection of attitudes, judgements and values that an individual holds with respect to his behaviour, his ability, his body, and his work as a person—in short how he perceives and evaluates himself. We form impression about ourselves just like we form impression about others. Each normal person experiences himself or herself as a distinct, continuous being or 'object' with clear body boundaries. In the course of maturation each individual develops attitudes towards that 'object' and calls it name 'I' or 'Me' or 'Myself'. This is the basis of 'self-concept'. Self-concepts involve an integration and organization of a tremendous amount of information. The roots of our self-concepts are the impression and evaluation that other people have of us in our interaction with them through the course of life. Popular methods used in the research on self-concept are self-oriented questionnaire or asking the subjects to rate themselves on a series of statements or a group of descriptive adjectives.

Several self-statements both direct and indirect are included in the self-rating scale to measure various aspects of the self-concept of women literacy workers. The rating scale is shown to the women literacy workers twice—before and after the literacy work. Some of the ratings to these statements by women literacy workers varied when presented for the second time after the literacy work. It is assumed that the difference in the disposition of women literacy workers is due to their active participation in the literacy work.

It can be seen from Table 6.11 that with regard to emotional balance, self-acceptance, self-confidence, self-esteem and social competence women literacy workers have shown an improvement in their self-image. More women literacy workers have shown an enhanced self-concept and showed the tendency of gaining empowerment with regard to these dimensions of self-image. Such an improvement is not seen with regard to open-mindedness and sense of reality.

Greater participation in social activities gives women opportunities to check the effectiveness of their own self-image.

Literacy work provides with ample chance for the literacy workers to check for themselves their temperament, openness to others' views and reality, the strength and weakness of their personality, self-regard, truthfulness of their beliefs and value system and above all their social competence.

Table 6.12 : Feeling of Security of women literacy workers

Feeling of Security	Respondents (N = 56)	
	Before	After
1 Highly secure, self-confident, gaining empowerment	11	12
2 Secure, moderately confident, marching towards empowerment	45	44

Every individual invariably craves for security. To be secured and happy, they must feel that they have anchorage, a place where they can stay safely. Similarly they should have people to share their joys and triumphs as well as sorrows and defeats. A person with feelings of security is usually well adjusted. Economic and political security assures safe shelter, comfort and nutrition. The feeling of insecurity or being tossed around is painful. It has its limits of endurance. Once, it grows beyond the limit the person may land into the zone of maladjusted behaviour. There are some factors responsible that would precipitate the feeling of insecurity. Effects of periodic unemployment as well as underemployment may lead to an insecure feeling in the persons. The rejection of children as well as overprotection of children by the parents could result in the feeling of insecurity. An insecure person may tend to have diffidence, shyness, worry, feelings of loneliness, dissatisfaction, suspicion, nervousness, discomfort, anger, mood change etc. as opposed to the secure person. The feeling of security is one of the indices of sound mental health. The feeling of security and insecurity are detected and assessed by administering the Maslow's S-I (Security-Insecurity) Inventory. This inventory is one of the widely used tools in assessing the feeling of security and insecurity and it has been used for the study with minor changes for suitable adaptation to the context.

The result of this exercise is given in Table 6.12. It can be seen from the table that there is no significant change in the sense of security, women literacy workers had, before as well as after the literacy work. All the women literacy workers have shown fairly moderate level of the sense of security prior to the entry into voluntary literacy work. With regard to the feeling of security at various social situations, the literacy workers are all above average and are marching towards empowerment. This higher level of the feeling of security may be one of the reasons for their voluntarism. This sense of security gave women literacy workers greater initiative to enter into literacy work. It requires a fair level of confidence and social competence on the part of the literacy workers to teach the illiterate women who are elder to them. It is like the daughters-in-law teaching their mothers-in-law. At least four women literacy workers had the fortune of teaching letters to their mothers-in-law. In Chandpur, when Shashi taught her mother-in-law how to read and write, she expressed that she got great satisfaction. What social experience is more rewarding than this for a woman in the rural Haryana? Mother-in-law has a very influencing status in the patriarchal families. When they appreciate the work of their daughters-in-law by attending literacy classes run by them, it is indeed an enriching and empowering experience for women literacy workers.

A monthly observation sheet for women literacy workers for 12 monthly observations is used to measure various aspects of social empowerment achieved by women literacy workers during the literacy work. This observation sheet is completed in the duration of 18 to 24 months. Literacy classes are sometimes not regularly held. During harvest seasons and during festivals, the classes are suspended and the researcher could not record the observation in a continuous term of 12 months. Some of the classes have not continued after 9 or 10 months, because the syllabus for the literacy classes has been completed before hand. The gaps in the observation sheet are filled by the methods of interpolation and moving averages.

The syllabus for literacy classes is divided into three grades and the entire programme is planned for a minimum of 6 months. The classes could not complete the syllabus within 6 months. The minimum duration taken to complete the syllabus is 9 months without break and one year with some occasional breaks of one and half months of harvesting and sowing season. In most of the cases the classes lasted for 12 to 16 months with a bread of 4 to 5 months. Constant encouragement and motivation is required for both the literacy workers as well as the participants to revive the classes once got suspended for one or two weeks and continue the classes till the evaluation phase.

Table 6.13 : Monthly observation : Attentiveness of the learners

Attentiveness of the learners	*Monthly Observation*											
	1st	*2nd*	*3rd*	*4th*	*5th*	*6th*	*7th*	*8th*	*9th*	*10th*	*11th*	*12th*
1 Very attentive (Value = 5)						2	4	6	5	11	6	19
2 Attentive (Value = 4)	4	6	8	15	15	25	22	21	22	18	25	24
3 Less attentive (Value = 3)	16	17	23	23	35	27	28	25	27	23	25	13
4 Distracted (Value = 2)	28	27	19	14	3	1	1	2	1	2		
5 Very Much distracted (Value = 1)	8	6	6	4	3	1	1	2	1	2		
Total respondents	56	56	56	56	56	56	56	56	56	56	56	56
Total value (weighed)	128	135	145	161	174	194	195	195	197	202	205	230
Average value of observation (upon 5 point scale)	2.29	2.41	2.59	2.88	3.11	3.46	3.48	3.48	3.52	3.61	3.66	4.11

The observation of the researcher has been in relation to attentiveness of the learners, discussion of women's issues in the classroom, singing and dancing in the class, dress of the worker and the interaction between the learners. The distribution of women literacy workers on a 5-point

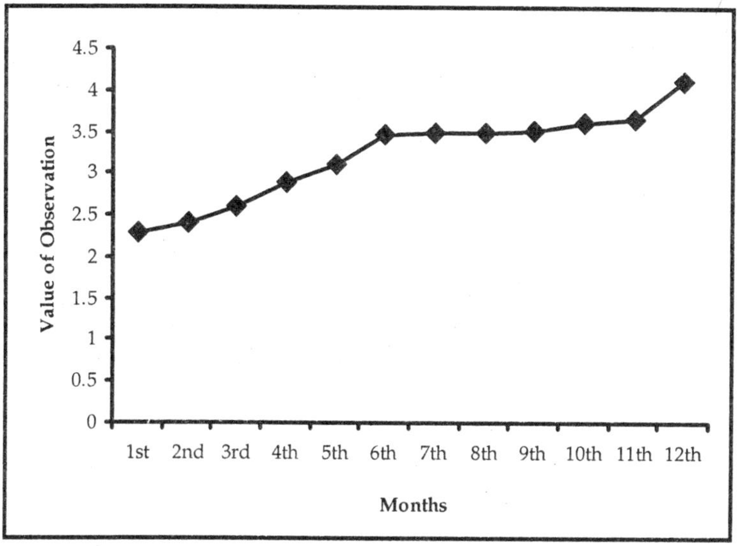

Chart 2 : Attentiveness of the learners

attentiveness scale over a series of 12 monthly observations is shown in the Chart 2. It can be seen from the chart that there is a gradual increasing level of attentiveness on the part of the learners over a period of 12 months. This increasing level of attentiveness is due to several factors like the increasing difficulty level of the lessons, the fear of final evaluation, the interesting nature of the reading materials, and above all the improving ability and skill of the literacy workers. This inference is related with the subject matter of the study under concern. Initially the literacy workers are unable to attract the attention of the learners and 50 per cent of women literacy workers are found distracted.

After completing 12 months of observation it is found that over 70 per cent of women literacy workers are attentive in the classes. Women literacy workers have definitely an important role in getting the attentiveness of majority of the learners in the literacy classes.

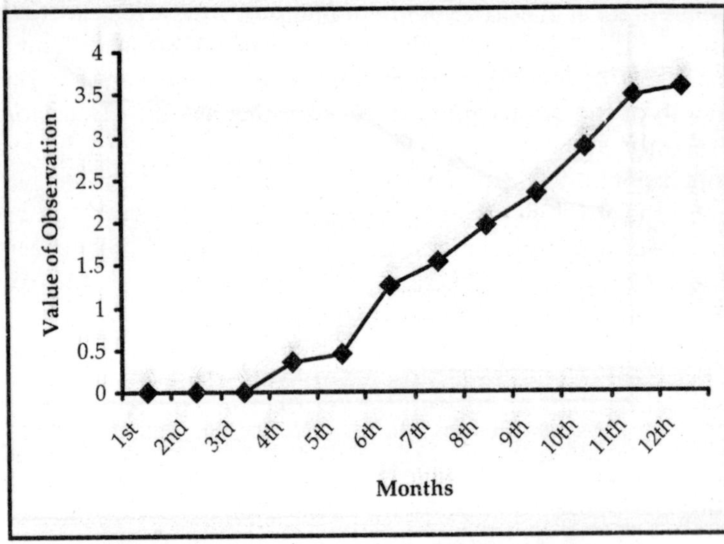

Chart 3 : Discussion of women's issues in the classroom

Table 6.14 : Discussion of women's issues in the classroom

Discussion of women's issues in the classroom	*Monthly Observation*											
	1st	*2nd*	*3rd*	*4th*	*5th*	*6th*	*7th*	*8th*	*9th*	*10th*	*11th*	*12th*
1 Yes (weightage = 5)				4	5	14	17	22	26	32	39	40
2 No (weightage = 0)	56	56	56	52	51	42	39	34	30	24	17	16
Total respondents	56	56	56	56	56	56	56	56	56	56	56	56
Total value (weighed)	0	0	0	20	25	70	85	110	130	160	195	200
Average value of observation (upon 5 point scale)	—	—	—	0.36	0.45	1.25	1.52	1.96	2.32	2.86	3.48	3.57

Discussion of women's issues like dowry, child marriage, mobility, reservation, etc. is not seen until the 6th month of the observation in the classes. Some of the issues like dowry and child marriage are mentioned in the reading materials and are the part of certain social awareness programmes held in the villages. Some discussions are initiated by the literacy workers and over 70 per cent of women literacy workers have meaningful discussion on women related issues by the 12th month of the observation. In most of the classes, discussions are only superfluous. Discussions did not lead to any conclusions and women literacy workers as well as the learners have the normal lifestyle at home after the classes. These discussions are on some incidents presented by the literacy worker and the reactions of women usually end with the expression of sympathy.

Table 6.15 : Singing and Dancing in the class

Singing and Dancing in the class	*Monthly Observation*											
	1st	*2nd*	*3rd*	*4th*	*5th*	*6th*	*7th*	*8th*	*9th*	*10th*	*11th*	*12th*
1. Mostly (value = 5)								11	5	9	7	17
2. Quite Often (value = 4)	3	6	5	14	13	20	29	21	29	23	30	19
3. Sometimes (value = 3)	17	15	25	30	35	32	27	20	22	24	19	16
4. Rarely (value = 2)	30	26	20	8	2	2						2
5. Never (value = 1)	6	9	6	4	6	2		4				2
Total respondents	56	56	56	56	56	56	56	56	56	56	56	56
Total value (weighed)	129	130	141	166	167	182	197	203	207	209	212	215
Average value of observation (upon 5 point scale)	2.30	2.32	2.52	2.96	2.98	3.25	3.52	3.63	3.70	3.73	3.79	3.84

Singing is a usual activity of the literacy class. Usually the class begins with a prayer song and ends with another prayer song. The learners have shown special interest in singing together and are also ready to dance along with the devotional songs if prompted. The frequency of these cultural events in the classes has increased by the end of 12th month. In the first month only 30 per cent of literacy classes have such activity while by 12th month over 90 per cent of the classes have these

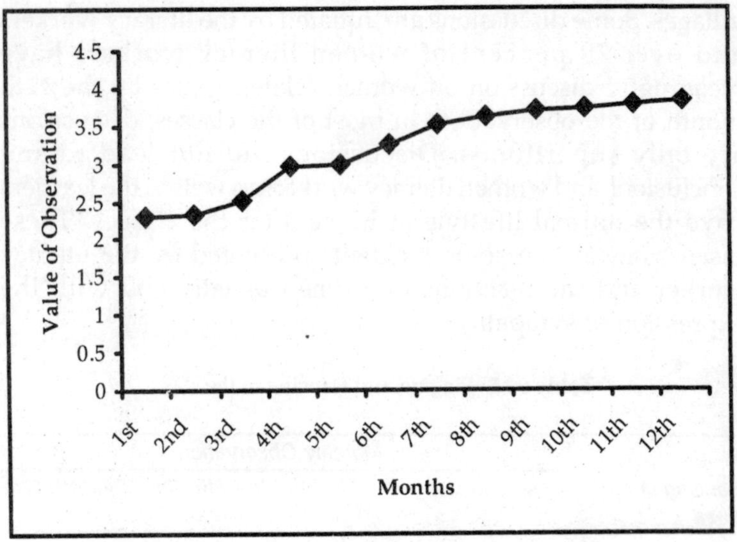

Chart 4 : Singing and Dancing in the Class

Table 6.16 : Dress of the worker

Dress of the worker	*Monthly Observation*											
	1st	*2nd*	*3rd*	*4th*	*5th*	*6th*	*7th*	*8th*	*9th*	*10th*	*11th*	*12th*
1. Formal (value = 5)								4	13	11	11	11
2. Informal but Special (value = 4)	6	3	9	13	14	19	30	25	18	20	19	24
3. Homely (value = 3)	12	18	27	33	35	31	26	27	20	22	26	21
4. Casual (value = 2)	30	29	15	8	2	3			2			
5. Shabby (value = 1)	8	6	5	2	5	3			3	3		
Total respondents	56	56	56	56	56	56	56	56	56	56	56	56
Total value (weighed)	128	130	152	169	170	178	198	201	204	204	209	214
Average value of observation (upon 5 point scale)	2.29	2.32	2.71	3.02	3.04	3.18	3.54	3.59	3.64	3.64	3.73	3.82

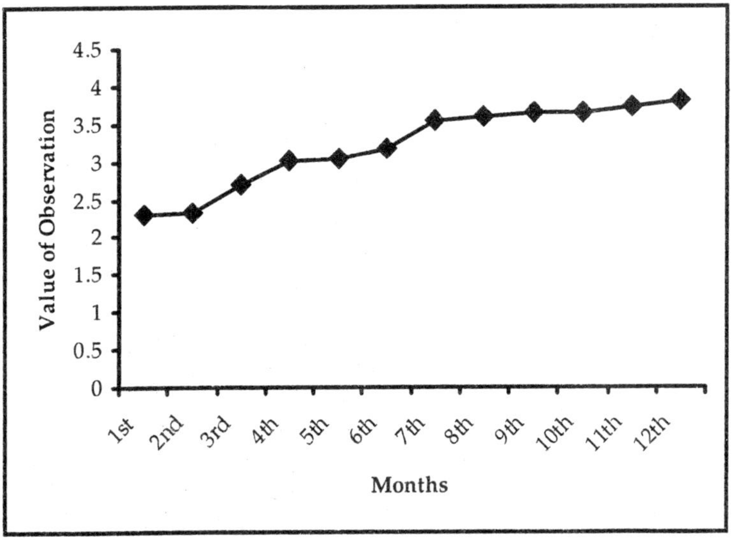

Chart 5 : Dress of the Worker (Unveiling of *Purdah*)

cultural activities. In Shajapur, the literacy workers and the learners are very much interested to show their singing and dancing in the classes before the visitors and the supervisors. These activities release the tension of the learners and allow them to relax in between their restless household activities. Some of the learners have attended the classes just for time pass and their participation is more active in the cultural activities than in the curriculum of the classes. Participation in these group programmes helps the literacy workers to improve their social competence.

The dress of the worker is an indicator of their seriousness in the literacy work and their self-confidence. In the beginning most of women literacy workers were in casual wear. By the end of the year the dressings of women literacy workers have become homely, special and in 20 per cent of the cases the dressing has become formal. Initially the literacy workers have to conduct the classes at their own houses and meet only the learners. Some of the classes are shifted from their own houses to some common places like *chaupal.*

Many outsiders started visiting the classes. The officers of the Block level literacy monitoring cell, supervisors of Gnan Prakashan Samiti, village animators and coordinators and the researcher started visiting the classes regularly. The literacy workers started wearing special dresses and towards the end, some of them have really been in formal dresses, because they are expecting the evaluation team of the literacy programmes at any moment. Along with the dressing the literacy workers have also exhibited formal ways of behaving. They could address the group and the supervisors in a polished way. Most of the classes started becoming serious with most of the learners practising writing on the slates and in the notebooks expecting a formal external evaluation. The informal set up of the classes is changed in most of the literacy classes towards the end. Initially the learners had gathered at the residence of the literacy workers just for a casual meeting and the classes were very informal. The first part of the syllabus (*Jatan Bhag 1*) is very easy and without much drill. The third part is more intensive and more serious.

Table 6.17 : Interaction between the learners

Interaction between the learners	*Monthly Observation*											
	1st	*2nd*	*3rd*	*4th*	*5th*	*6th*	*7th*	*8th*	*9th*	*10th*	*11th*	*12th*
1. Intimate (value = 5)								6	15	8	13	11
2. Good (value = 4)	5	3	7	13	13	17	29	24	14	25	22	21
3. Ordinary (value = 3)	13	19	26	34	33	33	27	26	22	23	18	24
4. Superficial (value = 2)	29	28	17	2	7	3			2			
5. Poor (value = 1)	9	6	6	7	3	3			3		3	
Total respondents	56	56	56	56	56	56	56	56	56	56	56	56
Total value (weighed)	126	131	146	165	168	176	197	204	204	209	210	211
Average value of observation (upon 5 point scale)	2.25	2.34	2.61	2.95	3.00	3.14	3.52	3.64	3.64	3.73	3.75	3.77

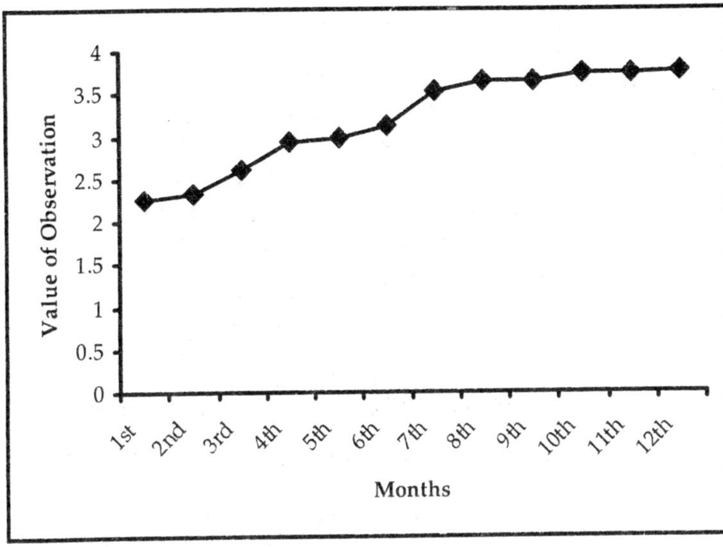

Chart 6 : Interaction between the learners

It is seen from the table that there is gradual improvement in the quality of interaction among the learners over the period of 12 months. In the first month 50 per cent of the classes witnessed superficial interaction among the learners. These interactions are very cordial and friendly but from the empowerment perspective, these interactions have not been deep and serious. The subject matter of the interactions at the initial sessions, were about the usefulness of literacy and the inconveniences at home for sparing time for literacy classes. Towards the end, the learners as well as women literacy workers have been talking about the same problems but with better insight and sympathy towards each other's situation.

It can be seen from the table that in the first month of the observation, only a few classes and their literacy workers have been observed as marching towards empowerment (value of observation is 1.83) as far as some social indicators of the classroom behaviour is concerned. These indicators are attentiveness of the learners, discussion of women's issues in the classroom, singing and dancing in the class, dress of the worker and the interaction between the learners. There has been a steady improvement in the classroom behaviour of the literacy workers and the learners in the classes. By the end of 12th month of the observation, majority of the literacy workers and their respective classes have been observed as marching towards empowerment (average value of observation has gradually increased from 1.83 to 3.82).

Table 6.18 : Estimate of Empowerment derived from the observed variables

Variables of Observation	*Months*											
	1st	*2nd*	*3rd*	*4th*	*5th*	*6th*	*7th*	*8th*	*9th*	*10th*	*11th*	*12th*
1. Attentiveness of the learners	2.29	2.41	2.59	2.88	3.11	3.46	3.48	3.48	3.52	3.61	3.66	4.11
2. Discussion of women's issues in the classroom	—	—	—	0.36	0.45	1.25	1.52	1.96	2.32	2.86	3.48	3.57
3. Singing and Dancing in the class	2.30	2.32	2.52	2.96	2.98	3.25	3.52	3.63	3.70	3.73	3.79	3.84
4. Dress of the worker (Un-veiling of *Purdah*)	2.29	2.32	2.71	3.02	3.04	3.18	3.54	3.59	3.64	3.64	3.73	3.82
5. Interaction between the learners	2.25	2.34	2.61	2.95	3.00	3.14	3.52	3.64	3.64	3.73	3.75	3.77
Total value	9.13	9.39	10.43	12.16	12.57	14.29	15.57	16.30	16.82	17.57	18.41	19.11
Average value (on 5 point scale)	1.83	1.88	2.09	2.43	2.51	2.86	3.11	3.26	3.36	3.51	3.68	3.82

It is further observed that the progress in the classroom behaviour is not carried to outside the classroom situation. Most of the women literacy workers behave in an empowered manner in the classroom and talk high about the need of women empowerment and the problems of empowerment. After the class they just behave in the traditional manner at home and in the neighbourhood.

It is also observed that the status of literacy workers has improved at home on account of literacy work. After noticing various people of high profile visiting the literacy workers and

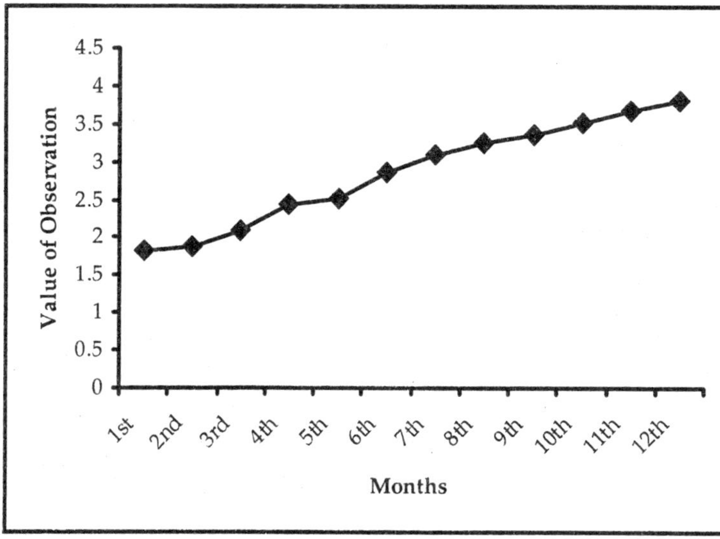

Chart 7 : Level of Empowerment over 12 months of Observation

the illiterate women of the neighbourhood respecting them the family members have realised the value of the literacy work in the village. The literacy workers have also realised their improved social status in the village and at home. The family members have recognised it and are happier to ask their opinion upon various household matters. The women in the neighbourhood are happy to invite the literacy workers to attend various functions held at their home. On the whole, it is observed by the researcher that the participation in the literacy work has definitely empowered the literacy workers as far as social participation and social status are concerned.

Economic Empowerment

Economic empowerment is relatively a long-term process. One year is too short a duration to measure the advancement of the literacy workers on economic empowerment scale. There has not occurred any change in the family income, personal earning and expenditure pattern of women literacy workers over the period of observation. Hardly any women literacy worker found out any alternative occupation or a new job. Women literacy workers are not promoted to any higher level of occupation. Therefore, women literacy workers did not become economically independent or no property rights are acquired by women literacy workers during the period of literacy work. Even if empirical evidence is not available about the economic empowerment of literacy workers, some indicators are examined in this section to know whether there occurred any of the progress of the literacy workers in the scale of economic empowerment.

Table 6.19 : Role of woman literacy workers in deciding financial matters

Role of women literacy workers in deciding financial matters	*Respondents (N = 56)*	
	Before	*After*
1. Very Significant Role	8	9
2. Significant Role	36	38
3. Very little role	6	2
4. No role, but informed	2	2
5. No role, not even informed	4	5

It is seen that there is no significant change visible with regard to the role of women literacy workers in household finance. In this table it is seen that just 3 women literacy workers have gained a better role in deciding financial matters of the family and one women literacy worker has actually lost the previous stand. It is the literacy worker who got married during the period of observation. However, it is important to notice that women literacy workers do have a significant role in the financial matters of the family before as well as after the period of observation. The higher educational status of women literacy workers is the primary reason for their good position at home.

It is seen from the table that there is practically no difference in position of decision-makers at home before and after the period of observation. In the case of a women literacy worker who got married during this period, the responsibility for monetary affairs at home shifted from father to husband. In all other families the situation remained unchanged. Similar situation is observed with regard to the occupational status of women literacy workers, income of women literacy workers, rights over their earnings, expenditure, savings and other economic indicators of empowerment.

Table 6.20 : Responsibility for Monetary Affairs at the Home of women literacy workers

Responsibility for monetary affairs at home	*Respondents (N = 56)*	
	Before	*After*
1 Self	7	7
2 Husband	15	16
3 Father	24	23
4 Mother-in-law	8	8
5 Any other	1	1

Political Empowerment

Unlike the economic empowerment the political empowerment has taken place at a faster rate in the case of women literacy workers. Social empowerment has immediately followed by political empowerment and finally, the economic empowerment. However, the momentum and the magnitude of these processes are rather slow. Not many indicators are available in the realm of political empowerment to estimate the improvement in the behaviour of women literacy workers. No changes are noticed with regard to the political representation of women literacy workers in the village Panchayats. Nobody lost or gained the right to vote during the period of observation. None of women literacy workers are elected as the member of headwoman during this period. Therefore, the scope of political empowerment of the literacy workers during the research period is limited. The following tables describe the political empowerment of women literacy workers during the period of observation.

Table 6.21 : Attending Gram Sabha Meetings by women literacy workers

Attending Gram Sabha meetings	*Respondents (N = 56)*	
	Before	*After*
1 Very often	5	1
2 Quite Often	9	3
3 Sometimes	7	41
4 Rarely	3	1
5 Never	29	10
6 NA/DK	1	

It is seen from the table that before the literacy work, more than 50 per cent of women literacy workers have never attended a Gram Sabha meeting. After the literacy work for one year, it is seen that over 90 per cent of women literacy workers have attended the Gram Sabha meeting at least once. They are asked to meet the *Sarpanch* and request for a common place to conduct literacy classes, and request him to announce the literacy programme in the village through public announcement system (*munadi*). In several such meetings with the *Sarpanch,* they are asked to appear in the Gram Sabha along with the block level or any other concerned authority of the literacy mission and talk directly to the people. Thus the literacy workers got the encouragement as well as opportunity to attend the Gram Sabha, which is otherwise attended only by male members of the family. The literacy workers are mostly the family members or the relatives of the *Sarpanch*. Therefore, the literacy workers are not hesitant to meet them. They are also ready to meet them with any issue of the neighbourhood whenever it is required. The illiterate women used to approach the literacy workers to accompany them to meet the *Sarpanch.*

Table 6.22 : Courage of women literacy workers to present common problems before civil authorities

Courage to present common problems before civil authorities	*Respondents (N = 56)*	
	Before	*After*
1 Yes, always ready	37	44
2 If necessary, we'll do	12	7
3 Can't say unless a situation comes	7	5

It can be seen from the table that more literacy workers showed readiness to present common problems before the civil authorities after the period of observation. Before the literacy work nearly 70 per cent of women literacy workers had the opinion that they were ever ready to approach the civil authorities for addressing any common problems. After the literacy work 80 per cent of women literacy workers have shown the readiness for the same. The remaining 20 per cent of women literacy workers have shown conditional preparedness to meet the civil authorities. All women literacy workers are thus willing to take the leadership in critical situations. After participating in the literacy work, women literacy workers are more exposed to the problems of illiterate women and the better-educated literacy workers are moved by the situation. They have accompanied the learners at various occasions to different civil authorities for solving their problems. These situations helped the literacy workers to act as leaders and representatives of the women in need. Thus it can be estimated that political participation of women literacy workers has improved after the 12 months' literacy work. It can also be concluded that the political and economic empowerment are slower than the social empowerment.

Concluding Remarks

The present study has been conducted over a period of one year, observing the behavioural changes in women literacy workers on a monthly basis and administering the key interview schedules before and after the literacy work of one year. It has been found that the literacy work has not significantly contributed to the achievement of empowerment. Empowerment is a long-term process, the progress of which is not visible within a short duration of one year. However, some changes are seen in the lives of literacy workers after participation in literacy work for one year. As compared with the situation of observing before the entry into literacy work, more women literacy workers have started moving out often. The number of women literacy workers observing *Purdah* has come down after one year of literacy work. More women literacy workers have expressed their willingness to meet any casualties in the villages coming to the forefront, after the participation in literacy work. The literacy workers have gained greater self-confidence and courage after the participation in the literacy work.

7

Problems in the Process of Empowerment

Empowerment of rural women is not an easy task. It is seen from the previous chapters that women literacy workers are aware of the low status of women and believe that men and women are to be treated equally in all walks of life. A great deal of awareness about the rights of women for equality and justice is imparted at different levels of the society beginning with educational institutions and in the community set up, at domestic, economic and political levels. However, women are not able to practice what they are aware of. In limited sense, at the personal level, women literacy workers can be considered as empowered in terms of knowledge and awareness, but at the practical level, both at home and outside home, they face several hardships. In other words, it is the external factors like restrictions at home and insecurity outside home that restrict the freedom and mobility of women. These restrictions at home are felt more in rural areas and problems of insecurity outside home are felt more in urban set up.

Restrictions at Home

There are certain restrictions that are traditionally imposed upon the women of India both in rural and urban set-up. Some of these restrictions are for moving outside home very often, going to (own) parents' house frequently, socialising with personal friends, interfering with financial matters of the family and observing *Purdah*. During the educational career, the girls are a bit relieved off these restrictions. There is a high level of school drop-outs among the girls in Haryana. Therefore, only a small percentage of women complete their schooling at higher secondary level and enter into college. Women literacy workers belong to this fortunate minority. All of them have completed their high school education.

The situation changes drastically soon after marriage. Whether literate or illiterate, educated or uneducated all women are forced to respect the restrictions. The following tables describe what women literacy workers do with regard to these restrictions.

From Table 7.1 it is seen that the most popular code of conduct for rural women is observation of *Purdah*. Even if both the Muslim and the Hindu women observe *Purdah*, there is significant difference in their observation. Muslim women often use *Burqa* whenever they go outside home. Hindu women use *Purdah* while they are in in-laws' house or when they move outside the village. It means that Hindu women do not use *Purdah* in their own house and in their own village. They used to cover their face with a part of their *sari* or *shawl* against all the strange men of the in-laws' house and other villagers.

Table 7.1 : Women literacy workers' opinion about the prevalence of general do's and don'ts for women in the society

Usual do's and don'ts for the women	*Opinion of women literacy workers*			
	Agree	*Disagree*	*NA/DK*	*Total*
1. Observing *Purdah*	53	3		56
2. Not interfering with financial matters	37	19		56
3. Not moving out very often	21	35		56
4. Not socialising with personal friends	21	33	2	56
5. Not going to (own) parents' house frequently	17	38	1	56

Almost 70 per cent of women literacy workers have the opinion that women are not to interfere with financial affairs of the family. Nearly 40 per cent of women literacy workers feel that women are not supposed to move out of home frequently and socialise with personal friends. Over 30 per cent of women literacy workers have expressed that women are not supposed to go to own house after marriage.

Table 7.2 : Opinion of women literacy workers about the restrictions

Sl. No.	*Opinion of Women literacy workers*	*Frequency*	*Percentage*
1.	Women must respect the custom and obey the elders	11	19.64
2.	Restrictions are discipline for women's life and respect them	2	3.57
3.	Give her right share and respect her likes and dislikes	2	3.57
4.	When men and women are treated equal, restriction vanish	3	5.36
5.	These restrictions are unjust and abandon them	4	7.14
6.	NA/DK	34	60.71
	Total	**56**	**100.00**

Nearly 20 per cent of women literacy workers are of the opinion that women must respect the custom and obey the elders and another 3.6 per cent of women literacy workers expressed that these restrictions are to be considered as the code of discipline for women's life and by respecting and upholding these restrictions would definitely protect women from both disgrace and physical hurt. Over 16 per cent of women literacy workers have expressed that the restrictions at home are unjust and are to be abandoned, women and men

Table 7.3 : Observation of do's and don'ts by women literacy workers

Observation of do's and don'ts by women literacy workers by themselves	*Agree*	*Disagree*	*NA/DK*	*Total*
1. Observing Purdah	38	6	12	56
2. Not interfering with financial matters	38	13	5	56
3. Not socialising with personal friends (peers)	23	27	6	56
4. Not moving outside the village very often	20	30	6	56
5. Not going to (own) parents' house frequently	18	25	13	56
6. Convincing family members about their problems	47	4	5	56
7. Not caring about do's and don'ts	48	6	2	56

are to be treated equal and the restrictions would vanish automatically, the society has to respect the likes and the dislikes of women and must be ready to give her the right share in the society. Over 60 per cent of women literacy workers have not expressed any comment on the restrictions at home.

While observing *Purdah,* women in Haryana cover their head and face below eyes. They do not cover their eyes. When they observe *Purdah* they do not look straight into the eyes of men and they will look down or sideways. There is also *Purdah* for voice. While observing *Purdah,* their voice will be low and they seldom appear in public. It is a custom, which steals away the self-esteem of women. As long as they observe *Purdah* they will feel that they occupy a lower position at in-laws' house. The system of *Purdah* effectively prevents women from occupying public offices and other visible positions. They will ever remain invisible members of the society. Their freedom of mobility, freedom of speech, self-expression and above all their rights to equality and rights against gender discrimination are grossly violated by this age-old custom.

It can be seen from the table that nearly 70 per cent of woman literacy workers do observe *Purdah* as if it is a well-established custom. 10 per cent of women literacy workers who are unmarried have not responded while 10 per cent of women literacy workers who are married told that they do not observe *Purdah* and do not face any pressure to observe the same. It is with this small section of women the process of empowerment begins.

Nearly 70 per cent of women literacy workers do not interfere with financial matters of the family while 20 per cent do interfere. Nearly 50 per cent of women literacy workers do not observe the restriction on their mobility and do move out of home for various purposes like meeting friends and meeting their own parents.

Over 80 per cent of women literacy workers do try to convince the futility of observing such code of conduct. Nearly 80 per cent of women literacy workers have expressed that they do not give much care or attention to these restrictions, have not given any serious thought to these restrictions, on the other hand they seem to be just observing them as if they are normal way of living in the villages. And it is observed by the investigator that when woman literacy workers get a chance to go to cities like Delhi, they tend to do away with *Purdah.*

Case Study 1

In her peer group Anita is regarded as a successful literacy worker in all Alipur. She is 25 years old and twelfth pass. She belongs to a *Gadariya* agricultural family. She is married and has a boy child. She is living along with her husband, father-in-law, mother-in-law and brother-in-law. She joined as a volunteer in the literacy campaign in 2000 and used to conduct the literacy classes in the public places—*Chaupal* and the village school. Not only is she educated, but also bold enough to work in the villages. She has faced tough resistance from her family members to the extent of physical torture. In spite of all these discouragement she continues to inspire the women of Alipur. Even if she is a daughter-in-law to the village she does not hesitate to move from house to house informing and educating the women about the usefulness of literacy. She is one of the early literacy workers in her village and 7 others joined as volunteers in the campaign due to her inspiration. The *Sarpanch* has been encouraging her. She fearlessly talked about the stupidity of *Purdah.* Over 110 illiterate women attended the literacy classes due to her persuasion. She has also participated in the organisation of *balwadi, balmela* and self-help groups. She is a source of strength for other women. She has really shown the strength of women power. She is considered as the backbone of SHG movement in Alipur. Even the *Sarpanch* used to consult her on various women related issues. She did not hesitate to tell in public the subjugation and exploitation of women by men. She is very much respected by all the villagers in and around Alipur.

Problems outside Home

There are several problems outside home for women that curtail her freedom and mobility. These problems are insecure streets and market places and increasing violence against women. These external factors prevent women from exercising their rights and thereby limit the scope of their empowerment. The lower literacy rate of women, the widening sex ratio, increasing migration of male workers, alcoholism and lack of precautions on the part of women are some of the contributing factors to the insecurity of women outside home. The feeling of insecurity among rural women depends on both objective and subjective factors. Subjective conditions refer to apprehension, fear, worries, and educational and occupational status of women literacy workers. Objective conditions are the situational factors, like past occurrences, bad experiences of close relatives and neighbours, etc. Some queries have been asked to woman literacy workers in this regard.

At least 16 per cent of women literacy workers are aware of problems faced by women of their village going outside home. Nearly one-fourth of women literacy workers don't know about any such happenings in their village. It is seen that majority of women literacy workers do not have any empirical evidence to show that women are unsafe outside her home. Only 16 per cent of women literacy workers have some incidence to show that women are in trouble when they are outside home.

Table 7.4 : Awareness of women literacy workers about incidents of violence against women happened outside home

Sl. No.	*Any trouble for women outside home*	*Frequency*	*Percentage*
1.	Lot of troubles for women outside home	9	16.07
2.	Don't know	13	23.21
3.	No troubles for women outside home	26	46.43
4.	Any other	3	5.36
5.	NA/DK	5	8.93
	Total	**56**	**100.00**

Nearly half of women literacy workers have not reported any incidence of violence or troubles for women going outside home. Even if only a minority have reported troubles happened to women in their village, more women literacy workers are of the opinion that women are not safe outside home.

Table 7.5 : Opinion of Women literacy workers regarding the Security of women outside home

Sl. No.	*Safety outside home*	*Frequency*	*Percentage*
1.	Confident women are safe outside home and progress in life	23	41.07
2.	Unless she is allowed to go out, can't say about her safety	15	26.79
3.	She is not safe, because society does not respect her body	10	17.86
4.	Women don't feel secure and self-confident outside home	6	10.71
5.	NA/DK	2	3.57
	Total	**56**	**100.00**

There are mixed responses to the question of the safety of women outside her home. Over 41 per cent of women literacy workers disclosed that the confident women are safe outside home and only brave women can progress in life. They believe that risk taking is the secret of success. They are very much aware of the happenings in the cities of sexual harassment of women who are mobile. Still they are of the opinion that unless she remains mobile she won't be able to progress in her education and career. Whatever happens she has to move out of home to secure what she deserves. Over one-fourth of women literacy workers resented about the lack of opportunity to go out of home. They had an interesting reply, 'unless she is allowed to go out, we can't say about their safety.' They are not sure about what would happen to them outside home. Their first concern is how to go outside home. Their mobility outside the four walls of house is restricted and they wish these restrictions simply vanish and they are allowed to just experience what would happen if they go outside home. Over 28 per cent of women literacy workers have confirmed to the conventional view that women are not safe outside home. Many of these women literacy workers feel that the society does not respect her body and there is chance for sexual harassment for women going out alone in the village. Others are of the opinion that women just don't feel secure and self-confident outside her home. These are women literacy workers who hold the view that the women are safe at home and going outside home is risky.

Table 7.6 : Woman literacy workers' readiness in facing the problems outside home

Sl. No.	*Facing troubles outside home*	*Frequency*	*Percentage*
1.	Bravely encounter, call police and get the criminal punished	13	23.21
2.	Come together, be stronger and help each other	29	51.79
3.	NA/DK	14	25.00
	Total	**56**	**100.00**

Table 7.6 shows women literacy workers' readiness in facing the problems outside home. It describes how women literacy workers would face the troubles outside home. Over half of women literacy workers have the opinion that the women should come together to help each other. Coming together empowers women. The literacy workers have come together in most of the villages to form self-help groups soon after the literacy work for one year. Sitting together, discussing about the problems of women, and learning from each other's experience make the literacy workers realise the strength of coming together to face troubles outside home. In the orientation programmes, the literacy workers have been motivated by what the women of Andhra Pradesh, Bangladesh, Rajasthan and Kerala achieved by coming together in self-help groups. The literacy workers believe that what a person cannot face alone can be dealt with collectively.

Nearly one-fourth of women literacy workers believe that they should bravely encounter, shout out for help, report to the police, and get the criminals punished. This is the conventional mode of facing troubles outside home. And 25 per cent of women literacy workers remained silent. Relatively less number of women literacy workers believe in the effectiveness of the conventional mode of facing the troubles. These methods are short-term solutions and the collective methods are long term and more effective strategies. Women are reluctant to request the assistance of police for protecting themselves. They often do not want to disclose any disgraceful events of their life before the police and getting the criminals punished is also considered secondary by women literacy workers. They are looking forward for a permanent solution for the troubles women face in the streets outside their home. This is possible from collective efforts on the part of the women supported and encouraged by the family members as well as the civil authorities. The collective efforts of the women can be the effective method to tackle the problems of alcoholism, eve teasing, exploitation and harassment at work place, unemployment, poverty, and others.

Table 7.7 : Opinion about the security of women outside home

Opinion about the security of women outside home	*Before*	*After*
1. Yes	9	20
2. I don't know	13	9
3. No	26	24
4. Any other	3	2
5. NA/DK	5	1

It is seen from the table that the opinion of women literacy workers about the security of women outside home has changed after the literacy work for one year. Only 16 per cent of the literacy workers believed that women are safe outside home before the literacy work. After the literacy work almost 40 per cent of women literacy workers expressed their belief in the safety of women outside home. After participating in the literacy work, moving in the village for inviting illiterate women for attending the literacy classes, and meeting the Panchayat members and other officers at various levels, the literacy workers gained greater confidence and their beliefs and attitudes have begun to change. They have started believing that the social situation outside home is not very dangerous as they thought it was earlier. Social competence is gained by increased participation in social activities especially by conducting various social programmes. Social attitudes are shaped by such enriching experiences and social interactions.

The finding of this table reinforces this fact. After conducting literacy classes for one year women literacy workers started thinking that the neighbourhood and the village situation is more friendly and safer than before.

Table 7.8 : Opinion of women literacy workers regarding their safety outside home

Safety outside home	*Respondents (N = 56)*	
	Before	*After*
1. Confident women are safe outside home and only they can progress in life	23	41
2. Unless she is allowed to go out, can't say about her safety	15	4
3. She is not safe, because society does not respect her body	10	8
4. Women don't feel secure and self-confident outside home	6	3

It is seen from the table that the number of the literacy workers who had the opinion that the women are not safe outside home has decreased from 30 per cent to 20 per cent. At least 15 literacy workers had the resentment that unless women are allowed to go out, nothing can be said about their safety. After the year's literacy work this number has come down to 4. This shows that more women literacy workers got opportunities to move outside home for various programmes and they have felt the village situation is rather friendly. Having more interaction with others in the village community, women literacy workers have found reasons to believe that the village situation is safer than what they thought it was before. It is learnt from this finding that fears and insecurity regarding social situations would vanish only when the women get more opportunity for social exposure and interaction with others in the villages. It is anonymity that breeds fears and social anxiety. Once the people get known to each other, social fears vanish. Their attitudes and thinking pattern begin to change. Literacy work has created ample opportunity to women literacy workers to meet many people and correct their prejudices about the situation outside home.

The number of woman literacy workers who held the opinion that confident women are safe outside home and only they can progress in life has increased from 40% to above 70%. Participation in the literacy work has increased the level of self-confidence of woman literacy workers. They have related the subjective feeling of self-confidence with the objective conditions affecting the safety of women outside home. In other words, these woman literacy workers have placed greater value to the subjective conditions over the situational factors of safety of women outside home. Another idea highlighted in this finding is the relationship between the feeling of self-confidence and the progress in life. By entering into literacy work, woman literacy workers had taken some risks in their life. This risk taking behaviour increased their courage and confidence to face strange social situation. They have started believing that only such risk-taking women would progress in life. Women sitting inside home would not achieve anything in their life. Empowerment of women is rather difficult for those who sit at home and hold that going outside home is not safe.

Case Study 2

Pinki Rani is a literacy worker in the village of Faizpur. She is 32 years old and is mother of five children—four girls and one boy. She is Thakur and is metric. She is from an agricultural family and her husband is a farmer. They have a nuclear family and their main source of income is their own agricultural farm. She joined as a volunteer in the literacy campaign in 2000 and took the literacy class in her house over nine months during 2000-01. She undertook the campaign in the midst of a heavy load of domestic work. Her eldest daughter is 12 years old and she has been asked to look after the younger children while she is taking the class. She has not been hesitant to move from house to house informing and educating the women about the usefulness of literacy. She is one of the early literacy workers in her village and 8 others joined as volunteers in the campaign due to her inspiration. Since she happened to be a daughter-in-law in Faizpur she has some resistance from her husband and his relatives for moving from house to house in the villages. Since the *Sarpanch* has been on her side she could undertake the literacy work fearlessly. Over 80 illiterate women have attended the literacy classes due to her persuasion. She has also participated in the organisation of *balwadi* and self-help groups. She is right now President of a self-help group. Initially she has been hesitant to move out of her house and visit other houses looking for other women. She has earned great respect from the women of the village who approach her for discussing upon various issues. She is a symbol of women empowerment in Faejpur.

Concluding Remarks

Empowerment of rural women is not an easy task. Even if a great deal of awareness about the rights of women for equality and justice is imparted at different levels, they are not able to practice what they are aware of. At the personal level women literacy workers can be considered as empowered but both at home and outside home, they face hardships. In other words, if the external factors like restrictions at home and insecurity outside home that restrict the freedom and mobility of women.

8

Social Participation, SHG Formation and Empowerment of Women Literacy Workers

It is found out from the study that there has not been much change in the behaviour of the literacy workers during their engagement in literacy work of one year. The literacy programme started in 2000 came to end by the beginning of 2003. The data collection for the research has been conducted during the same period. However, the field observation continued till date. The researcher has been keenly observing the social work interventions and the resulting changes in the condition of women literacy workers and the women participants of the literacy classes. It has been found that during 2000-2005, remarkable changes have taken place in the lives of women of the ten villages where the research has been conducted. The most important development observed is the formation of Self-Help Groups. Some of the findings of these observations are the basis for this chapter. Only observation and checking of the available records and reports have been used for this follow up. St. Joseph's Service Society (SJSS), an NGO working in the concerned villages facilitated this useful follow up.

San Joe Puram Women Empowerment Programme (SJPWEP)

San Joe Puram Women Empowerment Programme, the main community development project of SJSS has been running in the concerned villages since 2000. Literacy programme has been the first activity of this programme. In 2003 two major programmes have been launched in the concerned villages that facilitated the process of women empowerment. They have been the village library programmes as part of post-literacy campaign and organisation of self-help groups. There are 10 village libraries and 65 self-help groups at present in 10 villages. The literacy workers have been actively involved in the organisation of village libraries and the formation of self-help groups. The literacy workers have been also engaged in several other community development programmes such as running of *balwadies*, conducting *balmelas*, etc. They have also been exposed to various grassroots level training programmes during this period. As a result, remarkable changes have been observed with regard to the situation of women in the concerned villages.

San Joe Puram Women Empowerment Programme started in the year 2000 has undergone planning and action phases and at present it is in the transfer phase where the *locus of control* is being transferred from the organisation to the community. During the entire process of community organisation, several social work interventions have been planned and executed. Important programmes included in the community organisation process are socio-economic survey, literacy programmes, *balwadies, balmelas, mahila mandals*, post-literacy library programmes, and self-help group formation.

Training Programmes attended by Literacy Workers

Training is very important for the success of community organisation. Literacy workers have been the grassroots level workers and have been mostly volunteer girls, aged 15 to 25 years of age. There are 10 village animators and a coordinator who are selected from the village communities as the supervisors for the literacy programme. They are mostly women. There are two professional social workers and other supporting staff of the organisation at the top level to monitor the entire project of SJPWEP. Training sessions have been organised at three levels—at the top level for the managerial staff, at the intermediary level for the supervisory staff and at the community level for the voluntary staff, the literacy workers.

The resource persons from Universities and other resource centres have conducted at least three orientation programmes for the staff of the organisation in the first phase. Two professional social workers have been recruited for monitoring the community organisation programmes. There are full-time volunteer social workers and what they needed is professional knowledge and skills of community organisation.

After six months' on field training and orientation, the village animators (the supervisory staff at the intermediary level) have been prepared to venture out into the village community. Need based training modules have been planned and conducted to ten village animators and the village coordinator by the resource persons. Experts from the voluntary sector such as PRIA (Delhi) and AIFO (Bangalore) have given weeklong training to the local level workers on various skills of community work. The village animators and their supervisory staff members have been imparted training programme on the management of Self-Help Groups. The first task of the animators was to organise meetings of the villagers at different levels to recruit suitable volunteers for the community level work.

Training continued to the community level workers who are recruited from among the village community. Training programmes have been conducted for the village level leaders, women and SHG functionaries by Sarojini Naidu Centre for Women's Studies. Week long rural camps held by various Departments of Social Work exposed the village level workers as well as the local women leaders to professional skills of social work. Social awareness programmes on casteism, alcoholism, illiteracy, education of girls, child marriage, dowry, cleanliness and proper use of water have been conducted in the villages by different groups of student social workers. Training on reproductive health, participatory learning sessions, cultural programmes, street plays, house visits, cleanliness campaigns and Panchayat meetings have been conducted at regular intervals during the past three years.

Major training programmes given to the village animators, local level leaders and women of the self-help groups during 2002-2005 are the following :

- Balwadi Teachers' Training
- CBR Training on 'Four-fold Rehabilitation Strategy for the Disabled'
- CBR Training on Organisation of the Disabled
- CBR Training on SHG for the Disabled
- Gender Sensitisation Programmes
- Legal Literacy Programme
- Participatory Training programme for village librarians
- Training for Women Empowerment
- Training on Disability Management
- Training on Integrated Community Work—Balwadi, SHG and Literacy Work
- Training on Management of SHG
- Training on Motivation and Revival of Literacy Work
- Training on Reproductive Health
- Training on SHG Formation for the Disabled
- Training on Thrift and Credit Management
- Training Programme for Panchayati Raj Functionaries

Literacy workers have been active participants along with other women of the villages for all the above-mentioned programmes.

Community Development Programmes that Facilitated Empowerment of Literacy Workers

Major programmes, conducted after the literacy work, are *balwadi, balmela,* reading room, and self-help groups. Each of the programmes has progressively been organising the community as a responsible social entity, taking greater degree of control of their living. After the introduction of self-help groups, we have seen the people are growing capability of understanding and analysing various problems they face daily and plan out effective strategies for solving them. Literacy workers who have initiated the entire process of community organisation had the significant role in this empowering process. Women of the concerned ten villages have now a decisive role in various aspects of social life of their respective communities.

Impact of Literacy Programme in the Community

Improvement in literacy rate of women is the first indicator of women empowerment. The literacy condition of the villages is assessed by the animators by a formal socio-economic survey. The findings have been presented before the Panchayats. The poor literacy status of the women of the villages is exposed and the village Panchayats decided to intervene into the situation creatively. Literacy workers have been selected in the general body meeting of the Panchayat for every village. They are mostly girls and women who have passed at least matriculation. Every volunteer is requested to enrol at least 10 illiterate people of the age group of 15 to 35 from their neighbourhood. The venues were mostly the house of the literacy workers. Books, slates, chalks, black boards, charts and other teaching materials have been provided by the district literacy mission distributed through the NGO. The syllabus for the literacy programme is graded at three levels and the learner has to pass each grade successively. Tests have been conducted by both the organisations as well as the district level examiners. The entire course is spread for duration of six months to one year. The classes have been mostly held at noon hours, between 12 to 3 p.m. as per the convenience of women participants. Even if the adult literacy programme is targeted to men and women below 35 years of age, older people have also been welcome. It is found that the literacy programme has been moderately successful.

Usually the classes have been overcrowded. Women are often accompanied by their little children. Older people have attended the programme for a time pass. Literacy workers enjoyed teaching their elders sometimes including their own mothers and mothers-in-law. In one village the lady *Sarpanch* and her committee members who were illiterate attended the literacy classes.

The classes have been very interesting. Sometimes women sing in groups various *bhajans* and dance along with. Competitions have been organised to assess their reading and writing skills. Immense satisfaction is seen on the faces of women who could write their name and put signature for the first time. The immediate impact of the programme is the increasing enrolment of children especially girl children in the local school and the reducing school drop-out ratio. The villagers respected the literacy workers, admired the initiatives of the society, and better rapport is built-up with the local authorities.

Literacy programme started in the year 2000 in collaboration with National Literacy Mission, and Jana Chetana Kendra have made literate nearly 90 per cent of the illiterate men and women of the villages.

Case Study 3

Santhosh, 45 years, is the oldest literacy worker of Lehandola. She is one of the early literacy workers of her village. She is 10th pass and mother of two children. She belongs to *Gujar* agricultural family and lives with her husband and children. She joined as a volunteer in the literacy campaign in 2000 and took the literacy class in her house over 14 months during 2000-2001. Her sons are married and it is seen that sometimes her daughters-in-law also shoulder her responsibilities. She has set a new role model for all the mothers-in-law in the village. She is not hesitant to move from house to house informing and educating the women about the usefulness of literacy. She compelled 6 others to join as volunteers in the campaign. Over 70 illiterate women have attended the literacy classes due to her persuasion. She has also participated in the organisation of *balwadi* and self-help groups. Her success lies in organisation of anti-arrack movement in her village. She has effectively organised the entire women band of Lehandola against a liquor shop situated in her village, which has become the source of all the public nuisance. The movement is still on and she along with other women of the village has arrived at some settlement with the contractor of the liquor shop. She used to organise meetings of the women of the villages at the *Chaupal,* which has been otherwise reserved for only men. All have appreciated her presence of mind and courage and she remains as a source of empowerment to all the women of her village.

Reading Room

By the middle of year 2003, the first phase of literacy programme has been completed and the second phase started with the establishment of village libraries. The situational factor for the start of post-literacy programme has been an invitation from the Rajiv Gandhi Foundation (RGF) to join their village library programme. RGF financed for the procurement of furniture, books and TA for the librarian. Meetings have been held with the *Sarpanch,* Panchayat Samiti and the Gram Sabha for the legitimation of the programme. The rooms for the library have been arranged by the Panchayats. Village libraries have been established in 10 villages as a post-literacy programme.

Post-literacy programme is being conducted in collaboration with Rajiv Gandhi Foundation. Librarians (mostly women volunteers who have been the literacy workers) have been selected from respective villages. They have been paid travelling allowance of Rs. 200 per month. They have been given training by PRIA, Delhi. Since the need has been first expressed by the neo literates, there has been whole-hearted cooperation and participation of women in the library programme. Village Library Committees (VLC) has been formed for each library, having eight members including two women and one from the coordinating NGO. Each library has an average of 300 books, regional and national newspapers, magazines and sports materials. Activities centred at the village libraries include literacy programmes, organizing sports and cultural events, awareness programmes and activities for the development of the villages.

Village libraries are functioning two hours daily. Readership in each library has increased and many people are coming to the library to read daily newspapers. Village animators and librarians used to conduct house visits and organise meetings to encourage people to take maximum benefits of the library. Village library committees meet once a month.

With the establishment of village libraries, every village community had two centres of social activities or two community assets, viz. *balwadies* and libraries. Children have been the target groups for the *balwadies*. Youth and the adults have been the beneficiaries of the libraries. The recent trend shows that a large number of school going children are benefiting from the village libraries. The village libraries have been later on used as community centres for organising various training and awareness programmes. Thus the establishment of village libraries has accelerated the process of community organisation. The literacy workers who are selected as librarians have ample opportunities to read a number of useful books and to interact with the adult members of the community meaningfully. Some libraries are functioning as reading rooms and facilitate the learning of school going children. The literacy workers are assisting them in their studies. It has improved their teaching skills.

Balwadi

Balwadi programmes have been started in 2002 and have been conducted side by side with the literacy classes. One *balwadi* is established in each village. The need has been expressed by the participants of the literacy classes. The demand has been presented by the women themselves to the *Sarpanch* and the Committee. They allotted a common place (*Chaupal*) for the running of *balwadi*. Some of the literacy workers volunteered to be the *Balwadi* teachers. The *balwadies* did not have the nutrition component as the *anganwadies*. It has only the educational component. The children have been prepared to go to primary school. Each of the *balwadies* served as a play school and elicited great interest and participation of the children.

Balwadies are run in ten villages, from 9 a.m to 11 a.m. everyday. Attendance register of children is maintained in each *balwadi. Balwadies* ensure that children leaving *balwadies* are attending the local primary schools. Annual competitions for *Balwadi* children are held. Programmes include games, sports and cultural items and winners have been awarded prizes. Regular monitoring visits have been held to assess the functioning of the *balwadies*. Animators visit the parents to motivate them to send their children to *Balwadi* regularly. Very often it so happened that animators themselves had to go and call the children for *balwadi*. The success of the *balwadies* further enhanced the reputation of the agency in the villages and also nurtured greater degree of voluntarism among the women of the villages. The community level workers have been appreciated of their commitment for social service. They have been consulted upon various problems of the children. The volunteers and the literacy workers developed effective rapport with the parents of the *balwadi* children. The *balwadi* programme improved the human relation skills of the literacy workers.

Balmela

Literacy classes have become the platform for women to discuss various needs of the villages. The idea has been first discussed in the literacy classes 'to do something for the school going children during the summer holidays'. Conducting *balmelas* during the summer holidays has several advantages for both the organisation as well as the community. Objectives of *Balmela* are to gain access to the people of the villages, to bring the people together, to take the developmental activities to the people and to create awareness about the rights of the disabled, women empowerment, health and hygiene, etc. Various sports and cultural items have been held for different age groups for both boys and girls. *Balmela* help the children to develop their talents and qualities. *Balmela* is also a source of entertainment for the people of the village. It brings together people irrespective of their economic and social background.

Balmelas are held in the morning hours, 7 a.m. to 2 p.m. Since it is very hot during the day time, sports events are held early in the morning and the cultural events are held at noon hours. During the public meeting held thereafter, the villagers used to present some programmes to entertain the gatherings. The *balmelas* thus take the shape of *villagemelas*.

Table 8.1 : Participation of the people for Balmela in the village (2004)

Sl. No	Dates	Village	People participated	Children	Adults
1.	26-5-04	Lehandola	250	150	100
2.	27-5-04	Alipur	500	200	300
3.	28-5-04	Faizpur	200	125	75
4.	02-6-04	Gharoda	175	125	50
5.	03-6-04	Chandpur	200	150	50
6.	04-6-04	Raipur Kalan	225	150	75
7.	05-6-04	Imamuddinpur	80	65	15
8.	07-6-04	Shahajanpur	300	225	75
9.	08-6-04	Bahadurpur	100	80	20

This has been the fourth *balmela*. Speech competitions have been conducted this year. Each village is given a specific theme for speech, like alcoholism, dowry, hygiene, illiteracy, corruption and poverty. Large number of children gathered to participate in various competitions conducted. Most of the village *Sarpanchs* and councillors have also attended the *mela*.

Balmelas become full-time engagement for the kids as well as their parents. They spend several days for preparing the children for various events. Local schools are used as the venue of the programme. Women Literacy Workers, local teachers, *balwadi* teachers, village animators, local body members and other elders of the village come forward as volunteers. Local resources are mobilised in terms of tent, sound system, refreshment for the children, prizes etc. *Balmelas* have thus become an effective strategy for community organisation and the literacy workers have further improved their skills in the field with regard to community organisation.

Self-Help Groups (SHG)

The programme which elicited best cooperation and enthusiasm on the part of the learners of the literacy classes is the formation of SHG for women. The idea of self-help group formation has been given during the literacy classes with the objective of turning each learners' group into a *mahila mandal* after the literacy evaluation of the groups. However that did not take place. Self-help groups have been organised on the basis of the financial status of the members. Officers from Gurgaon Grameen Bank and the Block level extension workers (social educators) came forward to assist the organisation to hold preliminary meetings with the villagers and motivate them. The villagers have been issued two types of ration cards, viz. Yellow colour ration cards and Green colour ration cards on the basis of their gross family income. Families belonging to Below Poverty Line (BPL) have been issued Yellow cards. Women of these families have been given incentives to form Self-help groups such as margin money, interest free loans and subsidies. Issuing yellow or green cards has often been the discretion of the local body and it is found that there has been some kind of discrimination in the distribution of yellow cards. Several genuine families have been denied yellow cards. Therefore formation of groups of the green card holders has also been promoted by the organisation. Gram Sabha meetings as well as meetings of women have been conducted in each village separately. *Sarpanch*, Panchayat committee members, coordinators, village animators, experts from other agencies such as banks, block Panchayats and Universities have been invited for several such meetings and training programmes have been organised both at the community level as well as at a central location.

Several meetings have been held by women in the villages. Membership of a group varies from 10 to 20. The bye law has been discussed thoroughly, list of members has been finalised, group-wise meetings have been held several times, governing body has been elected, training has been given to the office bearers on book-keeping, maintaining minute books, and managing accounts, registers and minute books have been purchased, membership cards have been printed, seals and registers have been prepared, savings have been collected from the members, dates for regular monthly or fortnightly meetings have been agreed upon, formalities for opening bank accounts in the Grameen Bank have been completed and bank accounts have been opened and finally the self-help group is formed firmly. It has taken at least six months for the first group to open a bank account. Holding regular meetings, ensuring everyone's attendance and collection of regular savings are the most important as well as the most difficult tasks of the groups. It takes at least one year for a group to get consolidated. Once the group has accumulated considerable sum of savings in the bank, it will be easier to get the members' regular participation in various activities of the group. Until the groups are formed, group formation itself has been presented as the sole aim of the meetings. Once the groups are formed, higher objectives have been presented for them to work for. Two meetings have been scheduled every month—in the first and the third week of the month. The first meeting has been dedicated for the routine works of the groups such as collection of the savings, reading of the minutes, inter-loaning, preparing the records, assigning various responsibilities to the members etc. Every member is supposed to visit the bank in turn. The second meeting of month is dedicated for various activities, classes, training programmes and discussions. In the meetings, discussions are held on various matters such as approval of loan, collection of savings, repayment, group problems, absenteeism in the meetings, problems with office bearers etc. Awareness on TB, pre-natal and post-natal maternity care, disability, smoking, alcoholism, education, pulse polio, hygiene, various Government schemes and awareness on different other topics have been given in the meetings. Activities conducted by them include village cleaning, awareness on women education, maternity and child health.

Presently there are 65 SHGs for women. Annual turnover (savings and inter-loaning) has crossed Rs. 30 lakhs. Several groups (below poverty line) have received grants from the Government. Most of the groups have been linked with NABARD. SJSS has contributed matching grants to different groups to start income generation activities. Groups are engaged mainly in inter-loaning. All the groups hold regular meetings attended by village animators and coordinator.

Lehandola and Alipur the groups have campaigned against liquor shops. At present, the groups have formed a federation at the local level. The federation of the self-help groups is a powerful organisation of women that will positively exert pressure on the civil authorities. Recently the officials of NABARD, Ballabhgarh have appreciated the working of SHGs in the concerned villages and have initiated an intensive campaign for the formation of 100 SHGs in the nearby 30 villages in a period of 3 years. A marketing outlet has been opened at Tigaon with the assistance from NABARD for the sale of the products of SHGs who are the members of the federation.

Table 8.2 : Status of SHG in selected villages in Faridabad District (2005)

Sl. No.	*Village*	*Total SHGs*	*Membership*
1.	Faizupur	8	87
2.	Shahajanpur	8	85
3.	Chandpur	11	121
4.	Bahadurpur	8	82
5.	Lehandola	9	106
6.	Gharora	5	55
7.	Raipur	5	53
8.	Allipur	7	77
9.	Manjavali	1	12
10.	Shahupura	3	35
	Total	**65**	**713**

Self-help groups are proved to be grassroots level peoples' organisation to empower the weak, the marginalized, the poor and the down-trodden. Women of the families belonging to below poverty line are considered to be the main beneficiaries of the programme.

It has been found that formation of self-help groups is the highest form of community organisation. Initial stage of the group formation is difficult. It took almost six months to get the first group consolidated. Later on it has been easier. Seeing the successful functioning of some groups others have come forward to form themselves into groups. Faizpur has shown as example in this regard. Faizpur is a small village of

87 families, and all the families are now members of self-help groups. The first groups have required a lot of support, encouragement, training, motivation and constant guidance. Later on it is found that the groups that are formed later required less guidance and supervision. Women of the village have realised the advantages of group formation and have demanded less external support. This trend shows that the women of the villages are in the right path of empowerment. Even if inter-loaning is the main activity of the groups, some of them are able to take loans of Rs. 1 lakh and above for common enterprises. In the self-help groups are able to take up different problems of the villages, plan out actions, mobilise local resources, pressurise the civil authorities and take the control of the community organisation. With the establishment of a network of self-help groups it has shown a clear transfer of control of the process of community organisation from the agency to the community, which is the ultimate objective of community organisation.

Literacy workers have played a vital role in the formation and maintenance of SHGs for women. Most of the literacy workers are either office bearers or active members of SHG. For the first time, women started going to bank, negotiate for loans, buy buffalos, started giving loans to needy members, started going to civil authorities collectively to give petition to cancel the liquor contract in the villages, conducted demonstrations and rallies, and above all sat together for long hours in discussing various women related issues. During the literacy classes, the literacy workers had been sharing the successful campaigns conducted by women of Andhra Pradesh and Kerala. They have been inspired by the success stories of Narmada Bachao Andolan (NBA), Chipko movement, Anti-liquor campaigns etc. The literacy workers have really brought the mainstream women of the concerned villages in the path of empowerment.

Self-help groups have internal forces for their own sustainability. Once the self-help groups are formed and savings are deposited in the banks, which get accumulated every month the members of the group feel confident, more secure, united and empowered. Their solidarity among themselves and their loyalty towards the group tend to grow further. Once the group has secured subsidies and grants from other agencies, their common capital increases and it further nurtures their solidarity. Inter-loaning is the common activity of the groups. In the event of inter-loaning two members of the groups have to provide personal security, which in turn strengthens the factors of contracting among the group members. Consolidation of the group in the initial stage is a difficult task before the group members and once the group is consolidated the maintenance is much easier and its survival is quite natural. Follow up or any external monitoring has little relevance with regard to a well-established self-help group.

Participatory Monitoring

Participatory monitoring refers to the supervision, guidance, evaluation, and improvement of the process of community organisation by the community itself. In San Joe Puram Women Empowerment Programme, out of the 14 monitoring staff, 11 are from the village communities. Only three are from the organisation. Village animators are elected from the Gram Sabha. These animators were the first literacy workers of their respective villages. They are given training and awareness regarding various welfare programmes. Each animator has to conduct, supervise, monitor and evaluate the programmes held in her village. Animators gather once in week at the agency and share their experiences, learn from each other's experience and improve their own skills of supervision and monitoring. The experts from the agencies are present in such sessions. In addition to giving advices and guidance they go to the villages to assist the animators at their request.

Animators' meetings are held every week giving opportunity for all the staff in village work to meet together. During these meetings, animators and coordinators present weekly and monthly reports. Each village activity is discussed and assessed in the meetings. Necessary instructions and directions are given to the animators for better organisation of village activities. Inputs and awareness regarding various welfare schemes and programmes are given. The matters discussed include SHG meeting in different villages, functioning of the *balwadies*, visit of mobile health unit, formation of new groups, problems faced by the SHGs, happenings in the villages, house visits of the differently abled and patients, functioning of the village library etc.

Occasionally meetings are held at village level to evaluate the progress of various programmes. The suggestions of the villagers especially of the committee members are considered to improve the programmes. In the event of the resignation of a village animator, Gram Sabha is convened to elect new animator. Informal house visits by the animators, coordinator and agency supervisors help to evaluate the progress of the process of community organisation.

Case Study 4

Mamata Maheswari is 40 years old and mother of two children—a boy and a girl. She has completed her higher secondary education. Her husband runs a grocery shop adjacent to her house. She joined as a volunteer in the literacy campaign in 2000 and took two literacy classes in two different locations. Her village is sub-divided into three caste groups—Thakur *Mohella*, Muslim *Mohella* and Dalit *Mohella*. In spite of being a daughter-in-law in the village she used to visit all the houses in the villages breaking all the caste barriers. Her husband is a progressive minded man and did not discourage her initiatives. Sometimes she has faced resistance from the *Sarpanch*. She is one of the early literacy workers in Chandpur and 9 others joined as volunteers in the campaign due to her motivation. Over 100 illiterate women have attended the literacy classes due to her persuasion. She has also participated in the organisation of *balwadi* and self-help groups. She has been running the *balwadi* in her own house. Now both men and women regard her as a significant person in the village. Women of all the caste groups approach her for various suggestions and assistances.

Concluding Remarks

SHGs remain as agents of women empowerment for years to come. Initially much encouragement and several meetings have been required to convince the rural women the advantages of coming together to form SHGs. Now, the women who have not joined any groups so far are willingly coming forward to form SHGs. Women in general and the poor women in particular have realised the advantages of working together in the form of SHG and this trend is truly the sign of women empowerment. Literacy workers who have initiated the process of empowerment five years ago have been regarded as the torchbearers of this change in the concerned villages.

Literacy workers having been associated with the women empowerment programme right from the beginning have benefited much from the entire project. After five years of their continuous participation in the project, changes are seen in their personality, in their social attitudes, leadership behaviour, sense of social commitment, aptitude for social service, their social status in the neighbourhood, level of their participation in decision-making at all levels beginning from the family till the village Panchayats. These long-term impacts are the wider concern of the present study. Only vague and casual observations are made right now. A formal and systematic study would reveal the parameters of empowerment on a long-term basis. It opens up the scope for further research.

9

Conclusion

Summary of Findings

Analysing the available statistics and published reports, it is seen that rapid progress is achieved in the literacy level of the nation since independence. National Literacy Campaign launched in 1988 has significantly contributed to the improvement in the literacy level of the nation. However, regional disparity is vivid. The Scheduled Castes and Scheduled Tribes lag behind with regard to literacy level and their women are far behind the national average in this regard. Sex ratio continues to be declining especially with industrialised states. Haryana is above average in literacy level compared with the national literacy rate but is below average concerning sex ratio. Faridabad district where the study is held is better in literacy level, but poorer in sex ratio in comparison with the state averages.

Literacy work facilitates empowering women. Empowerment has been set as a challenging goal for the literacy workers. While conducting the literacy classes, they improve their social status, social competence, leadership qualities, self-esteem and self-confidence. They gain empowerment and bring other women in the path of empowerment. In this process they face several hardships and struggle to overcome them. Voluntarism shown by women literacy workers is the first sign of empowerment. While exploring various socio-economic factors of this voluntarism, it has been observed that women literacy workers belong to the best-educated women of the society. In this context it is found worthwhile to look into the socio-economic and demographic profile of women literacy workers.

While analysing the ***demographic profile of women literacy workers,*** it is observed that the literacy workers are from ten villages, mostly below the age of 25 years, unmarried and Hindu by religion. Among them, many are Dalit literacy workers. Analysing economic profile of women literacy workers, it is found that most of them belong to lower middle class families. Majority of women literacy workers live in semi-*pucca* or *pucca* houses with two or three rooms, have own agricultural land, have non-agricultural source of income, use traditional fuels for cooking, have traditional and modern assets and possess milch animals. Majority of women literacy workers have in their house, toilet facilities. Quite a few households have members who are either underemployed or unemployed. Majority of women literacy workers as well as the heads of the family are educated up to High School level. Most of the families of women literacy workers have school going children. Most of the families are medium size, i.e. is 4-6 members. Majority of women literacy workers belong to nuclear families. Most of the families are male dominated. Most of women literacy workers have access to various social infra-structural facilities like primary school, primary health centre, water supply, power supply, telecommunication media and public distribution system.

Social, Economic and Political Empowerment of Literacy Workers

Empowerment of women is a multi-dimensional concept. Social empowerment refers to development in attitudinal changes at the level of family, participation in decision-making at home, progressive changes in the educational status and increasing participation in various social activities. Economic empowerment refers to the participation of women in the paid work outside home. Political empowerment of women refers to their participation in political decision-making in the community and their representation at different levels of

Democratic Government, i.e. in Panchayat, Assembly and Parliament.

Prevalence of separate code of conduct for men and women is the indicator of discrimination and disempowerment. Majority of women literacy workers who are educated up to high school believe that there should not be any difference between men and women in the code of conduct. Majority of the unmarried women literacy workers do not admit the difference while 50 per cent of the married women literacy workers admit the difference. Majority of women literacy workers are secure and moderately confident with regard to optimism and open mindedness, self-confidence and sense of efficiency, self-esteem and sense of worthiness and sense of reality or beliefs and convictions while they are less secure and not so confident with regard to emotional balance, self-acceptance and social competence. At conceptual level most of women literacy workers are gaining empowerment with regard to sense of reality, self-esteem and self-confidence but require more attention with regard to emotional balance and social competence.

The proportion of married women with 'good' self-concept ('good' refers to a score between 151-200) is less compared to those who are unmarried. Four-fifth of women literacy workers do not have guilt feeling of being women. On the one hand majority of the women feel that they do not have to regret over their womanhood, and on the other hand, they feel proud on being women.

It has been found that all women literacy workers are above 'average' with regard to their sense of security. Above 80 per cent of women literacy workers feel secure and gain empowerment. Feeling of security is a sign of social competence. It is seen that unmarried women are more secure than the married ones. Out of 11 highly secure women literacy workers 10 are unmarried and only one is married. It shows that the married women feel less secure at the house of the husband. Majority of women literacy workers have 'average' level of self-concept as far as social competence is concerned and they need to gain empowerment. Women literacy workers with college education have a better self-concept regarding social competence in comparison with those who are educated up to secondary level.

Majority of women literacy workers are consulted by the heads of the families with regard to most of the decisions taken at home. In 15 families, women are decision-makers. For women literacy workers who are below the age of 20 years, fathers are decision-makers at home and for women literacy workers above the age of 20 husbands are decision-makers. In majority of the houses men are decision-makers and the role of women is secondary and supplementary and never has it been complementary.

In the houses of the married women literacy workers, most of the decision-makers are the husbands and in the houses of unmarried women literacy workers, fathers are decision-makers. In smaller families, women literacy workers or their husbands are the decision-makers while in larger families the parents are decision-makers. In 18 families where the heads of the family are daily wage labourers, 7 decision-makers are women. In families where women are engaged in non-agricultural occupations, women literacy workers get greater participation in decision-making. Where women are engaged in traditional occupation of agriculture, their participation in the decision-making of the family matters is very much limited. When women are engaged in non-agricultural occupations their income is made known to everyone in the family and their presence in the family is counted. Whenever any decision involving financial investment is taken, they are consulted. They sometimes rise to a prominent position and take independent decisions in the family, especially when they have a regular employment. Most of the families are nuclear families and 9 nuclear families have women as decision-makers. Only 3 medium size families have women in the key role for domestic decision-making. Nearly two-third of women literacy workers have opined that the married women have the responsibility to look after their own parents even after marriage. Over one-fourth of women literacy workers have the opinion that in no circumstances the parents would stay with their daughters after marriage. Nearly two-third of women literacy workers observe *Purdah* from the elders of the family. At least 14 per cent of women literacy workers do not observe *Purdah* from the elders of the family. In other terms the elders of these families do not enforce them to observe *Purdah*. Above 50 per cent of women literacy workers do not wish to leave the custom of *Purdah* as if this custom has proved to be useful for the safety of women. Only 16 per cent of women literacy workers wish to do away with *Purdah*. *Purdah* is not considered as a means to restrict the freedom of women by majority of women literacy workers. On the other hand, it is regarded as a precaution to protect women from eve teasing and other kinds of sexual harassment.

Literacy workers are the best-educated members of the family. All women literacy workers have opined that equal educational opportunity should be given both to boys and girls. Over four-fifth of women literacy workers have the best-qualified members other than themselves as literate and educated up to primary level. One-fifth of women literacy workers have opined that literacy programmes enable women read, write and count, render them knowledge and make them better qualified for better occupation. At least 12.5 per cent of women literacy workers believe that literacy programmes help them to manage home, learn saving, render self-confidence and live well. Nearly three-fourth of women literacy workers are aware of the effectiveness of literacy programmes in the lives of women. At least 46 women literacy workers who are educated up to high school have the best-educated member of the family who have reached up to primary level of education and 6 women literacy workers who are educated up to graduation have their best-educated family member educated up to high school. This finding shows that the aspiration of the best-educated member of the family is to educate the next generation at least one-step higher.

Over four-fifth of women literacy workers approve the stay of girls far away from home in pursuit of study or job. Women literacy workers who are unmarried are more willing to move out of home than the married ones. Out of 34 women literacy workers who are unmarried, 32 are ready to go far off places for higher studies or for job while only 15 out of 22 women literacy workers who are married are willing to do the same. At least 40 per cent of women literacy workers never go out of the village for seeing a film or attending any festivals. Out of the 22 women literacy workers who have never gone out of village for film or festivals, 18 are unmarried and only 4 are married. As many as 18 out of 22 married women literacy workers have gone out of village for any recreational purposes at least once while only 16 out of 34 unmarried women literacy workers have gone out of village for any recreation. The frequency of mobility of women literacy workers inside the village for any religious or village festivals is more compared to their mobility outside village for watching film or attending *Melas*. Over 93 per cent of women literacy workers have attended the religious or village festivals in the village at least once. Usually the family members go together to such religious festivals in the village. As would be expected telephone is the most popular means for communication followed by postal services. Nearly 90 per cent of women literacy workers have used telephone and postal services for communication.

Economic empowerment begins with career orientation for girls in the family. Over 90 per cent of women literacy workers have registered their opinion that equal job orientation is to be given to both boys and girls. One-fifth of the families of women literacy workers have employed women. Over 80 per cent of the families do not have earning women at home. At least 50 per cent of women literacy workers are agricultural daily wage workers. Nearly two-third of women literacy workers are undertaking double duties, one is domestic and household duty and the other is the agricultural and non-agricultural responsibility. Domestic duties are invariably the responsibility of women in rural Haryana. Four-fifth of women literacy workers have disclosed that they have significant role in deciding financial matters of the family.

Almost all women literacy workers have expressed that the household work should be treated as an occupation equal to any other occupation. In 70 per cent of the families, men are taking care of monetary affairs of the family. In 12.5 per cent of the families women literacy workers are taking care of the monetary affairs like saving and spending at home.

Political empowerment of women refers to equality in political representation and the exercise of the political rights. Nearly half of women literacy workers have attended the local level meeting at least once. One-fourth of women literacy workers have been attending the meetings often. All women literacy workers who have not attended the Gram Sabha are aged 20 years or less. All women literacy workers except one above the age of 25 have attended the Gram Sabha meetings at least once. Above 95 per cent of women literacy workers have opined that women have equal right to vote in election. At least 70 per cent of women literacy workers have expressed that women have freedom to stand for election. One-fourth of women literacy workers believe that women do not have equal right to contest for election. Two-third of women literacy workers are always ready to meet the civil authorities to address a common problem. Over one-fourth of women literacy workers are ready to meet the authorities if it is found necessary. Most of women literacy workers are ready to take the leadership in solving a common problem of the villagers. Over 70 per cent of women literacy workers have shown their willingness to take the leadership to face the natural calamities or any other casualties in the villages.

Role of Literacy work in Empowering Literacy Workers

The present study has been conducted over a period of one year, observing the behavioural changes in women literacy workers on a monthly basis and administering the key interview schedules before and after the literacy work of one year. It has been found that the literacy work has not significantly contributed to the achievement of empowerment. Empowerment is a long-term process, the progress of which is not visible within a short duration of one year.

At least 90 per cent of the family members have admitted the significant role of women literacy workers in the family matters before as well as after literacy work. Women literacy workers have shown increased autonomy with regard to savings but little improvement is visible with regard to purchase and ownership of property. This is due to their membership in the micro-credit union of women. More women literacy workers have realised the existence of restrictions on the freedom and mobility of women in rural areas.

As compared with the situation of observing before the entry into literacy work, more women literacy workers have started moving out often and started participating in the economic matters of the family. The number of women literacy workers observing *Purdah* has come down after one year of literacy work. No change is visible with regard to visiting parents' home. Four-fifth of women literacy workers have been trying to convince people about the problems of women before as well as after the literacy work. More women literacy workers have admitted the prevalence of differences in the code of conduct for men and women after the literacy work. More women literacy workers have expressed their willingness to meet any casualties in the villages coming to the forefront, after the participation in literacy work. At least 70 per cent of women literacy workers have shown this leadership trait and after the literacy work the number has risen to 80 per cent. The literacy workers have gained greater self-confidence and courage after the participation in the literacy work.

There is a marked change before and after the launch of NLC and in the situation of women literacy workers. More women literacy workers have realised the empowering role of literacy programmes in the lives of women. More family members and the village headmen have realised that the literacy programmes help women to read, write and count, make women alert and curious to learn, educate them about diseases, and help them to live well and manage home and savings and render self-confidence and power. There is considerable decrease in the number of women literacy workers who have been using *Purdah* in the villages. The number of women literacy workers who explicitly refused to observe *Purdah* has risen from 4 to 30. *Purdah* is a symbol of restriction upon the mobility and freedom of women and the empowered women would like to deny observing *Purdah*.

They have a fairly good concept regarding the empowerment of women before as well as after the literacy work. The changes visible are with regard to the behaviour rather than conceptual level. There is some improvement in the concept of women literacy workers of freedoms associated with empowerment after their participation in the literacy work. More women literacy workers have admitted that women must have more freedom to wear any dress of their choice, freedom to follow any hobby like embroidery, drawing, photography, etc., freedom in decision-making on significant matters such as purchase of household articles, education of children, employment of children, marriage of children, savings, income etc. freedom for ownership of property; freedom to earn and save and freedom for consumption of resources, freedom to visit bank and freedom to save or spend money; freedom to avail facilities, and freedom to exercise rights over one's own body and life after the duration of literacy work. The involvement of literacy workers in the voluntary literacy work has widened their understanding of women's rights. Women literacy workers did not show any change in their opinion regarding the freedom to participate as a voter in election, the freedom to participate as a contestant in election, freedom to participate in social organizations, freedom to exercise family planning methods and freedom to limit the number of children and freedom to feel proud of being a woman. The number of women literacy workers who subscribed for certain other freedoms associated with empowerment has virtually come down after the literacy work. These freedoms are the freedom to move out for recreational purposes such as going to exhibition, park, marriages, picnics, films etc. There is a significant change in the exercise of the freedom of mobility by women literacy workers after the literacy work. Before the participation in the literacy work only 50 per cent of women literacy workers have gone out of the village at least once. After the literacy work it is found that 75 per cent of women literacy workers have gone out of the village at least once. The participation of literacy workers in the village level social activities like, *balmela* (children's summer festival) and religious festivals has also improved. Participation in literacy work has enhanced the self-confidence of literacy workers and they have started participating in various public programmes held at village and block levels. With regard to emotional balance, self-acceptance, self-confidence, self-esteem and social competence women literacy workers have shown an improvement in their self-image. Such an improvement is not seen with regard to open-mindedness and sense of reality.

There is no significant change in the sense of security, women literacy workers before as well as after the literacy work. All women literacy workers have shown fairly moderate level of the sense of security and social competence prior to the entry into voluntary literacy work. This higher level of the feeling of security may be one of the reasons for their voluntarism.

A monthly observation schedule for each of women literacy workers over a period of 12 months have been used to measure various components of social empowerment achieved by women literacy workers during the literacy work. The observation of the investigator has been in relation to attentiveness of the learners, discussion of women's issues in the classroom, singing and dancing in the class, dress of the worker and the interaction between the learners. There is a gradual increasing level of attentiveness on the part of the learners over a period of 12 months. At least 70 per cent of women literacy workers have had meaningful discussion on women related issues by the 12th month of the observation. The frequency of the cultural events in the classes has increased by the end of 12th month. In the first month only 30 per cent of literacy classes have such activity while by 12th month over 90 per cent of the classes have these cultural activities. By the end of the year the dressings of women literacy workers have become homely, special and in 20 per cent of the cases the dressing has been formal. There is gradual improvement in the quality of interaction among the learners over the period of 12 months. Nearly two-third literacy classes and their literacy workers have been observed as marching towards empowerment as far as some social indicators of the classroom behaviour is concerned in the first month of the observation schedule. By the end of 12th month of the observation schedule

80 per cent of the literacy workers and their respective classes have been observed as moving towards empowerment.

It is to be noted that the progress in the classroom behaviour is not carried away to home. Just 3 women literacy workers have gained a better role in deciding financial matters of the family and one women literacy worker has actually lost the previous stand. However, it is important to notice that women literacy workers do have a significant role in the financial matters of the family before as well as after the period of observation. There is practically no difference in the position of decision-makers at home before and after the period of observation. Before the literacy work, more than 50 per cent of women literacy workers had never attended a Gram Sabha meeting. After the literacy work for one year, it is seen that over 90 per cent of women literacy workers have attended the Gram Sabha meeting at least once. More literacy workers have shown readiness to present common problems before the civil authorities after the period of observation. Before the literacy work nearly 70 per cent of women literacy workers opined that they had always been ready to approach the civil authorities for addressing any common problem. After the literacy work 80 per cent of women literacy workers have shown the readiness for the same. The remaining 20 per cent of women literacy workers have shown conditional preparedness to meet the civil authorities.

Problems in the Process of Empowerment

Empowerment of rural women is not an easy task. Even if a great deal of awareness about the rights of women for equality and justice is imparted at different levels, they are not able to practice what they are aware of. At the personal level women literacy workers can be considered as empowered but both at home and outside home, they face hardship. In other words, if the external factors like restrictions at home and insecurity outside home that restrict the freedom and mobility of women.

There are certain restrictions that are traditionally imposed upon the women of India both in rural and urban set-up. During the educational career, the girls are a bit relieved off these restrictions. Only a small percentage of women complete their schooling at higher secondary level and enter into college. Whether literate or illiterate, educated or uneducated all the women have to respect the restrictions. Most popular code of conduct of rural women is observation of *Purdah*.

Almost 70 per cent of women literacy workers have the opinion that women are not to interfere with financial affairs of the family. Nearly 40 per cent of women literacy workers feel that women are not supposed to move out of home frequently and socialise with personal friends. Over 30 per cent of women literacy workers have expressed that women are not supposed to go to own house after marriage. Nearly 50 per cent of women literacy workers have felt that the restrictions are prevalent in the Domestic World.

One-fifth of women literacy workers are of the opinion that women must respect the custom and obey the elders. Nearly 16 per cent of women literacy workers have expressed that the restrictions at home are unjust and are to be abandoned and another 3.6 per cent of women literacy workers expressed that these restrictions are to be considered as the code of discipline for women's life and by respecting and upholding these restrictions would definitely protect women from both disgrace and physical hurt. Over three-fourth of women literacy workers do observe *Purdah* as if it is a well-established custom. At least 10 per cent of women literacy workers who are married told that they do not observe *Purdah* and do not face any pressure to observe the same. It is with this small section of women the process of empowerment begins.

Nearly 70 per cent of women literacy workers do not interfere with financial matters of the family while 20 per cent do interfere. Half of women literacy workers do not observe the restriction on their mobility and do move out of home for various purposes. Four-fifth of women literacy workers do try to convince the futility of observing such code of conduct.

There are several problems outside home for women that curtail their freedom and mobility. These problems include insecure streets and market places, increasing crimes and violence against women. The lower literacy rate of women, the widening sex ratio, increasing migration of male workers, alcoholism and lack of precautions on the part of women are some of the contributing factors to the insecurity of women outside home.

Nearly half of women literacy workers have not reported any incidence of violence or troubles for women going outside home. Nearly one-fifth of women literacy workers are aware of problems faced by women of their village going outside home. Nearly one-fourth of women literacy workers do not know about any such happenings in their village. More than 40 per cent of women literacy workers think that the confident women are safe outside home. They believe that risk-taking is the secret of success. Over one-fourth of women literacy workers resent about the lack of opportunity to go out of home. Nearly one-third of women literacy workers have confirmed to the conventional view that women are not safe outside home.

Over half of women literacy workers have the opinion that the women should come together to help each other. Coming together empowers women. Sitting together, discussing about the problems of women, and learning from each other made the literacy workers realise the strength of coming together to face troubles outside home. Nearly one-fourth of women literacy workers believe that they should bravely encounter, shout out for help, report to the police, and get the criminals punished.

Only 16 per cent of the literacy workers believed that women are safe outside home before the literacy work. After the literacy work almost 40 per cent of women literacy workers have expressed their belief in the safety of women outside home. After participating in the literacy work, moving in the village for inviting illiterate women for attending the literacy classes, and meeting the Panchayat members and other officers at various levels, the literacy workers have gained greater confidence and their beliefs and attitudes have begun to change. The number of the literacy workers who have the opinion that the women are not safe outside home has decreased from 30 per cent to 20 per cent. At least 15 literacy workers have the resentment that unless women are allowed to go out, nothing can be said about their safety. After the year's literacy work this number has come down to 4. The number of woman literacy workers who hold the opinion that confident women are safe outside home and only they can progress in life has increased from 40 per cent to above 70 per cent.

Implications of the Findings of the Study

- Demographic profile shows that the literacy workers are 100 per cent literate and have reached at least high school level of education.
- The literacy workers are voluntary workers and have taken up the task of imparting literacy to the adult illiterate women without expecting any remuneration from the Government.
- The literacy workers have been found the best-educated members of the family.
- Social and educational profile of women literacy workers is better than the average women of the village.
- The literacy workers had a higher level of empowerment before taking up the voluntary literacy work. This voluntarism is an important variable to be studied. These volunteers belong to lower middle class families, well educated in comparison to the educational status of the women of Haryana state, and are motivated by the awareness that they are doing a good job in educating the adult illiterate women.
- Literacy work has facilitated the literacy workers to interfere meaningfully in the lives of the women of the neighbourhood.
- Literacy work has enhanced social status and respect of the literacy workers.
- Literacy work has opened up more opportunities for the literacy workers to move out of home.
- This study reveals that empowerment is essentially a personal phenomenon, manifest in the beliefs, values, feelings, and in social attitudes. The literacy workers

have shown a positive self-concept and a 'good' sense of security. This internal strength is related with their higher educational status and the recognition they got at home. The literacy workers have good self-esteem and have been very much appreciated for their good work and initiative for educating the illiterate women of the neighbourhood. They believe that their educational achievement is meaningless when majority of the women of their neighbourhood remain illiterate. These are truly the indicators of empowerment of women literacy workers have at the level of individual prior to the entry into the voluntary work.

- There are several situational factors that contribute to the voluntarism shown by the literacy workers. These factors are the encouragement given by family members, the Panchayat Council members, the members of the district and block level literacy council, respect and recognition given by the illiterate women of the neighbourhood, the orientation and training given by the block level resource team, continuous monitoring and support on the part of facilitating NGO, and above all the literacy workers have been motivated by the hope that voluntary participation in a Government sponsored literacy programme would help them to get a better job in the Government sector. It has been informed to the literacy workers that in the second phase of the literacy programme, the literacy workers would get a better participation and some honorarium. Village libraries are established now in the villages as part of post-literacy programmes and some of the literacy workers have been appointed as the librarians with a small sum as honorarium.
- Women literacy workers have a positive attitude towards the society and enjoy working voluntarily for the less fortunate ones in the village. Since they are better educated, literacy work has been a useful time pass for them. Many of the learners too find leisure between the unending household works by attending

literacy programme. Most of the literacy classes have a lot of fun, singing and group dancing. They too have prepared for cultural activities for the annual day. These social factors encourage the literacy workers to enjoy the literacy work.

- The literacy work has positive impact in the lives of the literacy workers. The continuous participation in conducting the literacy programmes nurtures the leadership qualities among literacy workers. The active involvement in the year-long literacy work has enhanced to the self-esteem, self-concept, self-confidence and social competence of the literacy workers. Their beliefs, values, attitudes and behaviour patterns have been modified due to literacy work. The role of literacy workers in the decision-making of the family affairs have increased. Their mobility in the village has also improved. Literacy work has contributed to the social empowerment of the literacy workers.
- Literacy work has not affected the economic status of women literacy workers. Economic empowerment is a long-term process and literacy work for a period of one year is not an adequate input to enhance to the economic participation of women literacy workers or in the acquisition of property rights. However the literacy workers have had a significant role in the financial matters of the family even before the literacy work. After the literacy work some of the literacy workers have actively involved in the formation of self-help groups bringing together the learners of the literacy classes. The literacy workers hold the executive posts of the self-help groups such as President, Secretary and the Treasurer. These groups have encouraged the women to collect savings and open bank account. They have started inter-loaning. Thus the literacy workers have access to credit. These developments could be assigned as the impact of literacy work. These are some of the main observations that come up as a result of present research work.

- With regard to the political empowerment of women literacy workers it can be seen that the voluntary participation in literacy work has not contributed much. Political participation of the literacy workers has not changed significantly during the period of observation. However, the level of political empowerment before the entry into literacy work has been significant compared to other women of the village. The literacy work has given the literacy workers more opportunities to meet the civil authorities face to face. Some of the literacy workers have started participating in the Gram Sabha meetings. Most of the literacy workers could attend at least one Gram Sabha meeting during the period of observation. This participation is not the sign of an active role in the local level politics. It has been mainly to announce the commencement of literacy work in the village.
- The leadership qualities of the literacy workers have improved, but the political impact of the same is not available. The literacy workers have taken active role in conducting various cultural programmes like *balmela* (children's summer festivals) and annual literacy day celebrations. They have also helped some women to meet the civil authorities to obtain pension, disability certificate and to open bank account. After the literacy work the literacy workers have been seen as the significant women of the locality and women of the neighbourhood have started approaching them for various kinds of help. It can be concluded that, at the grassroots level or at the village level, the literacy work has helped in some way to empower women politically.
- The problems in the path of empowerment of women are of two categories; restrictions at home and safety problems outside the home. Even if literacy workers have expressed their boldness to resist the restrictions verbally, it is seen that most of them observe these restrictions. They are bold in discussions but timid in practical level, because they want to avoid any friction

and tension at home. Even if women literacy workers have orally expressed higher level of self-confidence in moving outside home, they have not dared to go out in reality.

- In spite of all the problems in the path of empowerment it can be concluded that literacy work has boosted the process of great change in the lives of women of the villages of Haryana and this process of empowerment has initiated by the literacy work is still continuing through the formation of self-help groups, micro-credit formation and micro-enterprising movement.

Conclusions

This study has fulfilled all the objectives set for the study. The study has made an earnest attempt to understand the concept of empowerment and has revealed its social, economic and political dimensions in relation to women of Chandpur area in Haryana. Social empowerment of the literacy workers is studied under different categories such as personal level, at the level of family and at the level of social participation. At the personal level both the cognitive and emotional aspects are studied separately. It is found that the literacy workers are sound at the level of concept and above average at the level of family and the community with regard to indicators of social empowerment. The study has revealed the socio-economic aspect of the lives of the literacy workers. Women literacy workers are all from the lower middle class and none of them are from the higher or the lowest strata of the society. Women literacy workers belong to the group of the best-educated members of the family.

The study has also brought into light the impact of voluntary literacy work in the lives and aspiration of the literacy workers. The personality changes and growth among the literacy workers have been studied with the help of monthly study schedule. It is revealed that at the personal, family and the community level, women literacy workers have shown certain progress in the indicators of empowerment.

The study also attempts to suggest some measures for achieving more empowerment among women literacy workers.

Suggestions

- Literacy programmes under National Literacy Campaign are also means of empowering voluntary women literacy workers. The ongoing rural development programmes (Swarna Jayanti Gram Samridhi Yojana), meant for the families below poverty line focus on the empowerment of women through 'self-help groups'. A close observation of these programmes reveals that the women of villages of Haryana are hardly aware of the existence of such programmes. It shows that Governmental and Non-Governmental efforts for the empowerment of women are not properly propagated to the beneficiaries. Mass communication strategies, such as advertisement through Doordarshan and Akashvani, propagation in schools, announcements at railway stations, announcement at public gatherings of political parties, advertisement through posters and banners at public places, such as bus stands and hospitals, are to be adopted for the effective development communication.
- School drop-out girls are very high in Haryana. But, literacy workers are the exceptions to this general trend. Therefore, they are considered as the symbols of empowerment. It is the higher educational status that makes women literacy workers fit for becoming literacy workers and bring them in the path of empowerment. From this model it is learnt that investment in education of the women especially of the rural areas must receive the top priority in any strategy designed to empower women. Free and compulsory education for girls and women at the higher level is to be made mandatory. Reimbursement strategy is to be adopted for the implementation of educational and vocational scholarship schemes. Such schemes would encourage

women to take maximum benefits of the educational schemes for women.

- Literacy work is a voluntary work. It is heard from every corner in the village that the literacy workers should be remunerated for their services. Government should encourage such initiatives by paying some monetary rewards at least in the form of unemployment allowance. Government must have some incentives for the literacy workers.
- Training for capacity building, self-defence, leadership and assertiveness is to be imparted to girl students at high school and higher secondary level, so that they would assert their rights in various social situations, disclose the episodes of harassment and exploitation at home and work place, approach legal and police aid fearlessly, remind the male supervisors regarding their rights and extend support to the co-students and co-workers in need. Training for self-defence has been introduced in the cities but has not reached the rural areas of Haryana. Such type of empowerment education imparted at the high school level is likely to inculcate the spirit of voluntarism and social commitment among the students. They would more and more come forward to take up literacy campaign, formation of SHGs etc.

The follow up observation done by the researcher reveals that the literacy workers have shown some signs of empowerment in a period of 3 to 4 years. During this period the literacy workers have been exposed to various other social work interventions such as gender sensitisation programmes, legal literacy, organisation of *balwadi*, *balmela*, self-help groups and village libraries and have also been given a number of training-*cum*-social awareness programmes. They have been given inputs on reproductive health, prevention of female foeticide, importance of girl's education, inclusive education etc. All these exposures have a positive impact upon the lives of literacy workers who have been acting as middle level managers in the implementation of such programmes. After five years of their continuous participation in various women empowerment programmes starting with literacy campaign, changes are seen in their personality, in their social attitudes, leadership behaviour, sense of social commitment, aptitude for social service, their social status in the neighbourhood, level of their participation in decision-making at all levels beginning from the family till the village *panchayats*. It is, therefore, concluded that the process of women empowerment is a long term phenomenon and an isolated event like participation in literacy campaign does not really make significant changes in the lives of literacy workers unless accompanied by more challenging levels of social participation like participation in the SHG movement.

It is hard to define women empowerment, but easier to describe the behavioural characteristics of empowered women. Empowered women play a complementary role in the society, not a subsidiary role to men in the society. Empowered women have equal status in the society and their opinions and views are taken into consideration in planning, monitoring, implementation and evaluation of development plans at all levels of social organisation, beginning from the level of family, the smallest unit of society, till the level of state.

Empowerment is a dynamic concept. It is rather a process than a product. Empowerment takes place in the lives of women gradually as a result of their active involvement in social, religious and cultural activities and social movements. It is not a preconceived change but a bi-product of the sincere participation on the part of the women in various social, cultural, economic and political activities. It is primarily a long-term process. The researcher has studied both the short-term aspects and the long-term aspects of empowerment, in the sense that the study has brought out the factors responsible for the achievement of empowerment over a period of time.

National Policy for Women Empowerment, 2001
(Selected portion)

Article 1. Goal and Objectives (Art. 1.11)

The goal of this Policy is to bring about the advancement, development and empowerment of women. The Policy will be widely disseminated so as to encourage active participation of all stakeholders for achieving its goals. Specifically, the objectives of this Policy include :

(i) Creating an environment through positive economic and social policies for full development of women to enable them to realise their full potential;
(ii) The *de jure* and *de facto* enjoyment of all human rights and fundamental freedom by women on equal basis with men in all spheres—political, economic, social, cultural and civil;
(iii) Equal access to participation and decision-making of women in social, political and economic life of the nation;
(iv) Equal access to women to health care, quality education at all levels, career and vocational guidance, employment, equal remuneration, occupational health and safety, social security and public office etc.;
(v) Strengthening legal systems aimed at elimination of all forms of discrimination against women;
(vi) Changing societal attitudes and community practices by active participation and involvement of both men and women;

(vii) Mainstreaming a gender perspective in the development process;

(viii) Elimination of discrimination and all forms of violence against women and the girl child; and

(ix) Building and strengthening partnerships with civil society, particularly women's organisations.

Article 2. Judicial Legal Systems

2.1 Legal-judicial system will be made more responsive and gender sensitive to women's needs, especially in cases of domestic violence and personal assault.

2.2 The Policy would aim to encourage changes in personal laws such as those related to marriage, divorce, maintenance and guardianship so as to eliminate discrimination against women.

2.3 The Policy would aim to encourage changes in laws relating to ownership of property and inheritance by evolving consensus in order to make them gender just.

Article 3. Decision Making

Women's equality in power sharing and active participation in decision making, including decision making in political process at all levels will be ensured for the advancement of the goals of empowerment.

Article 4. Mainstreaming a Gender Perspective in the Development Process

Policies, programmes and systems will be established to ensure mainstreaming of women's perspectives in all developmental processes, as catalysts, participants and recipients. Wherever there are gaps in policies and programmes, women specific interventions would be undertaken to bridge these.

Article 5. Economic Empowerment of Women

5.1 *Poverty Eradication* : Steps will be taken for mobilisation of poor women and convergence of services, by offering them a range of economic and social options, along with necessary support measures to enhance their capabilities.

5.2 *Micro Credit* : In order to enhance women's access to credit for consumption and production, the establishment of new, and strengthening of existing micro credit mechanisms and micro-finance institution will be undertaken so that the outreach of credit is enhanced.

5.3 *Women and Economy* : Women's contribution to socio-economic development as producers and workers will be recognised in the formal and informal sectors (including home based workers) and appropriate policies relating to employment and to her working conditions will be drawn up. Such measures could include : (a) Reinterpretation and redefinition of conventional concepts of work wherever necessary, e.g. in the Census records, to reflect women's contribution as producers and workers. (b) Preparation of satellite and national accounts. (c) Development of appropriate methodologies for undertaking (a) and (b).

5.4 *Globalisation* : Strategies will be designed to enhance the capacity of women and empower them to meet the negative social and economic impacts, which may flow from the globalisation process.

5.5 *Women and Agriculture* : In view of the critical role of women in the agriculture and allied sectors, as producers, concentrated efforts will be made to ensure that benefits of training, extension and various programmes will reach them in proportion to their numbers. The programmes for training women in soil conservation, social forestry, dairy development and other occupations allied to agriculture like horticulture, livestock including small animal husbandry, poultry, fisheries etc. will be expanded to benefit women workers in the agriculture sector.

5.6 *Women and Industry* : The important role played by women in electronics, information technology and food processing and agro-industry and textiles has been crucial to the development of these sectors. They would be given comprehensive support in terms of labour legislations, social security and other support services to participate in various industrial sectors.

5.7 *Night Shift Work* : Women at present cannot work in night shift in factories even if they wish to. Suitable measures will be taken to enable women to work in night shift in factories. This will be accompanied with support services for security, transportation etc.

5.8 *Support Services* : The provision of support services for women, like child care facilities, including crèches at work places and educational institutions, homes for the aged and the disabled will be expanded and improved to create an enabling environment and to ensure their full cooperation in social, political and economic life.

Article 6. Social Empowerment of Women

6.1 *Education* : Equal access to education for women and girls will be ensured. Special measures will be taken to eliminate discrimination, universalise education, eradicate illiteracy, create a gender-sensitive educational system, increase enrolment and retention rates of girls and improve the quality of education to facilitate life-long learning as well as development of vocational/technical skills by women. Reducing the gender gap in secondary and higher education would be a focus area. Sectoral time targets in existing policies will be achieved, with special focus on girls and women, particularly those belonging to weaker sections including the Scheduled Castes/Scheduled Tribes/ Other Backward Classes/Minorities. Gender sensitive curricula would be developed at all levels of educational system in order to address sex stereotyping as one of the causes of gender discrimination.

6.2 *Health* : A holistic approach to women's health which include both nutrition and health services will be adopted and special attention will be given to the needs of women and the girls at all stages of the life cycle. The reduction of infant mortality and maternal mortality, which are sensitive indicators of human development, is a priority concern.

6.3 To effectively meet problems of infant and maternal mortality, and early marriage, the availability of good and accurate data at micro level on deaths, birth and marriages is required. Strict implementation registration of births and deaths would be ensured and registration of marriages would be made compulsory.

6.4 In accordance with the commitment of the National Population Policy (2000) to population stabilisation, this policy recognises the critical need of men and women to have access to safe, effective and affordable methods of family planning of their choice and the need to suitably address the issues of early marriages and spacing of children. Interventions such as spread of education, compulsory registration of marriage and special programmes like Balika Samriddhi Yojana should impact on delaying the age of marriage so that by 2010 child marriages are eliminated.

6.5 Women's traditional knowledge about health care and nutrition will be recognised through proper documentation and its use will be encouraged. The use of Indian and alternative systems of medicines will be enhanced within the framework of overall health infrastructure available for women.

6.6 *Nutrition* : In view of the high risk of malnutrition and disease that women face at all the three critical stages, viz. infancy and childhood, adolescent and reproductive phase, focused attention would be paid to meeting the nutritional needs of women at all stages of the life cycle. Special efforts will be made to tackle the problem of macro and micro nutrient deficiencies especially amongst pregnant and lactating women as it leads to various diseases and disabilities.

6.7 Intra-household discrimination in nutritional matters *vis-à-vis* girls and women will be sought to be ended through appropriate strategies.

6.8 Drinking Water and Sanitation : Special attention will be given to the needs of women in the provision of safe drinking water, sewage disposal, toilet facilities and sanitation within accessible reach of households, especially in rural areas and urban slums.

6.9 Housing and Shelter : Special attention will be given for providing adequate and safe housing and accommodation for women including single women, heads of households, working women, students, apprentices and trainees.

6.10 Environment : The vast majority of rural women still depend on the locally available non-commercial sources of energy such as animal dung, crop waste and fuel wood. In order to ensure the efficient use of these energy resources in an environmental friendly manner, the Policy will aim at promoting the programmes of non-conventional energy resources. Women will be involved in spreading the use of solar energy, biogas, smokeless *chulhas* and other rural application so as to have a visible impact of these measures in influencing eco-system and in changing the life styles of rural women.

6.11 Science and Technology : Programmes will be strengthened to bring about a greater involvement of women in science and technology. These will include measures to motivate girls to take up science and technology for higher education and also ensure that development projects with scientific and technical inputs involve women fully. Special measures would be taken for their training in areas where they have special skills like communication and information technology. Efforts to develop appropriate technologies suited to women's needs as well as to reduce their drudgery will be given a special focus too.

6.12 *Women in Difficult Circumstances* : Measures and programmes will be undertaken to provide the disadvantaged groups with special assistance. These groups include women in extreme poverty, destitute women, women in conflict situations, women affected by natural calamities, women in less developed regions, the disabled widows, elderly women, single women in difficult circumstances, women heading households, those displaced from employment, migrants, women who are victims of marital violence, deserted women, prostitutes etc.

Article 7. Violence Against Women

All forms of violence against women, physical and mental, whether at domestic or societal levels, including those arising from customs, traditions or accepted practices shall be dealt with effectively with a view to eliminate its incidence. Institutions and mechanisms/schemes for assistance will be created and strengthened for prevention of such violence, including sexual harassment at work place and customs like dowry; for the rehabilitation of the victims of violence and for taking effective action against the perpetrators of such violence. A special emphasis will also be laid on programmes and measures to deal with trafficking in women and girls.

Article 8. Rights of the Girl Child

All forms of discrimination against the girl child and violation of her rights shall be eliminated by undertaking strong measures both preventive and punitive within and outside the family. These would relate specifically to strict enforcement of laws against prenatal sex selection and the practices of female foeticide, female infanticide, child marriage, child abuse and child prostitution etc. Removal of discrimination in the treatment of the girl child within the family and outside and projection of a positive image of girl child will be actively fostered. There will be special emphasis on the needs of the girl child and earmarking of substantial investments in the areas relating to food and nutrition, health and education, and in vocational education. In implementing programmes for eliminating child labour, there will be a special focus on girl children.

Article 9. Mass Media

Media will be used to portray images consistent with human dignity of girls and women. The Policy will specifically strive to remove demeaning, degrading and negative conventional stereotypical images of women and violence against women. Private sector partners and media networks will be involved at all levels to ensure equal access for women particularly in the area of information and communication technologies. The media would be encouraged to develop codes of conduct, professional guidelines and other self-regulatory mechanisms to remove gender stereotypes and promote balanced portrayals of women and men.

Article 10. Operational Strategies

10.1 Action Plans : All Central and State Ministries will draw up time bound Action Plans for translating the Policy into a set of concrete actions, through a participatory process of consultation with Centre/State Departments of Women and Child Development and National/State Commissions for Women. The Plans will specifically include the following : —

(i) Measurable goals to be achieved by 2010,
(ii) Identification and commitment of resources,
(iii) Responsibilities for implementation of action points,
(iv) Structures and mechanisms to ensure efficient monitoring, review and gender impact assessment of action points and policies, and

(v) Introduction of a gender perspective in the Budgeting process.

10.2 In order to support better planning and programme formulation and adequate allocation of resources, Gender Development Indices (GDI) will be developed by networking with specialised agencies. Gender auditing and development of evaluation mechanisms will also be undertaken alongside.

10.3 Collection of gender disaggregated data will by all primary data collecting agencies of the Central and State Governments as well as Research and Academic Institutions in the Public and Private Sectors will be undertaken. All Ministries/Corporations/Banks and financial institutions etc. will be advised to collect, collate, disseminate and maintain/publish data related to programmes and benefits on a gender disaggregated basis.

Article 11. Institutional Mechanisms

11.1 Institutional mechanisms, to promote the advancement of women, which exist at the Central and State levels, will be strengthened. These will be through interventions as may be appropriate and will relate to, among others, provision of adequate resources, training and advocacy skills to effectively influence macro-policies, legislation, programmes etc. to achieve the empowerment of women.

11.2 National and State Councils will be formed to oversee the operationalisation of the Policy on a regular basis. The National Council will be headed by the Prime Minister and the State Councils by the Chief Ministers and will be broad in composition having representatives from the concerned Departments/ Ministries, National and State Commissions for Women, Social Welfare Boards, Representatives of Non-Governmental Organisations, Women's Organisations, Corporate Sector, Trade Unions, financing institutions, academics, experts and social activists etc. These bodies will review the progress made in implementing the Policy twice a year.

11.3 National and State Resource Centres on women will be established with mandates for collection and dissemination of information, undertaking research work, conducting surveys, implementing training and awareness generation programmes, etc. These Centres will link up with Women's Studies Centres and other research and academic institutions through suitable information networking systems.

11.4 While institutions at the district level will be strengthened, at the grassroots, women will be helped by Government through its programmes to organise and strengthen into Self-Help Groups (SHGs) at the Anganwadi/Village/Town level. The women's groups will be helped to institutionalise themselves into registered societies and to federate at the Panchayat/ Municipal level.

Article 12. Resource Management

12.1 Availability of adequate financial, human and market resources to implement the Policy will be managed by concerned departments, financial credit institutions and banks, private sector, civil society and other connected institutions. This process will include :

(a) Assessment of benefits flowing to women and resource allocation to the programmes relating to them through an exercise of gender Budgeting. Appropriate changes in policies will be made to optimise benefits to women under these schemes;

(b) Adequate resource allocation to develop and promote the policy outlined earlier based on (a) above by concerned departments;

(c) Developing synergy between personnel of Health, Rural Development at field level and other village level functionaries;

(d) Meeting credit needs by banks and financial credit institutions through suitable policy initiatives and development of new institutions in coordination with the Department of Women and Child Development.

12.2 The strategy of Women's Component Plan adopted in the Ninth Plan of ensuring that not less than 30% of benefits/funds flow to women from all Ministries and Departments will be implemented effectively so that the needs and interests of women and girls are addressed by all concerned sectors. The Department of Women and Child Development being the nodal Ministry will monitor and review the progress of the implementation of the Component Plan from time to time, in terms of both quality and quantity in collaboration with the Planning Commission.

12.3 Efforts will be made to channelise private sector investments too, to support programmes and projects for advancement of women.

Article 13. Legislation

13.1 The existing legislative structure will be reviewed and additional legislative measures taken by identified departments to implement the policy. This will involve a review of all existing laws including personal, customary and tribal laws, subordinate legislation, related rules as well as executive and administrative regulations to eliminate all gender discriminatory references. The process will be planned over a time period 2000-2003.

13.2 Effective implementation of legislation would be promoted by involving civil society and community. Appropriate changes in legislation will be undertaken, if necessary.

13.3 In addition, following other specific measures will be taken to implement the legislation effectively : —

(a) Strict enforcement of all relevant legal provisions and speedy redressal of grievances will be ensured, with a special focus on violence and gender related atrocities;
(b) Measures to prevent and punish sexual harassment at the place of work, protection for women workers in the organised/unorganised sector and strict enforcement of relevant laws such as Equal Remuneration Act and Minimum Wages Act will be undertaken;
(c) Crimes against women, their incidence, prevention, investigation, detection and prosecution will be regularly reviewed at all Crime Review fora and Conferences at the Central, State and District levels. Recognised, local, voluntary organisations will be authorised to lodge complaints and facilitate registration, investigations and legal proceedings related to violence and atrocities against girls and women;
(d) Women's Cells in Police Stations, Women Police Stations, Family Courts, Mahila Courts, Counselling Centres, Legal Aid Centres and Nyaya Panchayats will be strengthened and expanded to eliminate violence and atrocities against women;
(e) Widespread dissemination of information on all aspects of legal rights, human rights and other entitlements of women, through specially designed legal literacy programme and rights information programmes will be done.

Article 14. Gender Sensitisation

Training of personnel of executive, legislative and judicial wings of the State, with a special focus on policy and programme framers, implementation and development agencies, law enforcement machinery and the judiciary, as well as non-Governmental organisations will be undertaken. Other measures will include :

(a) Promoting societal awareness to gender issues and women's human rights;
(b) Review of curriculum and educational materials to include gender education and human rights issues;
(c) Removal of all references derogatory to the dignity of women from all public documents and legal instruments;
(d) Use of different forms of mass media to communicate social messages relating to women's equality and empowerment.

Article 15. Panchayati Raj Institutions

The 73rd and 74th Amendments (1993) to the Constitution of India have served as a breakthrough towards ensuring equal access and increased participation in political power structure for women. The PRIs will play a central role in the process of enhancing women's participation in public life. The PRIs and the local self-Governments will be actively involved in the implementation and execution of the National Policy for Women at the grassroots level.

Article 16. Partnership with the Voluntary Sector Organisations

The involvement of voluntary organisations, associations, federations, trade unions, non-governmental organisations, women's organisations, as well as institutions dealing with education, training and research will be ensured in the formulation, implementation, monitoring and review of all policies and programmes affecting women. Towards this end, they will be provided with appropriate support related to resources and capacity building and facilitated to participate actively in the process of the empowerment of women.

Article 17. International Cooperation

The Policy will aim at implementation of international obligations/commitments in all sectors on empowerment of women such as the Convention on All Forms of Discrimination Against Women (CFDAW), Convention on the Rights of the Child (CRC), International Conference on Population and Development (ICPD) and other such instruments. International, regional and sub-regional cooperation towards the empowerment of women will continue to be encouraged through sharing of experiences, exchange of ideas and technology, networking with institutions and organisations and through bilateral and multi-lateral partnerships.

ANNEXURE 2

Progress of Literacy Campaign in India

The Total Literacy Campaigns (TLC) model is accepted as the dominant strategy for eradication of adult illiteracy in India. These campaigns are area-specific, time-bound, volunteer-based, cost-effective and outcome-oriented. The thrust is on attainment of functional literacy through prescribed norms of literacy and numeracy. The learner is the focal point in the entire process and measurement of learning outcome is continuous, informal, participative and non-threatening.

The campaign is implemented in stages. The initiation of TLC begins with a process of consultation and consensus, involving political parties, teachers, students and voluntary groups. All sections of society are given due representation in planning and implementation of the programme. With the help of the core team so identified, the project is formulated. The campaigns are implemented through District-level Literacy Committees. They are registered under the Societies Registration Act as independent and autonomous bodies to provide a unified umbrella under which a number of individuals and organisations can work together. Leadership for the entire campaign is provided by the District Collector/ Chief Secretary and the Zila Parishad (District Council). The structure rests on three pillars—participatory people's committees, full-time functionaries and area coordinators. Government officials provide a support system, which provides with an interactive and a communicative process of management and implementation. The campaign is delivered through volunteers who work without any expectation of reward or incentive.

A detailed survey to identify and enumerate the non-literate people is conducted in the district with the help of volunteers. The social survey provides opportunities for the volunteers for personal contact and interaction. During the survey, more volunteer teachers and master trainers are identified.

Environment building is an important part of TLC. In the process of environment building mass mobilisation takes place through a multifaceted communication strategy, which creates the right environment and enthusiasm for teaching-learning activities. The success of TLC depends on the effectiveness with which all sections of society are mobilised. The basic objective of the environment building stage is to generate a sustained demand for literacy on the part of non-literates. Its momentum must not merely precede the campaign, but pervade throughout and even afterwards through post-literacy and continuing education phases. Environment building includes mobilising public opinion, creating community participation, sensitising educated sections of the community and recruiting them as volunteers, and mobilising and motivating non-literate people to become literate. Several media are utilised for environment building. Effective results have been obtained by using folk art forms, *jathas*, street plays, *nukkad nataks*, *bhajans* and *kirtans* as also *padyatras*, literacy walls, etc.

Training of the Task Force is conducted through key resource persons and master trainers—one master trainer for every 25 to 30 volunteer teachers, and one key resource person for every 25-30 master trainers. The key resource persons are trained first, who in turn train the master trainers. Finally, the master trainers train the volunteer teachers in batches. The materials for TLC are based on an innovative pedagogy called Improved Pace and Content of Learning (IPCL) that incorporates motivation-oriented teaching-learning material. Books suited for neo-literates and adults have been prepared after conducting adequate research.

A 3-grade primer is used for TLC. They are the three progressive sets of primers. Each grade corresponds to a different level of literacy. Each primer is an integrated one, in the sense that it combines workbook, exercise book, tools of evaluation of learning outcome, certification etc. The entire process is based on the principle of self-evaluation. The tests are simple and participative. Every learner is free to attain the desired level according to his/her convenience. It is, however, expected that a learner should be able to complete all the three primers within the overall duration of 200 hours spread over six to eight months. Monitoring and supervision of total literacy campaigns is done through a periodic system of reporting, and visits of the officials of the National Literacy Mission, State Directorates of Adult/Mass Education and the State Resource Centres. The management information system in a campaign is based on the twin principles of participation and correction. It has to be accountable, credible and instead of being enrolment-oriented, it has to be outcome-oriented.

Though the total literacy campaign is meant to impart functional literacy, it also disseminates a 'basket' of other socially relevant messages, such as enrolment and retention of children in schools, immunisation, propagation of small family norms, promotion of maternity and childcare, women's equality, and empowerment, peace and communal harmony. The achievement of total literacy campaigns has been slower in the Hindi speaking states of Bihar, Haryana, Punjab, Jharkhand and Uttar Pradesh. The conditions are different and demand innovative approaches. However, despite the slow take-off, the essence and the spirit of the campaign remain the same.

Success Story

An interesting episode of successful literacy campaign has taken place in South India in the year 1992. Kamarajar district in Tamil Nadu launched its total literacy campaigns on the 50th anniversary of the Quit India Movement and called it 'Quit Illiteracy Movement'. More than 1,000 performances of *jathas* have been held. An effigy of the demon of illiteracy is burnt. Buffaloes and elephants have been painted with literacy slogans and taken around on the streets, to create an interest in literacy. Letters and words have been hung from trees. There have been wall writings in many places. There is a monthly radio programme as well as a monthly newsletter on literacy. Amongst the learners are rickshaw-pullers, Muslim women and members of the nomadic gypsy tribe. Building on this, six campaigns have been integrated in the post-literacy stage—health, legal literacy, freedom struggle, disaster management, small savings and water management in agriculture. Libraries are also opened in each village (www.nlm.nic.in).

Post-Literacy Programmes

Literacy campaign is an ongoing programme. There is a genuine danger that neo-literates may regress into partial or total illiteracy unless timely action is undertaken to consolidate their learning skills. This is the rationale for Post-Literacy Programme (PLP). The National Literacy Mission has visualized the post-literacy programme as an extension of the Total Literacy Campaigns in the continuum of life-long education. Each Total Literacy Campaign is followed by the Post-literacy phase of one-year duration, to be implemented in a mission mode. A post-literacy programme envisages 40 hours of guided learning in contrast to 200 hours of teaching-learning during the Total literacy phase. Post-literacy is focused not merely on enhancing the learning skills of the neo-literates. Post-literacy seeks to ingrain the reading habit in the neo-literates and to make them use their literacy skills in their day-to-day existence. It also serves as an umbrella under which a host of developmental activities are undertaken. Skill development forms a major component of PLP.

Post-literacy phase is also the time when linkages with other development departments and schemes are sought in right earnest. Health, Rural Development and Environment are some of the areas in which this convergence is found. Jan Chetna Kendras or 'clusters' are being used as an 'open window' for dissemination of information on other development departments and schemes. Many districts have brought out simplified booklets on development schemes for neo-literates that have enabled them to make informed choices. The village library movement is an important initiative that has been launched in the post-literacy phase. There is a great scope for creation of a pool of literature by holding writers' workshops and by encouraging local talent to write stories including folk tales in the local languages, apart from encouraging neo-literate newsletters and magazines.

The post-literacy programme also undertakes a 'mopping up operation' to enable those who had dropped out of the campaign due to some unavoidable circumstances or have been unable to achieve the NLM norms, to attain the required level of performance through an intensive programme of remediation. In keeping with the belief that each district is unique and its requirements are district specific, the NLM has avoided offering a single model for post-literacy. Instead it has been left to the local genius of the Zila Saksharta Samiti (District Literacy Mission) to create a model, which suits the specific needs of the district and its learners.

To ensure that there is no time lag between the conclusion of the basic literacy phase and the start of post-literacy activities which could result in regression for neo-literates, NLM has laid a great deal of emphasis on the planning and launching of Post-Literacy Programmes which are sanctioned when 25% of the learners have completed Primer II. Thus the Total Literacy Phase and Post-Literacy Phase overlap in most districts.

A quick survey is undertaken at the launch of the post-literacy campaigns as the target group of post-literacy includes not only the neo-literates emerging out of the literacy campaigns but other learners at different levels of literacy as well. A system of external evaluation has been envisaged to assess the achievements of the district in fulfilling the goals of post-literacy. Post-literacy evaluation concentrates not merely on evaluating learning skills but also on other themes of post-literacy including convergence with other development programmes, skill up-gradation etc. In keeping with the NLM's thrust on transparency and objectivity, the agencies assigned to undertake the final evaluation are external. Post-literacy campaigns are successfully ensuring that neo-literates make a smooth transition from guided learning to self-learning, so that, they can proceed towards life-long education. They are treated as a preparatory stage for Continuing Education (CE).

Integrated Approach

Union Cabinet took some momentous decisions in its meeting held on 30th November, 1999. The Government has decided that an integrated approach to literacy would be followed. Since then, Total Literacy Campaigns and the Post Literacy Programme operated under one literacy Project. Literacy campaigns would continue to run in those areas where there are large pools of residual illiteracy. At the same time, for those who have crossed the basic learning phase, programmes of consolidation, remediation, vocational skills, integration with life skills and such other aspects would be considered the basic unit. The integrated proposal sought to effectively bring the activities of literacy campaigns under one 'Literacy Project' to achieve continuity, efficiency and convergence and to minimise unnecessary time lag between the two.

Continuing Education

The structure of the continuing education programme has been launched in 1995 as a fully funded centrally sponsored scheme. A continuing education centre is set up for a population of 2,000-2,500 so that it caters to the need of at least 500-1000 neo-literates. A nodal continuing education is set up for a cluster of 10-15 continuing education centres. The function of imparting basic literacy and transaction of literacy primers would be continued in the continuing education phase. The activity of teaching learning for basic literacy would be available not only to drop-outs and left-outs but also to new illiterate entrants in the age group of 15-35. The implementing agencies for continuing education centres or nodal continuing education centres are voluntary agencies, Mahila Mandals, Panchayati Raj Institutions, Nehru Yuvak Kendras, etc. The scheme also envisages convergence with the programmes of Nehru Yuvak Kendras, National Service Scheme, National Service Volunteer Scheme, etc., at the grassroots level.

The Scheme of Jan Shikshan Sansthan

The Scheme of Jan Shikshan Sansthan (JSS) or Institute of People's Education (formerly known as Shramik Vidyapeeth) was initially launched as a multi-faceted adult education programme aimed at improving the vocational skill and quality of life of workers and their family members. The first Jan Shikshan Sansthan (then called as Shramik Vidyapeeth) in the country has been established at Worli, Mumbai in the year 1967 and gradually the number had increased to 58 by the end of Eighth Five Year Plan, i.e. 1996-97. Fifty more Jan Shikshan Sansthans have been set up in the Ninth Five Year Plan period (1999-2003), taking the total number to 122. The programme has been evolved to respond to the educational and vocational training needs of numerous groups of adult and young people living in urban and industrial areas and for persons who had been migrating from rural to urban settings. Now with the emergence of millions of neo-literates through the total literacy campaigns launched across the length and breadth of the country and the transformation that has taken place in the economic and social set up over the years, the role and scope of these polyvalent educational institutes have widened manifold.

In the changed scenario, the focus of Jan Shikshan Sansthan is now shifting from industrial workers in urban areas to the numerous neo-literates throughout the country who are both unskilled and unemployed. Now, these Sansthans act as district level resource support agencies especially in regard to organization of vocational training and skill development programmes for the neo-literates and other target groups of the continuing education scheme. Hitherto the Jan Shikshan Sansthan Scheme was restricted to urban, semi-urban and industrial areas. Now, the area of operation has been extended to the entire district including rural areas also. As per the revised guidelines issued by the Government of India, at least 25% of the beneficiaries of the Jan Shikshan Sansthan should be neo-literates.

The JSSs offer around 255 different types of vocational courses—from candle and *agarbatti* making, sewing and embroidery to computer courses. In the year 2001-02 alone, around 14.78 lakh beneficiaries had been covered under various vocational training programmes, activities and other activities, of which around 60.98% are women. Earlier, the Jan Shikshan Sansthans have been being set up under the aegis of non-Governmental organizations, State Governments and Universiries. One Jan Shikshan Sansthan (in Delhi) is run directly under the Government of India. As per the revised guidelines issued by the Government of India, the Jan Shikshan Sansthans will function only under the non-Governmental organizations. Efforts have already been made to transfer all the Jan Shikshan Sansthans that run under the aegis of the State Governments to NGO sector.

ANNEXURE 3

Programmes for Women Empowerment under the Ministry of Women and Child Development

The Department of Women and Child Development was set up in the year 1985 as a part of the Ministry of Human Resource Development to give the much needed impetus to the holistic development of women and children. With effect from 30.01.2006, the Department has been upgraded to a Ministry under the independent charge of Smt. Renuka Chowdhury, Minister of State for Women and Child Development.

The broad mandate of the Ministry is to have holistic development of Women and Children. As a nodal Ministry for the advancement of women and children, the Ministry formulates plans, policies and programmes; enacts/amends legislation, guides and coordinates the efforts of both Governmental and non-Governmental organisations working in the field of Women and Child Development. Besides, playing its nodal role, the Ministry implements certain innovative programmes for women and children. These programmes cover welfare and support services, training for employment and income generation, awareness generation and gender sensitization. These programmes play a supplementary and complementary role to the other general developmental programmes in the sectors of health, education, rural development etc. All these efforts are directed to ensure that women are empowered both economically and socially and thus become equal partners in national development along with men (http ://wcd.nic.in).

At present the Ministry of Women and Child Development has mainly three schemes for the welfare and development of marginalized women. They are Swayamsidha, Swadhar and Support to Training and Employment Programmes for Women (STEP).

SWAYAMSIDHA or Integrated Women Empowerment Programme (IWEP)

SWAYAMSIDHA or Integrated Women Empowerment Programme (IWEP) is a recast of Indira Mahila Yojana (IMY) merged with Mahila Samriddhi Yojana. SWAYAMSIDHA is an integrated scheme for women's empowerment based on the formation of women into Self-Help Groups (SHGs). It aims at the holistic empowerment of women through awareness generation, economic empowerment and convergence of various schemes. The vision of SWAYAMSIDHA is to develop empowered women; who will demand their rights from family, community and Government; have increased access to, and control over, material, social and political resources; have enhanced awareness and improved skills; and be able to raise issues of common concern through mobilization and networking. Its coverage includes 650 Blocks, including the 238 erstwhile IMY Blocks, at a total cost of Rs. 116.30 crore to benefit about 9,30,000 women, with the formation of about 53,000 SHGs, about 26,500 Village Societies and 650 Block Societies. The achievements of SWAYAMSIDHA up to March 2006 are 67,971 women self-help groups, 9,89,485 beneficiaries, 6234 clusters and 387 federations (GOI, 2006 : 24-25).

Support to Training and Employment Programmes for Women (STEP)

Support to Training and Employment Programmes for Women (**STEP**) under the Ministry of Women and Child Development is to provide technical, institutional, organisational and social support to poor women working in selected sectors such as agriculture, dairy farming, small animal-husbandry, fisheries, trade and village industries, handlooms, handicrafts and sericulture. The programme is implemented through existing institutions such as cooperatives or voluntary organisations, which are to mobilise women and employ female workers to provide extension services. The programme focuses on households whose income is below the poverty line, including migrant labourers, unemployed, female-headed households, Scheduled Caste and Scheduled Tribe communities and crisis-stricken groups. The intermediary institutions are to ensure linkages with the mainstream economy and economic viability. Supportive services are to be provided through existing programmes wherever possible.

SWADHAR

SWADHAR scheme purports to address the specific vulnerability of women in difficult circumstances through a home-based holistic and integrated approach. The objectives of the scheme are: to provide primary need of shelter, food, clothing and care to the marginalized women/girls living in difficult circumstances; to provide emotional support and counselling to such women; to rehabilitate them socially and economically through education, awareness, skill upgradation and personality development through behavioural training etc.; to arrange for specific clinical, legal and other support for women/girls in need of those intervention by linking and networking with other organizations in both Government & Non-Government sector on case to case basis; to provide for helpline or other facilities to such women in distress; and to provide such other services as will be required for the support and rehabilitation to such women in distress. Beneficiaries of the scheme are widows deserted by their families; women prisoners released from jail; women survivors of natural disaster; trafficked women/girls or women/girl victims of sexual crimes; women victims of terrorist/extremist violence; mentally challenged women; women with HIV/AIDS; or similarly placed women in difficult circumstances (http://wcd.nic.in).

Other programmes intended for poverty alleviation and income generation for the rural as well as the poor are the

Swarna Jayanti Shahari Rozgar Yojana (SJSRY), Nehru Rozgar Yojana (NRY), Prime Minister's Integrated Urban Poverty Eradication Programme (PMIUPEP), Urban Basic Services for the Poor (UBSP), Urban Self-Employment Programme (USEP), Urban Wage Employment Programme (UWEP), Scheme for Development of Women and Children in the Urban Areas (DWCUA) and Swarnajayanti Gram Swarozgar Yojana (www.rdmin.nic.in). Some of these schemes are getting reshuffled or merged with other schemes.

Samakhya—Education for Women Empowerment (Selected Portion)

The most successful programme for women empowerment implemented by the Government of India is Mahila Samakhya.

1.1 The Problem

Why has education been inaccessible to rural women for centuries? Part of the answer lies on the supply side—there is clearly a lack of adequate and sensitive educational efforts to mobilise rural women, involve them in the educational process and help them reflect critically on their lives. The other side of the problem lies in women's own inability and lack of will to demand education; to assert themselves. One can begin to understand this inability by a simple analysis of the socio-economic milieu in which a majority of poor rural women exist :

* Caught up in daily struggles for fuel, fodder, and wage they have no time for anything else.
* Their well-defined social roles and norms of interaction leave little room for education and critical thinking.
* Going about their chores in isolation, they are unable to share their experience of oppression with other women, and are therefore unable to tap their collective strength.
* They are denied access to information and alienated from decision-making processes. Even when they relate to Government schemes, they do so as passive recipients.
* Victimised by schemes, which purport to address their health, education, and employment needs, they are

forced to view their environment with fear and suspicion.

* Systematically robbed of their confidence to think and learn without fear of failure, they are subsequently paralysed by their own low self-image.

As a result of these factors, women are caught in a vicious, self-perpetuating cycle; their inability to educate themselves perpetuates the stereotype that education is irrelevant to women.

1.2 The Objectives

The Mahila Samakhya project presupposes that education can be a decisive intervention towards women's equality. Its overall goal is to create circumstances to enable women to better understand their predicament, to move from a state of abject disempowerment towards a situation in which they can determine their own lives and influence their environment, and simultaneously create for themselves and their family an educational opportunity which serves the process of their development.

Within this framework, some of the specific objectives of Mahila Samakhya are as follow :

(a) Enhance the self-image and self-confidence of women.
(b) Enable them to recognise the worth of their contribution to society and the economy.
(c) Create an environment where women demand knowledge and information; thus empowering them to play a positive role in their own development and the development of society.
(d) Women's awareness and perception of their role in family and society coupled with a determination to participate in decision-making processes will almost always lead them to demand education for themselves and their children. This in turn will create an effective vocal demand for educational facilities in the concerned villages. In an environment where this demand is

articulated in a structured manner, specific inputs will be designed and introduced in order to meet their educational needs.

(e) Provide women with the necessary support structures to create time in their lives for education.

(f) Create informal educational structures, which respect women's pace and rhythm of learning, given the multiple demands of household, and changing agricultural seasons.

(g) Build mechanisms, which enable adolescent girls working in their homes, in agriculture and in the formal and informal sector, to get an opportunity for formal education.

(h) Revitalise the existing educational structure and build mechanisms to ensure that women monitor their own education and the education of their children.

(i) Create, through the MSKs a cadre of educated rural women; thereby promoting in rural areas an environment supportive to the goals of an women's project.

In the long run effective mobilisation for education will improve the capacity of the people to absorb various educational inputs. The critical difference between a state like Kerala with almost cent per cent literacy and Uttar Pradesh with a 41.75 per cent literacy rate is the community's recognition of the positive impact of education. Mahila Samakhya will thus, endeavour to generate this demand.

1.3 Non-Negotiable Principles

As the project inches towards these objectives, it has sought guidance not from targets, but from certain inviolable principles, which have been kept in mind at all stages of implementation :

(a) The initial phase, when women are consolidating their independent time and space is not hurried or short-circuited.

(b) Women participants in a village determine the form, nature, content, and timing of all the activities in their village.
(c) The role of project functionaries, officials, and other agencies is facilitative are not directive.
(d) Planning, decision-making and evaluation processes at all levels are accountable to the collective of village women.
(e) Education is understood as a process, which enables women to question, conceptualise, seek answers, act, reflect on their actions, and raise new questions. Education is not to be confused with mere literacy.
(f) Acceptance that as an "environment of learning" is being created, what women decide to learn first may not be reading and writing. Women's priorities for learning must always be respected.
(g) Acceptance that given the time, support, and catalysts for such reflection, women are of their own volition seeking knowledge with which to gain greater control over their lives.
(h) The educational process and methodology must be based on respect for women's existing knowledge, experience and skill.
(i) Every intervention and interaction occurring in the project must be a microcosm of the larger process of change; the environment of learning, the respect and equality the time and space, the room for individual uniqueness and variation must be experienced in every component of the project.
(j) A participatory selection process is followed to ensure that project functionaries at all levels are committed to working among poor women, and that they are free of caste/community prejudices.

2. Mahila Sanghas

2.1 *Sahayogini*

Women's groups known as Sanghas form the nuclei of the collective reflection/action envisaged by the Mahila Samakhya project. Functionaries known as Sahayoginis perform the initial catalytic function of organising a Sangh. The Sahayogini's initial work is to open dialogue with village women; discuss their problems and aspirations; encourage them to come together as a group; help them to negotiate an independent space for themselves in the village. As the Sangha gradually comes into its own, the Sahayoginis role shifts to being a supporter, guide, and information and feedback link between the Sangha and the support structures at the district level including the DIU.

The Sahayogini performs this initial catalytic and subsequently a supportive role for 10 village Sanghas, interacting with some more than others depending upon the level of motivation of the village women. Sahayoginis rare expected to live within the cluster of 10 villages they co-ordinate.

Potential candidates are identified by voluntary groups and social activities and now, with the expansion of the project, by other Sahayoginis working in nearby villages. The final selection is done through an orientation-*cum*-training programme with the participation of the DIU, Sahayoginis, trainers, and resource persons. Experienced Sakhis/Sahavakis may also be selected as Sahayoginis. Intensive trainings prepare the Sahayogini for her role.

The fundamental criteria for selecting a Sahayogini are her desire to work with rural women, and freedom from any caste/communal prejudices. Most Sahayoginis also have some basic, formal education (8th pass) although in Bidar District neo-literate Sakhis have also been appointed as Sahayoginis.

The most effective Sahayoginis tend to be women with the ability and generosity to devolve their own strengths and experiences to Sangha women. Unless a Sahayogini is able to evolve and explore new avenues of growth in tune with the Sangha, it will outgrow her. These criteria are being kept in mind in all subsequent Sahayogini selections.

2.2 *Sakhi (Known as Sahavaki in Karnataka State)*

Sakhis are village women who play a key role in activating their 'village Sangha'; they contribute the potential nucleus of a rural women's movement which will endure despite the future withdrawal of a project structure. The role of the Sakhi has been defined somewhat differently in each of the three states. Consequently, Sakhis have also been selected and come into active play at different states of Sangha formation in these states. This flexibility is necessary to match the diverse levels of awareness are responsiveness of women in the regions being covered under the project.

In Uttar Pradesh, Sakhis, identified almost simultaneously with the Sahayoginis, play a critical role in facilitating the Sahayogins initial contact with their village. They are thus involved in all states of building their village Sangha. They are trained and expected to facilitate meetings, and mobilise women around issues which effect their lives. For this (part-time) function they are given a small honorarium.

Keeping in mind some of the negative fall-outs of having a paid worker as the main catalyst for a village collective (alienation from the village community, been viewed and viewing themselves as "Government Servants" rather than as "Sangha Woman"), Gujarat and Karnataka States have experimented with different models of the Sakhi.

In Gujarat State, the Sakhi is viewed not as a "worker" but as a "learners" who will in turn share her training and exposure with the village. The honorarium paid to her is considered a scholarship for her learning period rather than a salary for work performed. This shift in terminology (from worker to learner) imbues the Sakhi's position with humility rather than arrogance. She does not know any better than the other women; she merely learns along with them. Here identity is first that of a village woman growing and evolving along with the Mahila Sangha, not an external facilitator alienated from the life processes of the village.

Sakhis are thus selected only six to eight months after the Sahayogini has initiated contact with the village and the nucleus of a Sangha is already in existence. The Sangha then selects and sends one or more women to be Sakhis. They are expected to use their training and exposure to help consolidate and strengthen their Sangha. As more and more women come forward to learn, the position is rotated annually.

In Karnataka, the Sahavaki's position is voluntary and there are usually a group of 1-5 articulate women with leadership skills who function as Sahavaki. Any Woman who participates in meetings, training or other event as a representative of her Sangha is known for that period as the Sahavaki. In a sense then all village women are Sahavakis to each other. The funds earmarked for Sahavaki honorarium are deposited in a bank account opened in the name of the Mahila Sangha, which collectively decides upon its use.

The Sakhis across all districts are the individuals who provide the project access to the pulse of village level processes and activities. They meet with their Sahayogini approximately four times a month, when she makes her village visits (approximately once every ten days). Sakhis from a cluster of ten villages together also have bi-monthly meetings with the Sahayogini. Sakhis are almost invariably illiterate.

2.3 *Sangha*

Through the collective efforts of Sahayoginis and Sakhis/ Sahavakis, Sanghas are gradually emerging. Starting as loose, informal issue-based gatherings of women, Sanghas have, in many places, metamorphosed into cohesive women's groups with a vision and identity, and in some places into autonomously registered entities. Here meetings are held regularly and problems are discussed systematically in terms of analysis, debate, information gathering and collective planning on the course of action. It is usually an instance of collective action, which transforms a loose gathering of women into a Sangha of collective intent.

Today, in approximately 1200 villages spread over 10 districts in three states women gather together to discuss all aspects of their lives and to explore, perhaps for the first time, their collective strength. They discuss problems ranging from fuel and childcare to questions of negative self-images and personal evolution. They address simply whatever they, as a group, chose to prioritise wages, ration cards or greater control over their bodies, as women are seeking solutions to their numerous problems; they invariably find themselves handicapped by illiteracy. The demand for literacy/ innumeracy is emerging as a logical corollary to Sangha women's increasing awareness and greater public participation.

3. Project Components

This project has tried to offer rural women the opportunity to reflect critically on their lives, to understand the socio-economic processes, which impinge upon it, to maximise individual and collective self-expression, and promote personal and political growth. The components of the project are designed to facilitate this collective reflections/action and to expand opportunities for basic education in rural areas.

3.1 Sangha Hut (Known variously as thikana, kutir, etcetera, depending upon the region)

In the original project design it was anticipated that a small hut with a specious veranda would be provided as a facility to help the Sangha come into its own. This would be metaphoric and literal 'space' in which women could meet in freedom. This component remains a part of the project but with a somewhat altered sequence of implementation; it will not precede the formation of the Sangha but will instead emerge from its strength. Experience has shown that unless the Sangha is a strong and cohesive enough entity for it to take on the responsibility of building and maintaining a hut, it will be accepted as yet another "services", destined to fall into misuse and disrepairs.

The demand for such a space is being voiced by gradually in keeping with women's growing consciousness as a collective with a distinct identity and independent needs. Where Sanghas have emerged strong, land for the hut has been identified at the initiative of the women.

3.2 Literacy

Creating a Demand

Literacy in the Mahila Samakhya scheme is not viewed as an end in itself, but as one part of an overall strategy of empowerment. The provision of additional infrastructure alone will not help unless a systematic effort is made to mobilise women and enthuse them to participate in the schooling process. Rather than impose AE or NFE in a didactic manner, an effort has been made to create a demand for literacy. Women will become literate in a more permanent way if they are allowed to seek it at their own time and pace. Forcing literacy on them or making it a condition of their participation only reduces interest and involvement.

Mahila Sanghas, collectively addressing themselves to problems of fuel, child-care and income generation, find that all problems are linked at a very fundamental level to the question of access to authentic information and hence to literacy. As women are shedding years of accumulated fear, shame, and gain collective strength through this Sangha, they are also regarding the confidence to reach out and acquire literacy skills without fear of failure.

Where the demand for literacy can be met by activating existing AE centres or creating new ones such centres will be provided. It does not, however, seem necessary or feasible to adhere only to a centre-based model for imparting literacy and numeric. Informal, individual teaching-learning sessions are frequently more participating and better suited to the needs of rural women, constrained as they are by low levels of confidence coupled with demands of child and changing agricultural seasons.

New Approaches to Literacy

Mahila Samakhya functionaries have conducted several small field experiments to understand and respect the pace and rhythm of learning of adult rural women :

(a) Open agenda literacy workshops have been held in Mysore District. No pre-determined literacy targets are set and the learners control the pace and method of their own instruction. New and more effective pedagogical methods to reach adult women are evolving. Conducted and closely monitored by the DIU and Sahayoginis, these workshops can provide the basis for replication of alternative literacy experiments on a larger scale.

(b) In Sabarkantha several workshops have initiated the long but necessary process of generating educational materials in local dialects.

(c) In Bidar District a series of small literacy workshops have sparked off a chain reaction of learning-teaching. Hundreds of women are being imparted literacy skills, which they in turn pass on to others in their villages. Each link in this chain transmits not only an alphabet she has recently learned but more importantly her enthusiasm and motivation to learn. Because the information is imparted piecemeal, the learner is never overwhelmed by the task before here; being taught by a neo-literate she is also not intimidated; and the teacher, herself a struggling neo-literate, is much more sensitive to the needs, and pace of learning of her student. The literacy experiment here is a microcosm of the process of empowerment envisioned by the Mahila Samakhya project—an organic transmission of power and knowledge, not a didactic imposition.

(d) Several DIU's (in Bidar, Saharanput, Varanasi, and Baroda) have, independent of each other, evolved a camp-based model for imparting literacy skills. In this model residential literacy camps (10-15 days) are interspersed with a follow-up period of learning (approx. one month) in the village itself. This model allows both structure and flexibility. Serious teaching-learning is concentrated in one phase and at the same time the learner is given the opportunity to absorb and consolidated her new-found knowledge at her own pace in her own daily routine. These literacy camps are planned in several Mahila Samakhya districts in the following year.

3.3 *Creative Centres for Children*

Rural Women's needs for childcare, pre-school, and NFE facilities for their children are frequently overlapping and interrelated. For example, a young girl attending an NFE Centre may be forced to bring along younger siblings who will simultaneously need childcare and pre-school instruction. These overlapping demands cannot be met by demarcating and separating out one component from the other. Instead an attempt is being made to evolve flexible models of childcare and NFE, more appropriately labelled "Creative Centres for Children". Here provision can be made for childcare, along with exercises in creative expression, educational games, and instruction in the three R's. In addition to providing children with quality care, these centres free women to participate in Sangha activities.

In Varanasi District over 25 such centres known as Udan Khatolas (flying magic carpets) are being attended by children of all ages. Two literate Sakhis from the village are trained to run the centre. One looks after the needs of pre-school children and the other is trained to look after the NFE component for the older age group (7-10). The Udan Khatolas are located within a basti (hamlet) to ensure that distance does not pose an impediment to younger children who need to attend the centre. The educational content of the centres are planned in conjunction with the Mahila Sanghas. In villages with more than one basti with a sizeable population of non-school going children there are two Udan Khatolas.

3.4 *Jana Shikshan Nilayan (JSN)*

The JSN under this project corresponds in its objectives to the scheme of the same name of the Department of Education (MHRD), but differs somewhat in its scope and facilities. While the objective is to provide women with post-literacy skills, Mahila Samakhya has not adopted the original JSN model of locating a post-literacy centre amid 4-5 contiguous villages.

Many functions of the centre in the original JSN model (classes for upgradation of literacy skills, discussion groups) are being performed by other educational inputs in the Mahila Samakhya project; above all, by the Mahila Sanghas themselves. In the system of a mobile library currently operative in Karnataka, the Sahayoginis and/or Sahavakis effectively function as the JSN Preraks. They collect books from the district office during their monthly meetings. They then distribute these books and other reading material monthly meetings. They then distribute these books and other reading material to the village women. The material is in the village itself and easily accessible to all. At the next monthly meeting, the books are exchanged. Where the need arises, there is a provision for full-time workers to function as Preraks.

3.5 Mahila Shikshan Kendra (MSK)

In recognition of the extreme dearth of innovative women-centred educational facilities in rural areas, Mahila Samakhya will try and set up MSKs (Women's Education Centres) in each district.

The main objectives of this institution are :

(i) Provide women opportunities for learning in the shortest period.
(ii) Create a pool of trained women who can work both within this project and other education and development programmes.
(iii) Provide a facility where women who have been marginalised by society (single woman, widows deserted, divorcees) can pursue education in a secure and stimulating atmosphere.

Where a competent voluntary agency can be identified to maintain and manage an MSK, there is provision for a low cost building in the Mahila Samakhya project.

3.6 District Resources Unit (DRU)

The DRU is an educational resources unit for AE and NFE to generate gender-sensitive educational material, develop innovative teaching modules for rural women, and train instructions in creative pedagogy. Funds for setting up DRUs will be provided in districts where there has been preparatory work to generate large-scale demand for education.

3.7 Support Services

Financial provision has been made for a few collective experiments relating to support services. As the Mahila Sanghas are addressing themselves to problems of access to fuel, fodder, drinking water, sanitation, they can use this provision for innovative solutions of their own choosing. For example, using village commons to grow fuel, fodder, trees, or organising a community bio-gas plant to pump drinking water are concrete steps to reduce the drudgery of rural women's lives.

In addition, the DIUs are co-ordinating with the block and district administration to provide such services by harnessing ongoing schemes like DWCRA, Jawahar Rozgar Yojana, training and credit schemes being organised by the Department for Women and Child and the Rural Development Department. An effort is being made to ensure that there is no duplication by keeping communication channels open and actively forging linkages with the administration at all levels.

3.8 Material Generation

Information as Empowerment

As women are seeking greater control over their lives, they are also articulating a need for information on a wide variety of subjects (health, agriculture, legal rights etc.). The information, which does exist, is not in a form or language readily accessible to rural women. The State and district units are attempting to address this lacuna by producing material in the form of booklets, manuals, audio-visuals and handbooks. Apart from providing a lasting gender-sensitive information resource, these materials will play an importing role in encouraging women to seek literacy, and in consolidating post-literacy programmes.

5. Facilitating Decentralisation

5.1 When the programme was being drafted, a great deal of attention was paid to the concept, approach to training procedure for selection of project staff and innumerable details regarding the kind of support structure required to nurture the programme in the initial phase.

5.2 However, when the Budget was being formulated, the conventional system of calculations to arrive at a comprehensive figure for the project was followed. We tried to estimate how many Mahila Sanghas, NFE centres, AE centres etc. would come up in each block of 100 villages. Similarly, estimates were calculated on the basis of annual addition of 100 villages per district. All the funds required for Mahila Sanghas, including huts, AE, NFE etc., was provided from the day one of the first year. Even though the project document and the notes on the financial pattern clearly stated that no targets will be imposed, in effect calculations were made on certain numbers of villages to be covered and a certain number of components per village. Funds to the Mahila Samakhya societies were released on the basis of this Budget. This resulted in some problems, namely :

5.2.1 No gestation period was provided for setting up the project structure. Obviously, the identification, selection and training of Sahayoginis would take time. Mahila Sanghas would need time to come together as a cohesive group. The project document went into great details on the need for time and space, and how services be delivered on demand only. Mahila Samakhya was seen as a programme that would generate a demand for education and a mechanism to increase women's participation in village level forums—including the village education committees/Educational inputs—called programme components in the project document was to be made to women if they wanted. The Budget did not reflect this.

5.2.2 Calculations were made for a cluster of 100 villages and all inputs were budgeted for. When the conceptual part of the project was designed to make room for regions/community specific innovations, there was little scope for variations in the Budget. The Mahila Samakhya Societies were thus hardened with enormous funds when their capacity to absorb them was limited. In the first year they were concentrating on selecting their teams, training them and getting the project infrastructure on the ground.

5.2.3 Executive Committees of MSS had the powers to monitor guide the programme but little financial flexibility. It was not clear if they could approve innovative educational activities that do not conform to approved patterns. Minor rules related to leave, delegation of financial powers etc. had to be approved by Government of India.

5.2.4 The financial pattern and the Budget was in effect top-down, whereas the programme was expected to take its cue from the village.

5.3. While Government of India appreciated the reasons for underutilisation of funds in the first year, it took some time before the inherent contradiction between the programme objectives and the financial pattern became apparent. In April 1990, these contradictions were discussed openly and it was felt that the entire financial pattern would necessarily undergo major changes in the VIII Plan period. The National Project office, therefore, concentrated on drafting revised financial patterns and system for the release of funds. As a stop gap arrangement the following changes were made and approved for Financial Year 1991-92.

5.3.1 The Executive Committee was fully empowered to consider any innovation and approve the same. As Government of India is represented in that committee, the decision of the Executive Committee would be treated as final.

5.3.2 The Executive Committee was fully empowered to appointed staff, regulate their working conditions (including leave rules) as long as the society does not exceed the total number of approved posts and do not increase the proportion of management costs.

5.3.3 Annual Budgets are to be prepared by each society on the basis of the plans made by each district. These Budgets should be based on the capacity of each district unit to take up activities or expand. If any district decides to harness the resources of an ongoing educational programme like Adult Education—then that district need not ask for funds for AD. Similarly, if a district team decides to take hut construction at a later date, they can do so. In the meeting of the NRG held on July 23, 1990, Education Secretary, Government of India urged the MS teams to promote innovative work in education.

5.4. Once this was done the entire project team heaved a sigh of relief. Many innovative Government sponsored programmes have not been able to introduce the necessary financial flexibility and they have to face innumerable problems. Too many controls and rigid financial patterns rob programmes of its initiative. Once the project staff at the state and district level feels they have no control over their own plans and that targets are handed to them by someone who is not aware of their working condition—then they loose interest. If Mahila Samakhya is to steer clear of this trap, it was imperative to respond to signals of distress and take corrective measures immediately.

5. 5 The financial patterns, pending approval for the VIII Plan period reflects this commitment. The following changes have been suggested.

5.5.1 While the staffing pattern of the National State, and District level project offices have been worked out in order to keep the management cost low; no such numbers, rules and limits have been stipulated for activities.

5.5.2 A lump sum has been provided in the Budget for all activities. The overall project Budget has not been based on any *de facto* targets taken as a based for calculations. Each state unit is expected to prepare its annual Budget based on the district plans. Funds will be released on the basis of these plans. The Executive Committees of the MSS has to approve and forewarned these plans/Budgets.

5.5.3 Financial patterns in the form of unit costs have been worked out with respect to Sahayoginis, Mahila Sanghas, Huts, Mahila Shikshan Kendras and District Resource Units for AE/NFE. The MSS cannot exceed the limits prescribed in these units' costs.

5.5.4 MSS can follow the approved financial patterns for AE, NFE, and Children's Centres. The Executive Committee has full powers to approve any innovative model keeping in view the reasonableness of the financial requirement. For example, if a district decides to adopt a camp based approach to literacy, the Excessive Committee if fully empowered to approve this. As it is chaired by the Education Secretary of the State, and the State Departments of Finance and Government of India are represented in the committee, its decisions will be treated as final.

5.5.5 The number of resource persons in each district has been linked to coverage. An additional resource person has been provided for every additional cluster of 100 villages. Similarly, if any distinct adopts the approved Government of India pattern for AE or NFE, they can provide additional staff on the lines of those schemes.

5.5.6 The responsibility of the National office is to ensure smooth flow of funds.

Samakhya literature reveals that literacy is not merely acquisition of the ability to read and write but empowerment for participation, autonomy and self-reliance.

Training for Empowerment (A module developed for the training of Mahila Samakhya Workers)

Training evolves spontaneously, as part of a shared experience. It is a journey, an interaction, a reflective process that brings about change. The word 'training' instantly brings to mind a formalised structured programme, where participants are sent to be instructed by experts in the field. Implicit in this notion of training is the involvement of two sets of people the trainers, who are knowledgeable, the participant who must be taught. In this scheme training is viewed as a didactic transfer of knowledge and information from the trainers to the trainees. But *training for empowerment is a participatory process,* which involves sharing of ideas and information, where everyone learns and teaches. Training attempts to breakdown traditional hierarchical relationships and establishes in their stead bonds based on mutual respect. This is not to say that trainers have no control over the content or events of the training, not that they are without certain powers, and privileges. The trainers' intervention is imperative, but it is shaped and structured by the dynamics of the group and the reality of the lives and circumstances facing the participants. This process involves the negation and reassessment of old biases and priorities on the part of the trainers, leading them as much as the trainees to a new understanding of self and society. *Sketch of a typical training programme for women empowerment* is given below.

Training begins with a collective process of reflection about women themselves, their lives, their beliefs, and their values. It is a collective process, which involves building :

- A sense of oneness among the women.
- A feeling sensitivity towards each others problems and lives.
- An environment in which women begin a process of questioning the social values by which they live.
- An understanding of empowerment whereby women struggle to resolve issues not in isolation but by creating forums for themselves at the village level.
- A deep sense of commitment and involvement to the cause without which it would be impossible to increase women's collective strength.

Creating an Environment of Trust

Attending training can be a daunting prospect. It is often the first time a woman is leaving her family, home and village, to go to an unfamiliar place to be with a group of unknown people, for sometimes as long as ten days. Not surprisingly, on the first day of any training one usually sees as hen-faced timid looking women with barely audible voices. Apprehension, fears, distrust are the dominant feelings among them. Many think the training is an examination and if they fail to answer the questions they will fail.

The initial task facing a trainer is to dispel this feeling and build an atmosphere of camaraderie. As a first step, the women must get to know each other, since the participants are usually from farflung villages, and the trainers from an even more alien urban environment. Games and creative exercises are frequently introduced to build trust, team spirit, to learn to question, and to understand certain conceptual issues. Discussions and reactions that follow the games set the tone and steer the dialogue. This kind of process creates an environment where women begin to talk about their lives. It is often the starting point for in-depth discussions on social attitudes, customs, the village power structures, caste, religious taboos, practise at child birth/death, marriage, widowhood etc.

Teaching Women to Question and Be Creative

Always taught to acquiesce, women initially find it difficult to ask questions. Exercises are introduced to replace this docility with assertiveness. For instance, a *'chunni'* (Scarf) or a piece of cloth is placed in the centre of the circle, and everyone in turn has to ask the woman next to her one question connected with the cloth. She must answer and ask the next person another question. Repetition is not encouraged. Eventually many questions are asked about the wearer of the *'chunni'*, the significance of *'chunni'* in our society, *'purdah'* the wages of the labourer and so on.

After a few days, initial fears are replaced by a newfound confidence. The women shed their inhibitions and demand explanations, such as—Will we benefit from this training? What will we get? How are these games going to help us to do our work?

Overcoming the apprehensions of their first days of training, women gradually begin questioning the structures of oppression that bind them and with which they will have to struggle. The starting point is a discussion on gender and the constraints faced by women. This involves the recognition that as women in our society we have accepted and internalised constraining and passive images of ourselves as devoted mothers and sisters, and obedient, wives and daughters. There is a chimney to let smoke out from the kitchen, but there is no outlet for women. They begin questioning this subordinate status of women, and simultaneously explored areas of women's strength.

Issues of domestic oppression and conflicts within the household, particularly with husbands, are clearly vexing for many of the women. Women work harder than men. Men can rest after a days work. Women must go on, take care of the children, take care of husbands, elders, the animals, and do household chores. After all that a man will ask what the women was doing at home.

The customs associated with widowhood are discriminatory against women. Why, when both men and women marry, only widowed women face discrimination. One explanation is that women are economic burdens and are therefore ill-treated. The treatment of widows is merely a continuation of society's largesse to womankind; it gave them constraints, fear, shame, loneliness, oppression, sadness, worry and tension. Such debates are a liberating experience for many women.

Understanding Social Realities and Analysing Social Inequalities

While gender issues are given importance in the training, a number of other vital problems are also addressed. It is imperative for the women to critically analyse caste and socio-economic structures, and to understand the state/district/block administrative machinery with which they interact on a daily basis.

This aspect of training sometimes begins with an experience known as the 'resource game' which raises issues of inequality, discrimination of justice. A chart paper and some crayons are placed in the centre of the circle. A group of three women are called and given 7 minutes to draw whatever they want, using as many colours as possible and utilising as much paper. During the next round a larger group of women are called and asked to repeat the process but are given fewer colours, less time and obviously less paper. For the third round and remaining women (a very large group) are called and the process is repeated. There are just a few crayons to be shared for approximately three minutes.

The game always generates feelings of tension and aggression. The last group of women feel cheated and are unwilling to accept this unfair arrangement. The discussion taken a natural turn towards the inequalities in society and the oppressive relationship between the rich and the poor, high and low castes, and men and women.

In order to initiate a process of questioning about poverty and access to Government services, trainers often enact a play called 'Rakku ki Kahani' (The story of Rakku). The play depicts the life of a poor woman, Rakku. She and her husband work as wage labourers for the local landlord. They have two children, one daughter who stays at home and does all the work and a little baby. One day the baby gets cholera. The play follows Rakku as she tries to save her baby's live through even conceivable hardship and injustice; abuse from the landlord, pawning her utensils at the moneylenders, being incorrectly diagnosed by the village doctor, bribing the Government hospital guard etc. Despite her most desperate efforts the baby dies.

The discussion goes through a series of complex questions about the structure of poverty and the ways of changing it. The women are encouraged to make a list of some reasons for the perpetuation of poverty. Usually they enlist the following :

1. Unemployment
2. Debt
3. Lack of information
4. Control over resources by the rich
5. Fear
6. Low wages

Fired with enthusiasm by such discussions, the women are eager to begin work to organise, educate, give information and generate income.

If the realities of caste are sobering, other barriers like education and literacy are more readily broken. Paper is identified with literacy. The same women, who make beautiful drawings on the walls of their houses, when asked to draw with crayons on paper, initially refuse saying that they are illiterate. However, they begin hesitantly but soon fill their posters with beautiful illustrations of houses, flowers, animals, peacocks and scenes from their daily lives.

Later they are asked to reflect upon the issues of education :

- Why is education necessary for the poor?
- Why are certain sections of society deprived of educational opportunities?
- What is the distinction between literacy and education?

The main points of the ensuing group discussions are :

- Everyone should have an opportunity for self-improvement.
- Poor people have practical knowledge based on the reality of their lives, but they have been denied access to formal education.
- Given access to educational opportunities they can improve their lot.
- Literacy is a tool while education is a life long process. An individual can be educated and not literate and literate but not educated.
- Education for the poor get poses a threat to the rich; they have a vested interest in keeping the poor illiterate and preoccupied only with basic issues of *'roti'* (food), *'kapada'* (clothing) and *'makan'* (shelter).
- Women and girls are discriminated against in seeking access to education.

Once the proper understanding of the discriminatory status of women is realised by women themselves, it will be easy to organise them to fight the discrimination and resist the exploitation. Since empowerment is an active process, there is little scope for external agents to intervene. Only women's groups can take any creative steps in this regard. Since the past one decade, self-help groups are on the rise. In Andhra Pradesh, Rajasthan, Kerala, West Bengal, Bihar, U.P., Haryana, Maharashtra and Gujarat, women are increasingly getting organised into Self-help groups and are in the path of empowerment.

Bibliography

Abraham, Taisha and Malashri Lal, *Female Empowerment : Impact of Literacy in Jaipur District, Rajasthan*, Har-Anand Publications (P.) Ltd., New Delhi, 1995.

Ahlawat, Neeraj, *Women Organizations and Social Networks*, Rawat Publications, Jaipur, 1995.

All India Adult Education Conference (50th Session), "Women's Empowerment and Gender Issues"—Working paper presented at Shegaon (Maharashtra) from December 19-22, 2001, *Indian Journal of Adult Education*, Vol. 63 (2), 2002.

Arya, Sadhna., '*Women, Gender Equality and the State*', Deep and Deep Publications, New Delhi, 2000.

Aruna Goel, *Education and Socio-Economic Perspectives of Women Development and Empowerment*, Deep & Deep Publications, New Delhi, 2004(1).

Aruna Goel, *Violence and Protective Measures for Women Development and Empowerment*, Deep & Deep Publications, New Delhi, 2004(2).

Azim, Saukath, *Muslim Women : Emerging Identity*, Rawat Publications, Jaipur, 1997.

Bisnath, Savitri and Diane Elson, "*Women's Empowerment Revisited*", UNIFEM—Progress of the World's Women Biennial Report, New York, 2001.

Busch, Noel Brigit and Deborah Valentine, "Empowerment Practice: A Focus On Battered Women", Emma Gross, (ed.), 'AFFILIA—*Journal Of Women And Social Work*', Vol.15 (1), Spring, 2000.

Chitkara, M.G., *Women and Social Transformation*, APH Publishing Corporation, New Delhi, 2001.

Cranney, Breda, *Local Environment and Lived Experience : The Mountain Women of Himachal Pradesh*, Sage Publications, New Delhi, 2001.

Croft, Suzy and Peter Beresford, "The Social Worker's Role in Empowerment", in Martin Davies (Ed.), *The Blackwell Encyclopaedia of Social Work*, Blackwell Publishers Ltd., Oxford, U.K., 2000.

Davar, Bhargavi V., (ed.), *Mental Health From A Gender Perspective*, Sage Publications, New Delhi, 2001.

Davies, Martin (ed.), *The Blackwell Encyclopaedia of Social Work*, Blackwell Publishers Ltd., Oxford, UK, 2000.

Devasia, Leelamma and V.V. Devassia (eds.), *Women in India—Equality, Social Justice and Development*, Indian Social Institute, New Delhi, 1990.

Digumarti, Bhaskara Rao, Dr. and Ms. Digumarti Pushpa Latha, *Women and International Action*, Discovery Publishing House, New Delhi, 1999.

Gonsalves, Lima, *Women and Human Rights*, APH Publishing Corporation, New Delhi, 2001.

Gopalan, Sarala, *Women and Employment in India*, Har-Anand Publications, Delhi, 1995.

Gutierrez, L.M., K. De Lois, and L. Glen Maye, "Understanding Empowerment Practice : Building On Practitioner Based Knowledge", *Families In Society*, Vol. 76 (9), 1995.

Iyer, Justice Krishna, "Human Right to Woman", in Kusum (ed.), *Women—March Towards Dignity—Social and Legal Perspective*, Regency Publications, New Delhi, 1993.

Jandhyala, B.G. Tilak, "Inequality in Education by Sex in India", in Chetana Kalbagh (ed.), *Women's Struggles for Equality and Emancipation*, Discovery Publishing House, New Delhi, 1992.

Jejeebhoy, Shireen J., *Women's Education, Autonomy, and Reproductive Behaviour : Experience from Developing Countries*, Vedams eBooks (P.) Ltd., New Delhi, 1995.

Jethmalani, Rani, *Kali's Yug : Empowerment, Law and Dowry Deaths*, Har-Anand Publications (P.) Ltd., New Delhi, 1995.

Joseph, Ammu and Kalpana Sharma, *Whose News? The Media and Women's Issues*, Sage Publications, New Delhi, 1994.

Kaldate, Sudha, "Educated Women, Equality and Role Conflict", in Leelamma Devasia and V.V. Devassia (eds.), *Women in India—Equality, Social Justice and Development*, Indian Social Institute, New Delhi, 1990.

Kapur, Promilla, *Socio-economic Empowerment of Women in the Family*—Paper presented at a 'Seminar on National Policy on Empowerment of Women-2001', held at SNCWS, Department of Social Work, JMI, on 7-8 March, New Delhi, 2002.

Karmakar, Sumati, *The Better Half : Mothers, Sisters, Wives and Homemakers*, Dominant Publishers and Distributors, New Delhi, 2001.

Kaushik, Susheela, *Empowerment of Women*—Inaugural Address at a 'Seminar on National Policy on Empowerment of Women-2001', held at SNCWS, Department of Social Work, JMI, on 7-8 March, New Delhi, 2002.

Khanna, S.K., *Women And the Human Rights*, Commonwealth Publishers, New Delhi, 1998.

Majumdar, Maya, *Protecting Our Women*, Vol. III, *Imperative of Empowerment; The Political Response*, Dominant Publishers and Distributors, New Delhi, 2001.

Mazumdar, Vina, *Key Note Address on National Policy on the Empowerment of Women, 2001*, Paper presented at a 'Seminar on National Policy on Empowerment of Women-2001', held at SNCWS, Department of Social Work, JMI, on 7-8 March, New Delhi, 2002.

Menno, Lattice, *Women Empowerment and Challenge of Change*, Concept Publishing Co., New Delhi, 1998.

Mir, G.Q., *Women Workers and the Law*, New Delhi, Anmol, 2002.

Mohanty, Manoranjan (ed.), *Class, Caste, Gender*, Sage Publications, New Delhi, 2004.

NCRB, *Crime in India*, Ministry of Home Affairs, New Delhi, 2005.

Narasaiah, Lakshmi M., *Women, Children and Poverty*, Discovery Publishing House, New Delhi, 2001.

Narasimham, Shakuntala, *Empowering Women—An Alternative Strategy from Rural India*, Sage Publications, New Delhi, 1999.

Nayak, Jessie B. Tellis (ed.), *Indian Womanhood : Then and Now*, Sat Prakashan Sanchar Kendra, Indore, 1983.

Pamecha, Suman, *Women on Economic Front*, Agrotech, Udaipur, 2002.

Pamei, T., "Women's Empowerment : A Study of Mahila Samakhya in Saharanpur", Lal Bahadur Shastri National Academy of Administration, Mussoorie, Government of India, *Reading Material For Training Programme On Indira Mahila Yojana*, Publications Division, New Delhi, 2001.

Pande, G.S., *Political Participation of Women in India : Implementation of 73rd and 74th Amendments*, New Royal Book Co., Lucknow, 2001.

Pruthi, Raj Kumar, Rameshwari Devi and Romila Pruthi (eds.), *Status and Position of Women : In Ancient, Medieval and Modern India*, Mangal Deep Publications, Jaipur, 2001.

Rajammal P. Devadas, G. Ramathilakam and K. Arulselvam, "Equality of Women through Education and Employment and Challenges to Social Justice", in Leelamma Devasia and V.V. Devassia (eds.), *Women in India—Equality, Social Justice and Development*, Indian Social Institute, New Delhi, 1990.

Roy, Debal Singha (ed.), *Social Development of Marginalised Groups*, Sage Publications, New Delhi, 2001.

Roy, Kalpana, *Women's Oppression and Protection of Law*, Rajat Publications, New Delhi, 1999.

Sachchidananda, "Social Development and Empowerment", in Debal Singha Roy (ed.), *Social Development of Marginalised Groups*, Sage Publications, New Delhi, 2001.

Saeed, Fouzia, *Taboo : The Hidden Culture of a Red Light Area*, Oxford University Press, New Delhi, 2001.

Sahay, Sarita, *Tribal Women in the New Profile : Vis-à-Vis their Non-Tribal Twins*, Anmol Publications, New Delhi, 2002.

Saxena, Kiran, *Women and Politics*, Gyan Publishing House, New Delhi, 2000.

Sherwani, Madeeha, "Why More Women Entering Workforce", in Chetana Kalbagh (ed.), *Women's Struggles for Equality and Emancipation*, Discovery Publishing House, New Delhi, 1992.

Shoma A. Chatterji, *The Indian Woman's Search for an Identity*, Vikas Publishing House Pvt. Ltd., New Delhi, 1988.

Siddiqui, G.A., *Fertility Status of Women*, New Delhi, Mohit, 2001.

Singh, Navinder K., *Role of Women Workers in the Tea Industry of North East India*, Classical Publishing Co., New Delhi, 2001.

Singh, Sukanya Nihal, *Prospectus for Women's Empowerment : Dynamics of Enablement*, Commonwealth, New Delhi, 2001.

UNDP, *Human Development Report 2005*, UNDP, New York, 2005.

Venkataiah, S., (ed.), *Women Education*, Anmol Publications, New Delhi, 2001.

Vidya, K.C., *Political Empowerment of Women at the Grassroots*, Kanishka Publishers, New Delhi, 1997.

Xaxa, Virginius, "Empowerment of Tribes", in Debal Singha Roy (ed.), *Social Development of Marginalised Groups*, Sage Publications, New Delhi, 2001.

Index